KEEPING BUSINESSES HEALTHY, HAPPY, AND LOCAL

Business Retention and Expansion Primer

Second Edition

Ginger Rich

Washington State Department of Community, Trade and Economic Development

Office of Trade & Economic Development

Washington State. Four borders. No boundaries.™

KENDALL/HUNT PUBLISHING COMPANY
4050 Westmark Drive   Dubuque, Iowa 52002

CONTENTS

LIST OF ATTACHMENTS

FOREWORD

It is critical to our state's economic vitality that we encourage our in-state businesses to thrive and grow. Retention of these businesses is equally as important than attracting out-of-state companies. Between 65 to 80 percent of all new jobs come from existing business expansions rather than from new site locations. It stands to reason that a balanced economic development program will include a strong focus on the retention and expansion of those businesses and industries presently located in the community.

The Washington Department of Community Trade and Economic Development (CTED) is proud of its award-winning Business and Job Retention Program. The technical assistance provided to businesses and community practitioners has provided a healthy environment to grow and expand. The Retention and Expansion Program, which began in 1988, has worked with over 2,160 companies and helped to retain or create over 31,000 jobs. This has resulted in the retention of more than 94 million in tax revenues.

Keeping Businesses Happy, Healthy, and Local: Business Retention and Expansion Primer by Ginger Rich, Program Manager for CTED's Business Retention and Expansion Program, is an important resource for any community that is serious about economic development. It lays out a strategy to help economic development practitioners identify the needs and concerns of existing businesses and develop plans and programs to assist them, thereby ensuring their economic health.

Community prosperity in Washington state depends on business vitality. Through research, experience, case studies, checklists, and sample forms, *Keeping Businesses Happy, Healthy, and Local: Business Retention and Expansion Primer* is another example of CTED's commitment to helping businesses thrive.

Martha Choe

Martha Choe
Director
Department of Community, Trade and Economic Development

PREFACE

The Washington State Business Retention and Expansion Program has made local capacity building one of the cornerstones of its mission. It holds semiannual technical assistance sessions and is committed to sharing retention and expansion tools and resources with local and state staff. Although numerous articles and books have been published about specific business retention and expansion components, program staff found no comprehensive manual that could assist practitioners in developing a successful BRE program. This primer is intended to do just that.

ACKNOWLEDGMENTS

The **contributing authors**, who provided their knowledge, insight and experience to this project, and other contributors, including **Russ Hindin**, Hindin/Owen/Engelke Inc., for information on nontraditional funding; and **Jim Mooney**, Development Services.

Evelyn Roehl, who helped edit our work so it could be submitted to the publisher.

Milt Priggee, editorial cartoonist for the *Spokesman-Review*, **and David Horsey**, editorial cartoonist for the *Seattle Post-Intelligencer*, for their art work.

Michael Tracy, President, Grays Harbor Development Association, for his assistance in helping to identify local issues and for contributions on primer content.

Special Thanks to

Maury Forman, Education and Training Director, Community Trade and Economic Development, for his help in editing and providing resource materials.

Howard Levens, past Program Director of the Washington State Business Retention and Expansion Program, for his valuable input on the program design and his vision for a BRE primer.

ABOUT THE AUTHOR

Ginger Rich is Program Manager for the Business Retention and Expansion Program of the Washington State Department of Community, Trade and Economic Development. Ginger has more than 30 years experience as a specialist assisting companies with their employment, environmental, training, and program management and in working with other state agencies. She has a Masters in Public Administration from the University of Washington and is a Certified Master BREI consultant. Ginger can be reached at (206) 256-6112; *http://edd.cted.wa.gov/bac/bre*, or *ginger@cted.wa.gov*.

CHAPTER 1

THE BASICS OF
BUSINESS RETENTION AND EXPANSION

CALVIN COOLIDGE WAS RIGHT

President Coolidge predicted in the 1930s that business would be better, or it would be worse. A variation for today's economy and for many of this nation's regions, state, and local communities might be: *Business will be better, or it will be gone.*

Nearly every day we read stories on the front page and in the business section of newspapers about companies restructuring, re-engineering, downsizing, right-sizing, or outsourcing. Not only is the basis of the American economy undergoing structural changes, but corporate America is also making structural changes in how it does business in the competitive world market.

Companies are also facing an accelerated pace of technological changes. These changes are happening in our state and local communities. We see old-time "blue chip" companies, as well as local home-grown businesses, experiencing downsizing. Downsizing has hurt thousands of subcontractors who support the large Fortune 500 companies. The ripple effect has caused the displacement of additional workers in the second-tier companies.

It is no longer "business as usual." Instead, we need to look for ways to strengthen public-private partnerships to address the economic changes taking place in America today.

This book is a primer for economic development professionals, local government, community leaders, citizens, and

others who share an interest in keeping hometown businesses vital, growing, and firmly rooted. It is an attempt to distill the elements of a successful business retention and expansion program down to the basics, and to provide tools to help individual communities design a program that best meets their needs.

RECRUITMENT—
ONLY HALF THE STORY

How do communities respond when local firms go out of business, relocate, or choose to expand their operations elsewhere? For many, the answer lies in finding new businesses to replace the ones that have gone under or gone away.

It's no surprise, then, that the economic development strategy with the most star power is recruitment. And why not? Results are tangible: when a new company comes to town or a new plant opens its doors, development professionals can take a bow and cut ribbons along with community leaders. They can point with pride when new jobs go up on the local tally sheet and new tax revenue is logged.

But, as important as it is, **recruitment is only** *part* **of a comprehensive, long-range economic development plan.** Progressive communities—like yours—need to balance strategies that woo companies that are relocating and expanding with organized efforts to **keep local businesses healthy, happy, and local.**

THE BASICS OF BRE

Advocates of retention and expansion programs know that 60-85 percent of all new jobs are created by existing businesses. The fact is, organizing a Business Retention and Expansion (BRE) program in your community is the smart strategy for holding on to what you have. But it requires new ways of viewing results. While expanding companies can have star power like a recruitment case, retention services frequently measure their success in what *didn't* happen—all those local businesses that:

  ▶ *didn't* pull up stakes and take their jobs with them;

  ▶ *didn't* choose an out-of-area expansion site, but opted instead to grow in the area;

  ▶ *didn't* succumb to the grass-is-greener syndrome or to the high-intensity wooing of other communities and stayed home.

BRE can be the foundation for all local economic development planning.

PRESERVING JOBS TO BUILD BETTER COMMUNITIES

The purpose of a business retention and expansion program is to encourage local businesses and industry to remain in a community and to continue to grow. Its aim is to keep businesses happy and strong so that they have no reason to leave or shut down.

Local companies are valuable resources their communities can't afford to ignore or lose. They generate jobs and create taxes.

In today's economy, it is critical not only to create jobs, but to create jobs that provide family/living wages. A community's inventory of living-wage jobs is one of the key yardsticks by which economic development initiatives are measured. The best prospects are often the ones currently in your community. These prospects can generate further employment gains, more new businesses, and tax revenues to boost local economies.

Small to mid-size firms provide a large percentage of the jobs. The backbone of employment in many communities are firms with 50 or fewer employees. They are the engines that power much of this nation's economic activity and job creation.

In economic development, the lifetime value of even a small employer can be substantial. Yet, as with any annual annuity, it is easily taken for granted. One must remember that:

  ▶ New employers are hard (read expensive) to get

  ▶ Increasing the value of current employers is more cost-effective than trying to recruit new employers

  ▶ New businesses are drawn to suppliers that provide good service to existing businesses.

```
LIFETIME VALUE
SMALL EMPLOYER

15 employees

$430,000 payroll
$  45,000 property tax
$  15,000 miscellaneous

$490,000 annual

$4.9 million over 10 years

$9.8 million
Lifetime Value
```

These programs are delivering value measured in increased levels of employment, expanded tax revenues, and stronger, more resilient local economies.

PREVIEW OF CHAPTERS 2 THROUGH 11

This primer can help a community establish its own successful BRE program. Here are some of the issues covered:

Chapter 2

How to develop a business retention and expansion program that can spur local economic development

The *Cheshire cat* said it all: If you don't know where you are and where you're going, it doesn't matter which road you take. Establishing program mission and goals and planning staffing and targeting services are critical for a BRE program.

How to expand awareness and build support for the BRE programs in your community

In matters of public policy, perception is more important than reality. The reality is that business retention and expansion programs are one of the most effective, cost-efficient ways to keep local economies healthy. Use the media, community forums, communications materials, training sessions, and local business testimonials to set that perception in cement.

At the core, BRE programs are grassroot ventures that require broad-based local buy-in from community leaders to be successful. Bring as many leaders as possible to the table to gain consensus on priorities, goals, strategies, turf issues, and responsibilities.

An active business retention and expansion program—whether it is statewide or locally organized—can pay big dividends to the state and local community. Businesses helped by a BRE program become the best sales tool and referral base for potential clients. As tax revenues from various sources are explored, do not overlook the potential tax base from existing companies. Public policy should ensure that these companies stay in business and grow, with increased sales revenues that have the potential to spawn additional employees and increased tax revenues in the future.

Business owners are usually critical of government and policies, which they believe hinder their company's ability to make a profit. This could be real or perceived, depending on a particular company's perspective. In Washington state, a proactive retention program has been viewed as a friend and advocate for business. Retention and expansion of existing companies and the related jobs is a good public policy and a good business decision.

Today, BRE programs operate in major metropolitan areas, county/regional, across state lines and in small, rural communities—all linked by the common goal of keeping business happy, healthy, and local.

WASHINGTON STATE'S BRE PROGRAM

Washington's successful Business Retention and Expansion Program helps expanding or troubled manufacturers. Since 1988, when it was funded by the Washington State Legislature as a one-year initiative, the program has helped more than 2,100 manufacturing firms, saved or created 31,240 jobs, and retained $94 million in tax revenues. During the past 14 years, the return on investment (ROI) was estimated to be $14 for every dollar of state expenditures. This ROI—in an area where small manufacturing and processing firms still drive the economic destinies of many communities—is significant.

The objectives of the BRE Program are to:

1) Establish early warning systems for identifying companies at-risk or considering expansion,

2) Retain a strong manufacturing and processing base in the state,

3) Build local capacity for business retention and expansion services, and

4) Coordinate state and local business and job retention and expansion activities.

The case studies in this book demonstrate how communities can mount effective programs and put together win-win deals to retain local businesses and keep them growing. County Economic Development Councils (EDCs) worked with the Washington state BRE Program to develop the strategies and put together programs that spurred solid growth and revitalized local economies.

Chapter 3

How to form solid public/private partnerships to support business retention programs

You can't do it all. It is important to include the necessary partners who can help retain and create jobs in the community. This chapter will help identify potential public and private sector partners who can help in planning, marketing, technical assistance, and financing.

Chapter 4

Where to go to find information about companies and industries

BRE staff should not waste a business-person's time by asking for information that is already available. Staff or volunteers must do their homework. Learn to tap sources that provide the best information.

Chapter 5

What early warning signs can help identify troubled companies in time to make a difference

Timing is crucial when making contact with at-risk businesses. In good economic times, local businesses may feel they have no need for technical assistance from BRE. When a business is about to go down for the third time, it may be too late to mount a rescue. Knowing how to be in the right place at the right time with the right solution is the key to saving businesses and jobs.

Chapter 6

How to take the pulse of local businesses

Maintaining an awareness of the local business climate is a critical part of local economic development statistic planning. A short mail or phone survey can help staff understand business concerns and provide early warning of firms that are either in trouble or that have expansion plans.

Chapter 7

How to mount an effective visitation program that demonstrates a community's support for local business

Depend on it: Companies will not care how much you know until they know how much you care. If local businesses are being battered by competition, beset by management problems, or considering a move to a location where the grass is greener, genuine problem-solving and technical assistance is in order.

Chapter 8

How to provide business assistance and broker federal, state, and private resources to expand and retain local business

The notorious Willy Sutton robbed banks because that's where the money was —bad judgment but undeniable logic. Knowing where the money and technical assistance resources are and helping local business tap such resources as revolving loans funds, venture capital, and community mortgage pools are key elements in any business retention and expansion program.

Chapter 9

How to help businesses address workforce issues

The 21st century is an economy built on ideas rather than physical capital. Access to skilled workforce continues to be one of the top priorities for business.

Chapter 10

How to assist local businesses to compete in the new digital economy

Competitive advantage in economic development used to be where the asphalt or rails crossed. Today, it is where the fiber optic lines intersect. Communities with high-speed Internet service can provide the redundant communications capacity critical for many companies.

Chapter 11

How to assess a community's business climate and craft smart community planning and incentive packages that keep local businesses healthy and local

What are the *real* problems plaguing at-risk companies or those vulnerable to wooing from other areas? Find the answers through local business visitations and a community task force before reaching for the community checkbook.

Chapter 12

How and when to use bankruptcy as a tool to save a business and restore it to economic health

Bankruptcy does not have to spell the end for a business, but, to paraphrase Sir Winston Churchill, it may mark the end of the beginning. Getting a business to rise Phoenix-like from the ashes of bankruptcy doesn't necessarily mean preserving the current name over the door.

Chapter 13

How to evaluate your business retention and expansion program to respond to changing priorities, fill gaps, integrate new strategies, and document successes

A variation on the Cheshire cat's logic: it helps to know where you've been when deciding where to go next. Not every BRE strategy is right for every community all the time. Take regular, organized looks backward at the program to determine what works, what doesn't, and what demonstrates value to the community.

In developing an economic development strategy for today and tomorrow, **keeping local businesses at home and growing in your community is a *very* smart idea.**

CHAPTER 2

GETTING STARTED
THE SMART STRATEGY FOR KEEPING WHAT YOU HAVE

Watch a small child sometime on a voyage of discovery under an apple tree. The child's arms are full of fruit, and the goal is clearly to take home as many apples as possible. But every time the child bends to pick up more, the apples already collected tumble. At some point she either gives into frustration and apples start flying, or begins to balance her effort of holding onto the fruit in the basket with that of adding to her stash.

Smart economic development programs in communities like yours need to work to keep the apples currently in the basket. To remain vital and growing, the local economy must be fueled by strong existing businesses that create jobs and maintain a stable tax base as well as by newly recruited firms.

A Business Retention and Expansion program—backed by effective sponsors, committed staff, and the full support of the community—can go a long way to:

▸ Create a long-range development strategy that fosters solid growth, expanded employment, and stable tax revenues.

▸ Help local businesses to grow and prosper in your community.

▸ Develop an early warning system for business closings, relocations, and layoffs.

▸ Build an informal communication network and cooperative spirit within your community.

▸ Demonstrate an actively pro-business attitude.

▸ Generate new economic growth and jobs.

SECURING COMMUNITY BUY-IN

It is absolutely essential to gain early and earnest commitment from as many elements of the community as possible. Bring them all to the table to lay out goals and objectives and clarify the geographic area to be covered by the proposed BRE program. Chapter 3 discusses potential partnerships and Chapter 7, on business visitations, highlights a successful approach for getting community leaders involved in your program.

To boost chances for positive public response, key contacts and business leaders in your community should be contacted personally and briefed on the program. Feel out the level of their support for a BRE program and identify allies and potential pockets of resistance. Consider presenting the program plan at a public meeting.

IDENTIFYING YOUR RETENTION AND EXPANSION PLAN

Today, a local firm not only has to compete with other firms in the community but also in the national and international markets. Competition for locally produced products and international competition are major determinants of the economic outlook for individual firms and collectively for the community. While you cannot control the marketplace, you can develop a strategic plan to maximize local growth potential and develop contingency plans to respond quickly to major plant closings or more positive business changes.

> *It is important for a BRE plan to be part of a comprehensive long-range strategy to support the local economy and build a better community. This means working with local ports, cities, and counties in their comprehensive plans.*

Mission

What is the key purpose of your program? Many BRE programs have identified their mission as *helping local business to operate, grow, create, and retain jobs.* The primary mission of the Washington State Business and Job Retention Program, for example, is "to identify at-risk and expanding firms and reduce the number of business closures, layoffs, failures, and out-of-area expansions that result in significant jobs losses to the state and local economy."

Program Goals

Examples of program goals that you may want to incorporate into your program include:

- Establish a local BRE committee or task force.

- Establish a business visitation program.

- Develop an early warning system/rapid response capacity.

- Optimize the use of business assistance resources.

- Facilitate job creation through business retention and expansion.

- Coordinate community education programs that allow for planned growth, infrastructure development, and a positive pro-business outlook.

Specific policy areas, such as regulations, transportation, and infrastructure, may need to be addressed before you can implement BRE goals. For example, helping local businesses to expand in a community with inadequate water or wastewater infrastructure systems, could create a major gap in local business confidence of the community's commitment to help them grow.

Strategies

Strategic planning requires carefully reviewing the local environment, developing alternative strategies, and evaluating and selecting the strategy most appropriate to local resources and preferences. The data collected in the surveys and business visitations is a good source of ideas. For example, does the community want to grow? Successful programs will help the community adapt governmental regulatory procedures, such as permit issuance, building inspections, and zoning, that take into consideration business timing and financial concerns.

While BRE programs are strongly encouraged to customize strategies that address specific community problems, the following strategies may be appropriate or may stimulate further thought:

1) Improving firm competitiveness by sharing information on state and federal programs.

2) Enhancing the attractiveness of the community by improving the available labor force.

3) Enhancing the quality of life in the county and community.

4) Developing strategic and contingency plans for local economic development.

5) Developing a support and assistance network to respond to immediate and ongoing retention and expansion problems and opportunities.

6) Providing management assistance and educational seminars to address the problems identified in the survey—seminars and workshops regarding the "how-to's" of management and marketing for owners/managers.

7) Improving the community's existing support services and infrastructure.

8) Developing issue-oriented task forces to examine the frequently-identified problems.

9) Establishing labor/management committees to iron out differences among companies and their unions.

10) Coordinating or co-sponsoring programs for training and retraining in new technologies and processes. (Example: One program worked with a community college to take a trailer with computers into rural areas to teach computer skills.)

Local Objectives

Write specific objectives for your local program to express desired outcomes, e.g.:

- *Retain _____ [number of] jobs by solving existing businesses problems.*

- *Increase _____ [number of] jobs by solving problems of existing businesses.*

- *Improve the business climate; demonstrate commitment to existing business.*

- *Increase wage levels by ____%.*

- *Create _____ [number of] jobs above the county average annual wage.*

- *Provide network opportunities for firms to work together to solve common problems.*

- *Provide a unified business voice in dealing with legislative issues.*

- *Attract local investment in the community.*

- *Correct business climate liabilities and capitalize on assets.*

- *Address _____ [number] infrastructure needs.*

Geographic Area Served

Will your program be city-, county-, or regionwide? There is an economy of scale that needs to be considered in each. The Washington state program found that smaller rural areas have a harder time building trust or sharing confidential information on risky businesses because of the close-knit relationships found in these communities. On the other hand, large urban area programs may have difficulty with marketing, as they do not have the same visibility with business. Your community needs to decide what would work best.

Industries Targeted

A strong local program needs to identify its targeted clients or sectors. Depending on the size of your program, you may not be able to assist all existing companies in the community. To be better able to utilize your local program's staffing and financial resources, consider the following questions:

— Do you know the number and types (industry groups) of the businesses in your community?

— Has your community identified what the strategic industry sectors are in the local economy? The largest employer?

— Who are the major employers or strategic sectors in your local community?

— Which industries have significant growth potential?

— Who contributes to the local tax base?

— Are there local land use issues that will affect business growth?

— Should you target companies by size or sales level? (One community, for example, targeted businesses with fewer than 250 employees and sales less than $25 million.)

— Has a particular industry/business area had problems that need to be explored or dealt with immediately?

Sources to help identify your major industry/business groups include local Employment Security Department staff, chambers of commerce, business associations, Internet, Better Business Bureau, and Private Industry Councils. In Washington state, the Labor Market Information Center (LMIC) provides data on occupational wages, employment trends, industry employment, and labor force dynamics and other information. Contact LMIC at *1-800-215-1617* or their homepage, *www.wa.gov/esd/lmea.*

TARGETED INDUSTRY QUESTIONS

► Does current regulatory and tax structure favor retention and expansion of targeted businesses?

► Will local suppliers, vendors, and distribution infrastructure favor the cost-efficient operation of targeted businesses?

► Does the local workforce meet the needs of targeted businesses, or will retraining be needed?

► Will expansion of the operation of targeted businesses pose a threat to the quality of life in your community?

► Do targeted businesses have a long-term commitment to this community, or do they have a reputation for moving around for relocation incentives?

► Will targeted businesses provide family-wage jobs that contribute to stable tax revenues and a strong local economy?

► Will the presence of targeted businesses in this community draw others in linked industries?

Manufacturing Sector

Many successful BRE programs focus on manufacturing companies because of the higher economic impact. Manufacturing and processing jobs tend to be better paying and create more additional jobs in local communities.

- On average, each $1 million in final sales in manufacturing is associated with 13.6 jobs in manufacturing—both the jobs to produce the final product and the intermediate products that go into it—and 8.4 jobs in other sectors, such as raw materials and services. (SOURCE: *The Facts About Modern Manufacturing*)
- 75 manufacturing jobs trigger $2.6 million in first-year spending by employees. (SOURCE: U.S. Bureau of Labor Statistics)
- Manufacturing jobs stimulate the economy 1.3 times more than service jobs. (SOURCE: Congressional Research Service)

(See Attachment 2-1, which identifies employment multipliers by industry sector.)

The Washington State Business Retention and Expansion Program (BRE) chose to target primary manufacturing industries, such as primary metals manufacturers, foundries, metal and plastic extruders, float glass facilities, and the wood products industry, including dimensional lumber, plywood facilities, and pulp and paper facilities. The program also works with food processing facilities.

A good way to determine your strategic sector is to create a directory of manufacturers, possibly partnering with other groups in your community. The contact you have with manufacturers will hopefully result in a favorable first impression of your program and allow you to get quick up-to-date information on companies in your area. Data to collect includes: contact information, employment base, product sector, product lines, and import/export data.

Other Strategic Sectors

Another reason that BRE programs may focus on manufacturing firms is that communities find it more difficult to assist retail and service firms that are in trouble or wishing to expand, often because their problems are caused by market demand or customer traffic. However, if you have a small manufacturing base in your local community, it is important to identify your local community's strategic economic sectors. Some communities target manufacturing firms and large nonmanufacturing firms (more than 50 employees) because of their economic impact. In your business visitations, you may wish to target manufacturing and do a sampling of the rest of the retail and service businesses in order to get a better understanding of the business issues facing your community.

One area that may be overlooked is the supplier base needed to maintain the strategic sector businesses. If there is a large business near your community that provides jobs and is a major procurer of products from local firms, it may be worth visiting.

Industry Clusters

Cluster strategies can be an attractive alternative to sector strategies for economic development organizations. *Clusters* are geographic concentrations of interconnected companies, specialized suppliers, service providers, firms in related industries, and association institutions (i.e., universities, standards agencies, and trade associations) in particular fields that compete but also cooperate. A cluster consists of the firms in an industry, the related firms in other industries, and private and public institutions that are important suppliers, customers, or regulators of the industry.

Clusters often foster a competitive economic advantage because of an unusually high number of firms and jobs in an industry within a geographic area. For example,

Central and Southeast Washington have obvious clusters in agriculture and food processing, with many employers and jobs in these fields, which gives them a competitive advantage over other regions in the nation. A large network of related firms and institutions also contribute to the industry cluster, which increases the likelihood of further growth in the industry, including the spinoff of new businesses. Through clusters, new types of dialogue can take place among firms, government agencies, and institutions that can strengthen natural groupings of firms.

Economic development strategies can be crafted to enhance the competitiveness and growth prospects of clusters if sufficient information is available concerning the composition and competitive status of a cluster. Paul Summers, in his concept paper for Washington state, identified several forms of cluster-based economic development strategies. Depending on the status of a cluster, workforce, marketing, or technical assistance initiatives may be welcomed. Cluster growth patterns may also help state agencies establish priorities for infrastructure investments, and the land use preferences of clusters may provide useful guidance to growth management planning. The state could also encourage regional consortia of local economic development organizations focused on projects with leading clusters in particular parts of the state.

Tools to Identify Clusters

One key tool for identifying clusters is an input-output table—an empirical characterization of the relationships among industries in an economy. Edward Bergman, in *Targeting North Carolina Manufacturing* (1996), used factor analysis to identify relatively tight linkages among groups of sectors in the national input-output table to come up with 23 "benchmark clusters" for the U.S. economy. (See Attachment 2-2.)

Another measurement tool is Location Coefficients (LCs). LCs measure regional competitive advantage by comparing the relative concentration of a given cluster in a region as compared to the nation. LCs greater than one indicate a local concentration more dense than the national concentration of the industry. When an LC is much greater than one, the cluster is assumed to have significant competitive advantage, and it is likely to be an exporter of goods or services outside the region. Absent other information, an LC much less than one is indicates a locally focused industry or one that lacks competitive advantage. An example of Washington regions with high location coefficients are North Puget Sound, with 29.5 for aerospace; King County, with 4.0 for software and 3.0 for biotechnology; and Southeast, with 5.3 for food processing.

Remember: You Can't Help Everyone

Realistically, staffing limitations may mean you cannot provide in-depth assistance to all firms needing help. It is important to remember that most BRE programs provide business counseling but do not have business consultants who can work full time for the company. (Attachment 2-3 provides some additional issues local staff may want to consider in prioritizing companies to assist.)

STAFFING

No community is too small to have an effective program. Although smaller communities generally have far fewer resources for economic development, they also have less businesses. Programs can vary from one part-time person and use of a small volunteer team in small communities to one or more full-time staff dedicated to retention, expansion, and survey efforts with clerical staff support in larger areas. Depending on the level of participation, BRE programs can be time-consuming and require trained professional staff. Serious consideration should be given to also using resource partners as a way to stretch scarce local resources (Chapter 3).

Areas to consider include:

— How will information and technical assistance be provided to the businesses identified to be targeted?

— Will the staff's role be to provide information, help develop or influence policies to help retain businesses, provide hands-on technical assistance, refer business to technical assistance providers, manage training, or a combination of services?

— Will you use workshops and forums to provide basic technical assistance to multiple businesses?

Staff roles used by various BRE programs include:

Program Manager/Coordinator: This person is responsible for managing the program full-time, on a daily basis. A candidate for this important position would ideally be professionally skilled in administration and experienced as a manager of program organization, training, volunteer recruitment, media relations, and information analysis. If the program is using a visitation coordinator model, the manager would share survey administrative chores with the coordinator as well as managing media contacts and community outreach initiatives. This person recruits committee/task force members and serves as the liaison if there is a state program.

Technical Specialist: Many BRE programs engage the services of an economic development professional familiar with state and federal programs and skilled in technical assistance models. The specialist can: provide counsel to at-risk firms identified in business visitation sessions or through the early warning program; offer technical insight and assistance to companies that are ex-

panding; and act as an intermediary to obtain federal, state, regional and local assistance. Candidates should have experience working with businesses, accounting and finance institutions, governments, regulatory agencies, and development organizations. (Attachment 2-4 provides job descriptions of a combined manager/technical specialist position.)

Survey Program Coordinator: Programs that utilize the business visitations volunteer/task force model (Chapter 7) often appoint a volunteer survey coordinator. The selection of your program coordinator is a key decision, because he or she will be the program's point person in the community in dealing with task force members. Look for a person well known and respected within the community who is familiar with business, civic, and economic development issues. Many programs turn to retired local business executives who know the community, are familiar with local issues, have a broad range of contacts and bring credibility to the position and the BRE program. (Attachment 2-5.)

The coordinator, who may be a volunteer, will chair task force meetings and work with BRE staff on follow-up tasks to help resolve problems which surface in business visits.

Volunteers/Interviewers: To enhance business input, many programs recruit volunteers from the ranks of local businesses or professional service providers for visits with companies in their community. Retired executives, again because of their experience and credibility with the business community also make good visitation candidates. Be candid about how much time will be required of volunteers for training and the actual visits. Also be sure to stress the importance of confidentiality as,

WHO SHOULD BE ON YOUR
LOCAL ADVISORY COMMITTEE OR TASK FORCE?

Creating a broad-based BRE task force can bring together a cross-section of your community. That means including people who may not have previously seen themselves as allies. Assume that most will come to the table with an independent agenda, but emphasize that all share a common goal: to preserve your community's economic health by keeping businesses local and growing. This group can help foster ongoing communication about available services and specific business issues, develop a better understanding of economic development, and identify issues that need action.

Membership could include:

▶ **Business leaders from the community,** ranging from top management of large companies to successful small business owners.

▶ **Service providers** such as attorneys, certified public accountants, financial institutions, insurance professionals, real estate professionals, consultants, and others with client relationships among local businesses.

▶ **Economic development professionals.**

▶ **Leaders of business-oriented organizations,** such as Chambers of Commerce, Better Business Bureaus, local business incubators, small business development centers, business networks and associations, and others.

▶ Representatives from **local school systems, colleges, and universities.**

▶ **Elected and appointed public officials** and **administrators from regulatory agencies.**

▶ Representatives of **local labor unions.**

▶ Representatives from local **utility service providers.**

over the long haul, it can make or break a BRE program. (See Attachment 2-6 for sample job description.)

Local Advisory Committee/Task Force Members: Local BRE programs play a critical role in fostering coordination of the retention and expansion activities in their communities. Some programs operate on the "Lone Ranger" model, with staff focusing on the short-term, individual "let's-make-a-deal" goal of solving a specific company's problem; but they often do not address the underlying barrier or structure that causes specific problems. The most successful

BRE programs go beyond short-term goals of solving firms' immediate problems and begin a process of dialogue and coalition building with community and political leaders from different disciplines. A proven coordination vehicle is the establishment of a local advisory committee or task force. This may be a separate committee or an expansion of an existing local committee which hås the same goals as the BRE program.

An effective committee or task force, with members who represent different elements within the community, can be one of your most valuable resources in solving problems for local businesses and in mounting efforts to save at-risk companies and jobs. This public-private partnership can utilize civic, professional, and personal contacts who work with BRE staff to seek workable solutions. If your program uses the volunteer visitation model, one of the responsibilities of your task force is to help recruit volunteers to visit local firms and conduct the long survey. (See Attachment 2-7 for sample job description.)

OTHER STRATEGIC PLANNING CHOICES

Survey Approach

In addition to the kinds of business targeted to be surveyed, your plan needs to address how frequently businesses will be surveyed and survey methodology (mail or visitation) and if distributed through a "phased" or "blitz" approach.

It is important to determine what will be done with the information when the survey is finished. Focusing on all surveys as a whole can give you a wealth of information. Developing a database from the survey information will make trend analysis and company profiling much easier. A report or analysis of the information will help identify sector trends and community problems. Chapter 6 and 7 discuss surveying in more detail.

Office Location

Once you have identified your targeted industries and geographic area, take time to consider where the program's office is located:

- Is it convenient for the businesses you wish to target?

- Is it in a neutral location that can help foster positive discussions between the different players who may have turf or jurisdictional differences?

- Is there adequate parking?

- Is there office space for confidential one-on-one meetings?

- Is there a conference room that can hold a number of people? (Having conference room meeting space can be important to the public/private partnership.)

Technical Applications

After the office space issues and service objectives have been developed, identify your technical capabilities and computer hardware and software needs:

- What type of computer hardware will be used—a personal computer that is "IBM compatible" or a Macintosh?

- Will you have stand-alone computers or be networked?

- What software applications will be used—word processing, database, fax/modem; Microsoft Office, IBM, ACT, Winfax, etc.?

In today's information explosion, the Internet is an excellent source for computerized or hard copy information such as labor statistics, community planning documents, zoning maps and requirements, land availability, infrastructure maps and long-range plans. To access Internet and World Wide Web, you will need a modem, telephone line and open an account with an Internet service network or general net accounts with e-mail capabilities: CompuServe, America On-Line, Microsoft Net, etc.

Make sure you check with your primary partners which computer systems they use. If you share information, it is important for your systems to be compatible.

MARKETING:
GETTING THE WORD OUT

There is no one "best" way to get the word out about your program. Positive word-of-mouth and media coverage are the most effective ways of spreading your key messages throughout the community to build awareness of business retention and expansion as an issue and to gain widespread support for establishing a working BRE program.

Media and program approaches to market your program include:

▸ **Press releases** — Newspapers run and electronic media air the most newsworthy items. The extent to which your BRE program is perceived as having a significant affect on the lives of local citizens, is the extent to which it will earn local coverage. Releases should position the program as a benefit to the community and one which has a broad range of local support. *(See Attachments 2-8 and 2-9 for sample press releases.) Remember that confidentiality needs to be maintained while working with at-risk businesses.*

▸ **Editorial Board Meetings** — The media influences public opinion through its handling of news stories and the opinions it expresses in its editorial pages and prints in its commentaries. Meet with local editors to educate them on the benefits of business retention and expansion programs in general and yours in particular. Give them the information they need to make positive editorial comment.

▸ **Authored Articles** — Another tool to get your key messages out to the public are articles outlining the benefits of business retention and expansion programs and submitted for publication by influential contacts involved with your program.

▸ **Letters to the Editor** — Highlight business growth in area by getting a small cadre of your supporters to write letters that reiterate key messages to the editors of local and regional newspapers and magazines. These will build the perception of broad local awareness and support for your BRE program and its goals and objectives.

▸ **Relationship Building** — Get to know print, TV, and radio reporters and editors who cover economic development issues. Keep them apprised of your progress, and personally invite them to all meetings for which you seek coverage. Arrange exclusive interviews with local influential contacts who support your program.

▸ **Speeches** — Give speeches at service clubs and trade association meetings, such as accountants, mechanical contractors, manufacturing associations, Rotary Club, Kiwanis Club, etc. Guest shots on local TV and radio public affairs programs serve the same purpose.

▸ **Newsletter** — Create a newsletter to be sent to local industries to explain the community's programs and activities.

Generally, mass-market mailings to businesses are ineffective, as company executives are frequently burdened by paperwork. Companies need specific information when they are in trouble or considering expansions. To use the common industry term, they need to get "just-in-time" information.

TELLING YOUR STORY

BRE becomes mainstream when its "story" is told repeatedly or compellingly by its practitioners. A good BRE story —

- emphasizes that the home game is important because that's where most of the points are scored;

- is told repeatedly in various ways;

- is backed by evidence; and

- connects the present with the future through an action plan.

Examples of BRE stories could include:

▸ Existing businesses create most jobs.

▸ As existing business specialists, we visit each local business every M years.

▸ X businesses are expanding, creating Y jobs. To help them, we are/will....

▸ Z businesses report difficulty finding skilled workers. Together with local educational institutions, we are....

▸ We have identified an industry with import substitution potential. We are/will....

SECURING THE RIGHT SPONSOR

Businesses want to work with staff who understand their needs. The sponsor and advocate of a local BRE program can be any group or organization that can provide necessary credibility, funding, support, and leadership. A business organization, such as an economic development organization or chamber of commerce, can speak the same language as the firms with which they work. Other potential sponsors include county extension offices, university extension centers, other private and civic organizations, county or city government, utilities, and banks. At the local level, a private non-profit organization may more easily navigate the retention/expansion waters than a public organization which must adhere to many rules and regulations. In some cases, funding may come directly from a state development office or regional agency, local government, or utilities. *It is critical that the organization selected has the visibility and trust of local businesses.*

ONE SIZE DOESN'T FIT ALL

Business retention and expansion programs should be organized to fit the needs of each community to take maximum advantage of public and private sector resources and help keep local businesses local.

Build your program on a base of solid public support generated by effective communication strategies and all-community buy-in. Build it from the grassroots up.

CAUTION!
Don't get stuck in the process of organizing and determining a course of action. Make a realistic work plan, then quickly begin using the available financial and human resources to get the tasks accomplished.

DIRECT EMPLOYMENT MULTIPLIER
AND AVERAGE WASHINGTON STATE WAGES

Sector	Employment Multiplier*	Average Wage**
Ag/Forest/Fishing	2.0	$23,840
Mining	3.5	$41,980
Construction	3.0	$42,560
Manufacturing	4.2	$40,820
Transport/Utilities	3.8	$39,090
Wholesale/Retail	2.0	$37,520
Finance/Insurance/Real Estate	3.7	$39,210
Services	2.1	$37,680

* The Employment Multipliers are estimates of the total number of jobs generated in the economy per new job in that sector. These figures include that same initial job. The multipliers are from the Impact Analysis For Planning (Implan) model. (Implan is a microcomputer program that performs regional input/output analysis, developed by USDA Forest Service Land Management System Group and Minnesota Implan Group.)
  SOURCE: Resource Division, Washington State Department of Revenue, April 2002.

** Mean average annual wage for industry.
  SOURCE: Washington State Department of Employment Security, May 2002.

BENCHMARK CLUSTERS
FOR THE U.S. ECONOMY

Cluster	Number of Linked Sectors (4-digit SIC)	Cluster	Number of Linked Sectors (4-digit SIC)
1. Metalworking	93	13. Aerospace	5
2. Vehicle manufacturing	35	14. Feed products	5
3. Chemicals & rubber	20	15. Platemaking & typesetting	4
4. Electronics & computers	25	16. Aluminum	4
5. Packaged foods	21	17. Brake products	4
6. Printing & publishing	21	18. Concrete/Cement/Brick	3
7. Wood products	16	19. Earthenware products	5
8. Knitted goods	13	20. Tobacco products	4
9. Fabricated textile products	12	21. Dairy products	3
10. Nonferrous metals	8	22. Petroleum	3
11. Canned & bottled goods	6	23. Meat products	2
12. Leather goods	6		

SOURCES: Bergman, et al., *Targeting North Carolina Manufacturing*, 1996, p. 9.
Summers, *The Cluster Approach to Economic Development*, 2000, p. 4.

FACTORS FOR TARGETING SERVICES:
IS THIS A PRIORITY COMPANY?

It is important to determine what criteria should be used to evaluate what companies qualify as being a priority, i.e., number of employees, sales, assets, net worth, tax base, share of local employment base, profit, type of industry, etc. In rural areas, you may be able to assist all companies, but in medium-size and larger urban areas, you may only be able to assist companies that are "significant to the local community." The interpretation of this phrase varies among the local areas. A general guide for priority businesses:

SIZE	Number of Employees	Annual Sales
Large Urban Centers	*50-75*	*$3-5 million*
Medium Urban Centers	*10-35*	*$1-2 million*
Rural Counties	*all companies*	

The above criteria may be waived if the company has a specialty product (niche) in the market.

WAGE RATES

How do the wages compare to your community's average annual wage?

FINANCIAL STATUS

Review the company's financial statement to determine the depth of assistance need and if company can be helped. Compare the business to other companies in its industry in the following areas:

- ► Cash flow—the amount of cash available to pay short-term debts.

- ► Debt/equity ratio—the ratio of debt in relation to the company assets.

(See Chapter 4 for sources of industry comparisons of cash flow and debt/equity ratios.)

Assets should always be greater than debt.

Job Description A

MANAGER/TECHNICAL SPECIALIST

Objective: To provide technical and management assistance to XXX County manufacturing companies. Responsible for the local industry expansion and retention program as a client case manager.

Typical Duties:

1. Provide wide-ranging assistance to business and industry.

2. Manage the case load for the local industry expansion and retention program, including all ancillary duties as defined in the annual program of work. This can include: writing, managing, and assuring compliance of contracts for funding.

3. Conduct surveys and visitations at local industry firms to support the local industry program objectives as well as maintain the local industry files, including profiles on local manufacturing firms. This includes maintaining the "Early Warning Team" and other programs to identify "at-risk" firms.

4. Cooperate with local service provider to coordinate the provision of local services to industry firms, including referrals to service providers.

5. Participate in advising firms, and/or local communities, on state and/or federal finance programs and information on state tax deferral/ exemption/credit programs in support of economic development projects.

6. Participate in the community relations effort with emphasis on local business assistance.

7. May participate in or conduct technical training, including possible seminars, to encourage improvement of services or products in support of expansion and retention functions.

8. Advise and support other community agencies in promoting enhanced workforce and vocational training.

9. Provide leadership in establishing and promoting an industry recognition program.

10. Participate in developing legislative issues in support of local industry needs.

11. Monitor the retention and expansion functions to identify possible program improvements.

Position Requirements:

1. Have an understanding of the nature and operation of businesses.

2. Must have some consulting experience in assisting a business at the management planning and/or issues resolution level.

3. Excellent oral and written communication skills; including ability to conduct interviews and make presentations to small and large audiences.

4. Ability to work effectively with senior company management and maintain company confidentiality requirements.

5. Ability to work with a large variety of area service providers, governmental entities, and business leaders.

6. Working knowledge of and ability to use computer applications.

Position Requirements (continued):

7. Ability to handle a reasonable number of tasks simultaneously, and to work independently with little direction or supervision.

8. Bachelor's degree in business administration, finance, marketing, public policy, or similar educational background. Appropriate long-term experience may be substituted at Board's discretion.

9. Willingness to travel and work a flexible schedule, including some weekends and evenings.

10. Ability to coordinate and schedule use of program resources in a professional team setting.

Desired Skills and Experience:

1. Knowledge and experience with industrial business development.

2. Knowledge of and working relationship with the regional business community.

3. Business management experience.

4. Economic development experience.

~ ~

Job Description B

MANAGER/TECHNICAL SPECIALIST

Directs, coordinates and markets business assistance programs operated by the Economic Development Association.

DUTIES AND RESPONSIBILITIES:

Business Development

- Direct, coordinate and market business assistance programs.
- Provide technical assistance (finance, management, marketing, business planning, employee training) to new and expanding companies and to industrial and manufacturing firms facing layoffs or closure.
- Analyze and structure financing for businesses.
- Provide business credit analysis for companies.
- Coordinate the service of professional volunteers to work with firms.
- Work with federal and state agencies to bring their programs and services to the local level.

Operations Management

- Prepare and manage annual budget of $XXX,XXX.
- Research, write and submit grant proposals.
- Solicit service-in-kind and other contributions for fund-raising.

Marketing and Communications

- Plan and conduct public relations and marketing programs to create and maintain favorable public image and to keep public informed of the organization's services and accomplishments.
- Promote goodwill through publicity efforts such as speeches, exhibits, and question/answer sessions.
- Represent employer during community projects and at public, social, and business gatherings.
- Coordinate and support volunteers in fund raising events and activities including dinners, special events, and membership drives.

Community Education

- Develop ongoing business development training programs.
- Secure sponsorship funding for seminars and workshops.
- Coordinate informational sessions on numerous topics for businesses.
- Develop job-skills training programs for businesses.

Human Resource Management

- Hire, train, and supervise office personnel.
- Develop and recommend to the board of directors long and short-range plans for old and new programs and services.
- Prepare program budgets related to physical, financial, and human resources accountable for control of these resources.

JOB RELATED SKILLS AND QUALITIES:

- Excellent communication skills.
- The ability to read and understand business plans and financial reports.
- Good supervisory skills.
- Problem solving/conflict resolution skills.

Must have the ability to maintain strict confidentiality in business dealings. Must be flexible and have positive enthusiastic style in dealing with the public. Must be able to work 40 plus hours per week.

EDUCATION/WORK EXPERIENCE:

Bachelor's degree in business administration, political science, economics, or allied field. Should have experience in business and industry, banking, economic development, or local government. Preferred experience in program management, administrative experience, or managing a business.

Job Description C

SURVEY COORDINATOR

The Program Coordinator will spend most of his/her time in contact with governmental and private sector leaders, as well as local organizations involved in the design and execution of the local Business Retention and Expansion Program.

The Program Coordinator serves as staff to the business retention and expansion task force to promote business retention as a focus of the business community and major organizations within the community, such as chambers of commerce, service clubs, labor organizations, and educational institutions.

The Program Coordinator will be responsible for orchestrating the various resources needed to complete the project and will be supported by the sponsoring organization, private sector experts, and local government staff to gather business information, identify business concerns, and resolve business problems.

Job Duties:

- Meet with state BRE staff and the business retention and expansion task force to outline scope of the project.

- Work with Task Force to contact major business organizations within the program area to publicize program, recruit interviewers and obtain support.

- Establish "base listing" of companies to be contacted. Information is usually available through local records and should be purified to insure it is current.

- Establish staff/volunteer requirements based on the number of firms to be contacted.

- Draft support letters for mayor's and/or board of supervisors' signatures.

- Meet with representatives of the business retention and expansion task force to localize survey and arrange for interviewer training.

- Coordinate company interviews (i.e., ensure personalized letters from the mayor, chamber of commerce, and sponsoring organization are sent to first firms to be interviewed; assign interviewers to firms).

- Track progress of interviewers and coordinate preparation of subsequent interview schedules with associated mailings.

- Coordinate training for technical support (local government and private sector experts) to respond to business needs.

- Track incoming surveys for "red flags" (items for immediate attention or action by any level of government). Track local government response to assure that it is timely. If action is needed at the state level, contact staff at the state.

- Coordinate company data (i.e., file cards on each firm with records of interviewers, follow-up).

- Work with BRE task force to identify ongoing process for gathering business information.

SOURCE: *California Business Retention and Expansion Program Manual*

Job Description D

VISITATION VOLUNTEER

An important element of the Business Retention and Expansion Program is the interviewer who will gather information from local businesses.

REQUIREMENTS OR QUALIFICATIONS

The interviewer is the direct link to the business and will represent the program. Interviewers should demonstrate:

- Maturity and willingness to take on responsibilities
- Good communication skills
- A commitment to completing surveys
- A genuine interest in the community
- Ability to maintain confidentiality of interview information

DUTIES AND RESPONSIBILITIES

Interviewers will be responsible for:

- Setting up appointments
- Conducting the interview
- Completing and returning the survey to the coordinator along with a cover sheet indicating follow-up required

TIME COMMITMENT

Attend two-hour orientation on visitations and conduct two to three interviews.
Each interview will take approximately one hour. Travel should be minimal.

BENEFITS

Benefits available to interviewers include:

- Development of listening and interview skills
- Contact with local business and political leaders
- Opportunity to make a contribution to the community
- Acquire knowledge about the local economy
- Opportunities to make an impact on future policy

SOURCE: California Business Retention and Expansion Program Manual

Job Description E

TASK FORCE MEMBER

Purpose

The purpose of the Business Retention and Expansion Program task force is to determine program direction and policy issues and to interpret goals and programs for the community.

Responsibilities of Task Force Members

This listing is intended to describe the range of responsibilities of the task force. Individual members will be expected to perform all tasks, but not necessarily simultaneously.

General Responsibilities

— Know and understand duties and responsibilities of task force members and interviewers.
— Attend and participate in full task force meetings and serve on subcommittees as needed.
— Be a spokesperson or advocate for the program.
— Encourage working relationships between the public and private sectors.

Administration

— Provide input and make recommendations on program policies.
— Make recommendations on goals and objectives, and assist in establishing priorities for implementation.
— Provide assistance in ensuring continued support of the program.
— Review and make recommendations..
— Evaluate the work of the interviewers and task force members and make recommendations on improving the program.

Community Relations

— Provide effective community relations which interpret the program to the total community and pursue a policy of community involvement in the activities and direction of the program.
— Interpret, informally, the work of the task force in day-to-day contacts and, formally, when requested.
— Promote increased visibility for the program.

Direct Service and Assistance

— Assist in the development and implementation of the program.
— Provide leadership, expertise or experience in specific areas and aspects of the program.
— Provide professional and technical service to the program and be available to members and interviewers for consultation on matters of common concern.
— Work on special projects and activities.

Time Commitment

The time commitment will vary for individuals depending on the availability of members, current activities of the program and specific talents and skills needed to carry out those activities.

The minimum time commitment will involve preparation for and attendance at task force meetings, review and commentary on materials sent to members, and consultation with other members relating to the program, when requested.

SOURCE: California Business Retention and Expansion Program Manual

N E W S   R E L E A S E
[on your letterhead]

FOR IMMEDIATE RELEASE
[Date]

CONTACT: [Name of BRE spokesperson]
[Telephone, fax numbers]

[COMMUNITY] APPLIES TO FORM BUSINESS RETENTION AND EXPANSION PROGRAM

[Community, State] — [Sponsoring Agency] has applied to sponsor a Business Retention and Expansion Program designed to stimulate economic development and growth by assisting local companies.

"[Insert quote from the sponsoring agency or the BRE coordinator about the objectives or expectations and industries to be targeted of the program]," said [name] of [organization]. If the application is accepted by the state economic development agency, the program will begin in [month and year], according to [name].

Before the program can assist local companies, the staff must identify business needs, concerns and problems, according to [name], [title] at [organization]. Under the new BRE program, local volunteers [or staff members] will visit and survey [community] businesses. Information will be reviewed by [coordinator, assistant coordinator and task force members] to identify needs and solve business problems.

[Insert quote on the confidentiality of the program], said [name].

If approved, the total cost of the BRE program is estimated to be $[_____], but the community will pay only $[_____]. State sponsors will cover the remaining cost.

SOURCE: *Business Retention and Expansion in the Western U.S.: People and Planning Can Make a Difference*, U.S. West Foundation Grant/Utah State University.

NEWS RELEASE
[on your letterhead]

FOR IMMEDIATE RELEASE
[Date]

CONTACT: [Name]
[Telephone, fax numbers]

COMMUNITY GAINS ACCEPTANCE FOR BUSINESS RETENTION AND EXPANSION PROGRAM

[Community, State] — [Community]'s application to form a business retention and expansion program has been accepted by [agency], which will sponsor the new economic development program.

"[Insert quote from sponsoring agency expressing enthusiasm for the program and potential benefits for the community]," said [name, title] of [sponsoring agency].

The main objective of the new BRE program is to help existing businesses here in [community] become more competitive, according to [name, title] of [sponsoring agency]. "Assisting firms to be more productive and profitable increases the chances that they will stay and expand here in the community," [name] added.

The focus of the new program is on retaining and expanding companies that already call [Community] home, rather than attracting new ones, because existing businesses account for about 40 to 70 percent of all new jobs.

To begin the process of assisting local companies, staff [volunteers] will visit about [number] local firms in [month] to gather information. These visitations will use a questionnaire prepared by the BRE program to identify needs and to respond to concerns and problems within the local business environment. This information be used to seek solutions and help maintain a stable workforce.

"[Insert quote here from the local business, staff, or committee on the benefits of the program to local business and the community]."

SOURCE: *Business Retention and Expansion in the Western U.S.: People and Planning Can Make a Difference*, U.S. West Foundation Grant/Utah State University.

CHAPTER 3

PARTNERSHIPS
RETENTION/EXPANSION IS NOT A SOLO SPORT

If, as the community's retention and expansion professional, you are the quarterback, coach, cheerleader, and manager in creating and playing the game, consider a time out. There's too much at stake to be a maverick and on the ball all by yourself.

From the very outset, you need to identify and include necessary and appropriate partners for your BRE program. Successful retention and expansion of business is the result of numerous community partners acting to help: 1) identify troubled or expanding firms, 2) provide technical assistance or problem solving with firms, 3) solve problems that hinder continued operation or the expansion of companies in your community, and 4) finance your program.

The synergy of partners acting together can help both retain and create critical jobs in your community.

Who are your potential partners? Some will be obvious and, hopefully, others will generate new ideas for you to utilize. Partner roles vary from helping program staff to directly helping business. No retention and expansion deal will need all of these partners. But with experience you will learn how and when to put your best team in the field. Listed below are different types of retention and expansion partners, separated into the private and public sectors:

PRIVATE SECTOR:
1. Financial/Legal
2. Utilities/Tele-communications
3. Real Estate Brokers
4. Associations
5. Media
6. Business
7. Consultants

PRIVATE/PUBLIC:
1. Labor
2. Education/Workforce Providers
3. Manufacturing Extension

PUBLIC SECTOR:
1. Federal
2. State
3. Local

ROLES OF PARTNERS

Levels of Involvement: <u>H</u>igh <u>M</u>edium <u>L</u>ow

	Early Warning	Marketing	Technical Assistance	Business Financing	Program Funding
PRIVATE SECTOR: **Accountants**	L	H-M	M		Membership
Attorneys	L	H-M	M		Membership
Institutional Lenders	M	H	H-M	H	H-M
Real Estate Brokers	H		M		
Electrical/Gas Companies; Telecommunications	M	H	H-M		H
Water/Sanitary Sewer			H		
Associations	H	H-M	H	L	L
Media	M	H			Membership
Business Leaders	H-M	H		L-M	Membership
Consultants			H	H	
PRIVATE/PUBLIC: **Labor**	H-M	M	M	L	L
Education	M	M	H		
Workforce Providers	H	H	H		M
Manufacturing Extension		H	H		H
PUBLIC: **Federal Government**	L	L	H	H	L-M
State Government	H-M	H	H	H	H
Elected Officials Local Government	M-H	M-H	M-H	L	H

INVITE PRIVATE SECTOR PARTNERS TO PLAY

Seven private-sector partner categories should be considered as possible investors and significant partners in your retention and expansion program. Participation as an investor is an indirect way for the private sector to be your partner. Other ways in which the private sector can be partners in your retention and expansion program are detailed on the following pages.

FINANCIAL/LEGAL PARTNERS

Accountants

Accountants can provide technical assistance for both your BRE program and for the local firms in a number of ways:

▸ If a company is considering expansion in another community, a local CPA firm can prepare a brief *report or study* comparing your state and local taxes with those of your competitors. Have them do comparisons of a variety of your target industries and company sizes. If taxes are higher in your community, for example, you will need to develop materials that show the benefits gained by higher taxes or other significant benefits of doing business in your community.

▸ Accountants work with troubled companies and can be a good source for *early warning* of local firms that are considering out-of-area expansion or whose continued operation is at risk. Because of confidentiality, accountants may be unable to give you specific company names but can refer the firms to your program or help the program identify community barriers facing a number of firms.

▸ Accountants can help BRE staff understand the different financial statements and basic financial ratios.

▸ The large national accounting firms often publish newsletters to keep businesses updated on key accounting issues. Even if there isn't a local office for one of the national companies in your geographic area, they may be willing to put you on a mailing list as part of their marketing and public relations efforts.

▸ Some programs have formal agreements with accountants to be *technical assistance* providers. (See Attachment 8-2, Sample Fee For Service Agreement.)

Attorneys

Attorneys are not used nearly as much as accountants, but they can: contribute sound advice; assist with procedures for changing corporate structure; identify land use rules and regulations regarding zoning, permitting, and development; and assist with industrial revenue bonds and tax increment financing and bankruptcy.

▸ Attorneys who counsel troubled companies may be good *early warning sources*. They may know which firms are considering out-of-area expansion or whose continued operation is at risk. Because of confidentiality, attorneys may not share company names, but they may refer firms to your program.

▸ Large national law firms often publish newsletters to keep businesses updated on key legal issues. For example, Perkins Coie distributes *Washington Employment Law Letter*, published by M. Lee Smith Publishers. Visit their web site at *www.mleesmith.com* for similar publications in other states.

▸ In Washington, some attorneys have provided initial *counsel on a pro-bono basis*. Market the pro-bono time provided by these professionals as community incentives to companies. As with accountants, you may be able to negotiate a sliding scale fee for technical assistance. (See Attachment 8-2.)

Institutional Lenders: Banks, Savings and Loans, and Thrifts

Bankers can be an asset to your retention and expansion program in the following ways:

▸ Discussing *financing* for the company's capital equipment, building loans, operating capital, inventory, lines of credit, etc.

▸ Orienting program staff or businesses on *public and private sector financing* (revolving loan funds, SBA 7A, SBA 504, HUD, block grants, etc.).

▸ Giving feedback on *business plans*, as well as helping staff prioritize time to be spent on "real" companies and risky ventures.

▸ Serving as *early warning* resource persons. They know who is becoming delinquent in payments or having cash flow problems; however, because of confidentiality issues, the bank may not be able to share names of troubled firms. But they can be valuable partners in marketing the BRE program and referring businesses to your program.

UTILITIES PARTNERS

Electrical/Gas Companies

Many large electrical/gas companies have key staff designated to enhance economic development efforts. Because of their long-term investment in local infrastructure, utilities have an interest in maintaining and growing their client base. Retention and expansion is usually a component of their strategies. Typical ways they can help your program include:

▸ Printing of program marketing materials.

▸ Preparing cost comparisons between your city and the company's other location.

▸ Lending insight into the health of the firm. Although information is confidential, field customer service staff can refer business to the program.

▸ Helping you and your company review the capabilities of any industrial/commercial building to see if it fits their power needs.

▸ Reducing costs through discounts and rate reductions.

▸ Working with firms to improve energy efficiency.

Most utilities will help an expanding company design a cost-effective energy approach for a new building, and they may assist existing companies in reducing their power costs through new products and incentives. Many utilities have special energy-saving programs, so have your utility representative explain these programs.

Telecommunications

Telecommunications is more than just your local dial tone or long-distance telephone company. Telecommunications is truly the infrastructure of the future. Both manufacturing and back office operations demand the best in digital switching stations, fiber optics, dual back-up capabilities, etc. From fax lines to sophisticated CNC machine computer systems, the telecommunications operators can assist you, and the businesses you assist, in designing a program to meet their needs. Most telecommunication companies will help by reviewing the capabilities the company needs with respect to specific industrial/commercial buildings.

Ask your largest telecommunication provider to compile a brief study or report which discusses all of the telecommunications capabilities within their service area. Make this report handy for general inquiries from major telecommunications users. (See Chapter 10, Telecommunications.)

Water/Sanitary Sewer Companies

Many areas in your community or county will be served by private water and sanitary sewer companies.

- Introduce yourself to the key district staff for the relevant water and/or sanitary companies (i.e., those districts that serve your commercial/industrial companies).

- Larger districts typically have professional engineering and marketing staffs to assist you and your companies in water/wastewater capacity and design issues.

REAL ESTATE BROKERS

Real estate brokers can refer companies that are delinquent in rent payments, renegotiating leases, or experiencing problems with their expansion plans, and help identify potential sites for companies considering expansion.

ASSOCIATION PARTNERS

Associations or organizations in every community can be helpful to the retention and expansion effort. The most obvious are:

- **Chambers of Commerce** — Good resources for identifying community volunteers for the survey process. They should also be financial investors in your program. Chambers also have resources, such as brochures or videos, available for businesses.

- **Manufacturing associations and networks** — Good sources of information for prospects in their needs for industrial suppliers or sub-suppliers.

  In some places, such as predominately rural areas, there may not be an association or network with whom you can become partners. This would be an excellent opportunity for BRE staff to help organize an appropriate association, especially when there are sectors of more than three types of companies that can work together for the advancement of all of the companies. Examples of industries for which associations can be formed are:

  ▸ *Metalworking and machine shops*
  ▸ *Wood products manufacturers*
  ▸ *Food processing*
  ▸ *Aerospace suppliers*
  ▸ *General manufacturing*

  Oftentimes, after a group has been created, it takes on a life of its own. The members may work on issues that affect them as a business sector, such as ISO 9000 training and implementation, workforce training, and marketing.

- **Port and redevelopment districts** — Unique legislative units of government that offer financing or development opportunities.

- **Industry associations** — Membership organizations that help employers with personnel laws, hiring and firing practices, personnel handbooks, training seminars, wage surveys, etc. These types of organizations can provide prevailing wage information.

- **Regional partnerships** — Consider a regional (multiple city or county) service area that has the advantage of leveraging additional staffing and technical resources to assist businesses.

MEDIA PARTNERS

While the media is not a partner in the traditional sense as others cited above, it does play a very important role in any community. Establish guidelines and develop a working relationship with both broadcast and print media, including television and radio stations, daily newspapers, and the respective news departments of business publications. Meet with local business reporters on a regular basis to establish your credibility as a business information source. Send them press releases on expanding companies and BRE staff activities. Generate positive stories on retention or expansion successes.

If the media does get wind of a troubled company or possible expansion before an official announcement by that company, do not confirm or deny it. Simply tell them you cannot respond to their inquiry and will do your best to personally give them a story when one develops. Stress the importance of confidentiality and how the community could lose a business if they don't maintain their confidence in the organization.

BUSINESS PARTNERS

The best salespersons are businesses that have received services. They can be enlisted as ambassadors to give peer-to-peer recommendations of the program. An excellent spokesperson is often a plant manager who has found the area to be a profitable place. An existing business that is unhappy, of course, is not likely to expand or to recommend the area to others.

Businesses also can be good sources of information on major changes in an industry or with suppliers.

CONSULTANTS

Consultants who work directly with businesses on a regular basis can also be good sources for identifying industry and community issues that affect the ability of those local businesses to survive and grow.

Consider asking consultants to serve on an ad hoc committee to advise program staff regarding the needs of existing businesses. These would include:

— priorities that should be addressed

— type of assistance needed most by local businesses

— assessment of tax abatement programs that really work

— assessment of transportation system and local business's transportation needs

You may want to compile an inventory of local consultants on key retention topics.

PRIVATE/PUBLIC:
WORKFORCE PARTNERS

When surveyed, the majority of companies identify **workforce** as one of their primary needs and problem areas. Knowing that labor availability, productivity, and costs are paramount to companies, program staff needs to respond accordingly with partners. Labor costs account for the majority of the operating costs for businesses. Three critical workforce partners are the labor, workforce, and education sectors.

LABOR

- **Local apprenticeship programs** — Although apprenticeships may not be practical for an at-risk firm, they may be a valuable incentive for an expanding company. Check with your state apprenticeship coordinator (in Washington: (360) 902-5324).

- **Labor unions** — Unions can help identify workforce training issues. Additionally, labor unions are at the plant sites and can be valuable *early warning sources*. Workers are able to observe signs of a business that is at risk, such as a decline in the quality of maintenance, lack of reinvestment, management shakeups or instability, changes in ownership structure, and loss of major customers.

Some BRE programs work with a business/labor group to help resolve problems at specific sites or to help problem-solve in industries experiencing structural changes.

WORKFORCE

Workforce training is a collaborative effort between the program team; local education experts; schools; and statewide, county, or regional resources. Workers can be trained or retrained through courses provided on an ongoing basis, or with classes that are customized to the unique needs of a particular business. By partnering to train workers, communities are able to support the growth of local businesses that might otherwise move to locations with a differently-skilled labor force. Also, as businesses close, workers can be retrained and directed to other companies where their new skills can be used.

In addition to education (discussed below), there are two primary public sector workforce partners:

- **Workforce Development Councils** — regional councils responsible for providing workforce development planning and coordination in their region.
- **One-Stop Centers** (WorkSource in Washington) — offer resources for job seekers and employers.

(See Chapter 9 for information.)

EDUCATION

Educational institutions are concerned about the quality and quantity of the local labor force. Businesses need employees with specific knowledge, ability, and skills. They prefer communities where the labor force is known for high productivity, low absenteeism, and loyalty. Access to ongoing training or continued education through community and technical colleges is an important benefit for companies and employees.

Education partners are found in both the private and public sectors. **Technical/vocational colleges or institutions** are major partners. Talk to public and private sector educational institutions. Community college systems are likely to be the primary providers of employment training programs for most retention and expansion companies, so establish close working relationships with the administration and trainers at those colleges. Also tap the resources of your state university systems. They create

an ongoing pool of workers as well as provide research and development opportunities for collaboration and cooperation with companies. BRE staff may wish to work with these partners to develop a strategy for workforce development to:

- identify employer workforce needs and feed it back to the schools
- help build vocational training capacity in targeted industries
- help retrain workers who have been laid off

Many major universities have research centers or technology centers that can assist companies with technical problems or with development of new technologies that might make firms more competitive.

OTHER PUBLIC/PRIVATE:

MANUFACTURING EXTENSION PROGRAM (MEP)

In Washington state, a majority of BRE contractors have entered into matching agreements with Washington Manufacturing Programs (Washington's MEP) to better serve manufacturing firms in their area by providing information to help them become more competitive.

GET PUBLIC SECTOR PARTNERS IN THE GAME

Public sector partners are just as important as the private sector partners. However, there are fewer options to choose from to help on a regular basis, as compared to private sector partners. Government partners primarily will be involved as technical assistance partners. (Their technical assistance role is explained in Chapter 8.)

Three levels of public sector involvement are critical to the success of productive partnerships for retention and expansion programs: federal, state and local governments.

FEDERAL GOVERNMENT

Federal partners primarily provide technical and financial assistance for the business (see Chapter 8). Federal funding is moving more toward a block grant approach. Consequently, more programs and authority will be given to the state and local government levels.

STATE GOVERNMENT

Elected Officials

State senators and representatives can be important partners in retention and expansion efforts. Their role is to set policy for the state's economic future. In the state budgeting process, they can impact the level of funding available from the state to support local programs. They can also help address barriers to business retention and expansion. For example, in 1995 the State of Washington passed legislation to exempt sales tax on equipment purchases by manufacturers. This helped local manufacturers in retention and expansion efforts.

The most obvious state-elected official who can help is the Governor. When dealing with out-of-state corporate offices in a retention or expansion case, the Governor's Office may be helpful in tipping the scale in decisions to continue operations. You may not always be able to use the Governor, especially if there is another community in the state competing for the same company to expand into their community, because the Governor cannot show favoritism. However, when only one community in the state is being considered, the Governor can write, call, or visit the prospect. Use this resource wisely, and save the Governor's time for companies that will affect the State most.

State Departments

Department of Trade and Economic Development

Every state has a department to address economic development issues. It is important to know which state staff can provide technical assistance for retention and expansion problems, and to ensure that they know local retention and expansion strategy. Get linked into the networks and resources which they can leverage to help retain or expand local businesses. (For Washington state agency information, visit *www.access.wa.gov*.)

This department may offer community, trade, and economic growth initiatives, as well as administer and fund various state financing authorities, loan programs, industrial revenue bond funds, boards of development, etc. If the program is located in a rural area and/or has a limited budget, the dDepartment's staff can help develop the best strategies for that community.

Washington State publishes the *Washington State Business Resource Directory*. This directory of public and private resources is organized by programs and county and available at *http://edd.cted.wa.gov/bac/bizdir/local.htm*.

Other State Agencies

Also be aware of other state departments that can assist in your retention and expansion efforts. Get to know the other agencies who handle retention and expansion issues, such as:

- **One-Stop Centers** (WorkSource for Washington state), to help screen, train, and place employees.

- **Department of Revenue**, for tax credits or deferrals, taxation issues, and program referrals.

- **Department of Ecology**, for environmental compliance issues. Meet with local ecology staff to discuss any potential infrastructure barriers to expansion. For example, if the local wastewater system is at capacity, all expansion plans will be on hold until the system is upgraded.

- **Department of Agriculture** and **Cooperative Extension Services**, for food processing businesses.
- **Small Business Development Centers**, supported by the U.S. Small Business Administration, can be a major player in providing technical assistance to business. These programs are usually located in state population centers and geared to help emerging and entrepreneurial businesses succeed.

For Washington state agency information, visit *www.access.wa.gov.*

LOCAL GOVERNMENT

Local government partners will probably be more familiar than state government partners. They should be—and usually are—very important to retention and expansion success.

Elected Officials

Elected officials partners include city council members, the mayor, and county commissioners. These partners should know and have copies of the retention and expansion strategy. Many local officials are also business people and are aware of the issues first-hand.

Make sure that elected officials receive progress reports on retention and expansion activities. If they are funders of your program, don't just see them at budget time. Invite them to all press conferences or open houses at which a retention and expansion success is celebrated.

Local Departments

Just as elected officials are involved in your retention and expansion strategy, progress reports, and press conferences, apply the same efforts in working with the city manager or supervisor and county executive officer. These two officials will drive your public budget requests and pave the way through the various bureaucratic departments for the benefit of companies. In addition to the senior executives for the city and county, develop personal relationships with the planning director, public works director, and community development director. Close communication and partnership is a must.

Finding just the right partner is a possibility in just about any community. Be resourceful in building a project team.

PARTNERSHIP CASE STUDY:

PACIFIC CIRCUITS

An overconfident announcement by a company poised to relocate may still signal opportunity, as it did in the case of Pacific Circuits, Inc. Owned by Trey Coley, the company has been in business since 1978, employs 400 people, and grosses annual sales of $50 million. Pacific Circuits builds customer-designed and specific "boards" for such items as computers, medical devices, and telecommunications equipment—even fish finders. Customers supply the company with computer-aided drafting information, and Coley's staff uses that information to generate hole placement that will ultimately generate images for circuit boards.

The foundation of a deal to keep this growing manufacturing firm with a workforce of 400 from expanding outside its home state was literally laid down over a cup of morning coffee. The CEO of Pacific Circuits wanted to expand his company, but not at its present urban location. A relocation site in a neighboring state, which taxes neither capital equipment purchases nor manufacturing products, was starting to look good. The company figured they could save $1 million in sales tax annually on a new plant and equipment if it moved out of state.

BRE staff read about Pacific Circuits' proposed move in the business pages of a major newspaper from the other side of the state. The paper quoted economic development professionals as welcoming the company to their state. But the director of the Washington State's Business Retention and Expansion Program didn't believe the move was a done deal. So he picked up the phone.

The next morning staff met with the company CEO. During the conversation he learned three things that laid the groundwork for the retention deal:

▶ **The company's last expansion at its current location had dragged on interminably and came in over budget.** A building permit had taken 14 months to obtain for an operation that needed to be up and running in 18 months. Compliance with environmental regulations involved in the expansion contributed to delays. Additionally, the city had done little to streamline the process and had not mounted a campaign to retain the company.

▶ **Company management really had no particular desire to expand out of state.** Moving and travel costs for management and employees, plus training of new workers, would be hard on the company's bottom line.

▶ The president liked Idaho's plan for tax breaks and an offer to share some of the costs associated with hiring and training new people. **But what came through in his talk with BRE staff was a genuine desire to locate his company in a community that valued its presence and contribution to the local economy.** He also wanted help finding an appropriate site and a one-stop process for permitting and moving the building of the new plant along.

When the company's CEO was asked to consider taking a look at a community located just one and a half hours from his current operation, he agreed.

▶

BRE staff made contact with the Economic Development Association of Skagit County in northwestern Washington. The state had classified the county as economically distressed, had exempted local businesses from sales tax on plants and equipment, and issued them business and occupational (B & O) tax credits in return for creating new jobs.

The most important aspect in the expansion of Pacific Circuits was the receptiveness and cooperation of the entire Skagit County community. The Economic Development Association, in partnership with many organizations and agencies, worked to expedite all the issues—site location, wastewater discharge permits, general regulatory issues and building and occupancy permits, assistance with financing issues, coordination of tax and business incentives, and assistance with labor and training.

"The Skagit community is well organized, cooperative, and focused on the need to create jobs. The permitting process is streamlined to allow good projects to happen with dispatch," said Executive Director Don Wick.

Principally, strong cooperation on the project came from the cities of Anacortes and Burlington and from the Ports of Skagit County and Anacortes, from the Department of Community, Trade and Economic Development, the Department of Ecology, the Department of Employment Security, the Private Industry Council, and Skagit Valley College.

As Port of Skagit County Director Jerry Heller said, "This is a good example of cooperation among many public officials working to generate capital investment and new jobs within the county."

Nearly one year after the first meeting with the CEO, Pacific Circuits cut the ribbon on its new, $14-million, 71,000 square-foot plant near the Skagit County community of Burlington. The relocation will add about 35 more employees and, over the next three years may increase to as many as 500, making it a solid new corporate citizen in the area. In the relocation deal, Pacific Circuits received tax credits and deferrals, along with training incentive funds provided for dislocated timber workers.

Like all deals, the Pacific Circuits relocation project had its glitches. But the partnership among the Skagit County business community, the local economic development council, the Port of Skagit County and the State kept the process on track, on budget, and on time.

Pacific Circuits is a classic case of a BRE effort starting late, but moving fast to identify the real issues and working tirelessly to put a good deal together.

•

An active early warning system can alert your BRE team to a company's dissatisfaction with the local business environment and possible interest in expanding or relocating out of your area. Monitoring local and regional daily newspapers and business journals can spotlight opportunities in other communities.

The key is to persevere. Even relocation plans that appear to indicate a done deal may still be open to negotiation.

CHAPTER 4

BUSINESS/INDUSTRY INFORMATION
SCOUTING OUT YOUR LOCAL BUSINESSES

CLOSE ENCOUNTERS OF THE BUSINESS KIND

The goal of a successful BRE program is more than saving companies. It's also understanding the companies that will drive your community's economic engine.

While most new jobs will be created by local companies, there is surprisingly few information exchanges between local and county government and companies. Input from employers is becoming even more crucial as larger companies "outsource" production. How well do you know your businesses?

YOUR MOTHER WAS RIGHT: DO YOUR HOMEWORK

Asking the right questions has a lot to do with getting the right answers—the answers that will help identify expanding and troubled local companies and move on to proposing alternatives and solutions. Every community economic development organization needs to be able to do its own in-house research. Following is a short list of some of the standard data sources that are available in most libraries or can be obtained on CD-ROM or by online services. Some of these sources overlap, but by cross-referencing and comparing them it is possible to obtain an excellent composite analysis.

BUSINESS INFORMATION DUE DILIGENCE

Prior to a major business visitation or technical assistance session:

- Spend some quality time with public documents and publications that reveal how a targeted company has done in the past and where it may be headed in the future.

- Develop a working knowledge of the industries to which the targeted company belongs.

- Tap an informal network of information sources to determine how the company is viewed locally (i.e., civic ties, involvement in the community, interaction with local government, and compliance with local, state, or federal regulations).

- Create a profile of the company's CEO. Their personality will often be reflected in the company's corporate culture.

GETTING THE GOSPEL ACCORDING TO THE COMPANY

In conducting due diligence on a publicly held company, start with its annual report. This publication will be available upon request from most companies, or on file at your local library.

Make sure you are on the mailing list of large publicly held businesses within your community to receive the company's annual report (or yearly business summary). This report is targeted to shareholders, so expect some varnished truths about losses, employment problems, product glitches, and other issues. Annual reports can provide the following information:

— Who sits on the company's board of directors and in its executive offices.

— Where its headquarters and branch operations are located.

— What kinds of acquisitions the company has made, whether they offer access to new markets and new products, and whether they're in line with the local plant's production.

— Which divisions or plants have yielded the highest or lowest profit rates. If the local plant is on the low side, its long-term viability may be at risk.

— Where the company is spending its capital and how much has been earmarked for your local plant.

— Whether the company is spending resources on research and development.

— What's in the new-product pipeline, and whether markets are expanding or contracting.

— What level of dividends the company is paying. An unusually high dividend could indicate disinvestment in critical growth and development areas.

— Where the company's long-term loans are held. Public sector loans—industrial revenue bonds, urban development action grants or other public financing—can sometimes be used to deter a company from shutting down local plants.

Early warning of retention issues, such as if a local plant is identified as a marginal profit center, may be found in the company's annual report.

Note: You can purchase a database of the branches and subsidiaries in your geographic area from Dun & Bradstreet. Dial 1-800-234-3867.

ADD GOVERNMENT-REQUIRED REPORTS TO YOUR STASH

The U.S. Securities and Exchange Commission (SEC) requires publicly held companies to file annual 10-K reports and proxy statements containing detailed financial information. Here's a sample of the information these documents will yield:

▸ A description of the company's markets and major product lines, as well as indications of where it stands among prime competitors.

▸ A rundown of the company's labor relations, including work stoppages, strikes, and layoffs.

▸ A listing of plant closures and indications of future shutdowns.

▸ Other factors affecting the business's success, such as outstanding lawsuits that involve allegations of environmental abuse, unsafe or defective products, low- or no-interest loans to executives, pay levels of officers, and more.

Publicly held companies also must file brief quarterly reports with the SEC detailing recent financial information, including acquisitions, restructuring, or other strategic initiatives. The SEC's data search system, Electronic Data Gathering Analysis and Retrieval System (EDGAR), is found on the Internet at *www.sec.gov*.

GETTING THE LOWDOWN ON PRIVATE COMPANIES

Privately held companies are not required by law to disclose their business results in annual reports or in filings with the SEC. Generating information on these operations means digging in trade and business journals, traditional financial publications, government industry reports, newspapers, and periodicals. The best place to begin is your local library.

ANALYSIS OF TARGET COMPANIES

The references below are in hard copy directories available in libraries or by purchase. Most of them are also available on CD-ROM as well as online database services, such as the comprehensive Dialogue Information Services, Inc. (developed by Lockheed), which offers access to most business information databases.

Moody's Industrial Manual

This is one of the true gems in the business. In addition to providing extensive information about public companies listed on the major stock exchanges, it also describes their facilities by location, size, type, and how much space is leased vs. owned. The biweekly updates have a special listing in the index for new company expansions. It is an excellent source of information on geographical patterns of company locations,

which may provide clues on future location patterns as well. Visit *www.fisonline.com/a/lucent.pdf*, or *http://wncln.appstate.edu/search/t?moodystindustrialmanual*.

Dun & Bradstreet Million Dollar Directory

There are several kinds of D&B directories, but the *Million Dollar Directory* serves most company research requirements. In addition to basic information, it also gives company performance data and describes market coverage. It includes both public and private companies, but the information on private firms should be viewed with caution, as it is provided by the firms themselves and may not be entirely objective. Visit *www.dnbmdd.com/mddi/*.

Hoover Pros Plus

This website has up-to-date biographical data on company officers and directors. The information can provide economic development staff with a thorough grounding in the people who run a company or guide its strategy. Visit *www.hoovers.com/hoov/about/detail*.

InfoUSA Sales & Marketing Leads

InfoUSA gathers data from multiple sources, such as 5,200 Yellow Pages and Business White Pages directories; federal, state, city, and county government data, bankruptcy records, leading business magazines, and more. Its database includes nearly every business, no matter how small, large, or newly established. Reports include useful marketing information such as contact names, number of employees, and fax numbers. Visit *www.infousa.com/homesite/da.html*.

Standard & Poors Corporations

This directory is similar to the D&B directory in that it provides basic information about major companies. Visit *http:// products.dialog.com/products/oddatas/sandp. htm.*

State Directories of Manufacturers

If the market area is within one state, or a region comprised of a few states, then the various state directories of manufacturers can be an excellent source of company data. In the western U.S., the Database Publishing Company produces manufacturers registers for Arizona, California, Nevada, Oregon, Utah, and Washington. For California, they also provide information on service companies, technology companies, wholesalers, and firms engaged in international trade. Their information is available in hard copy, floppy disks, and CD-ROM. They also provide a compilation of database services to assist in transferring the data to a marketing program. These directories are published with the support and cooperation of the respective state economic development agencies. Visit website *http:// manufacturersnews.com/products.asp.*

Consider creating your own regional Directory of Manufacturers.

TRADE JOURNALS AND BUSINESS PUBLICATIONS

Look for information on specific industries in trade journals and business publications, as well as interviews with top management, that can give insight into a company's strategies, its financial condition, and where it stands among competitors. Many stories will focus on a company's ability to generate profit and what management should be doing to take profitability to higher levels.

Business Magazines:

Fortune, Forbes, Business Week, and *Inc.* publish annual performance charts of changes in sales, profits, employment, and other indicators for various sectors of the economy. *Fortune,* for example, ranks the top 25 industries in order of their sales growth from the previous year, using medians for all companies in each industry (not industry averages). While these are short-term changes, the list offers insights into which industries are likely to be looking at capital expansion budgets.

While not all areas have the size of businesses that may be featured in these publications, they can help provide information on the targeted industries.

Regional Business Journals:

Don't overlook local business publications, such as, *Daily Journal of Commerce, Washington CEO Magazine, Puget Sound Business Journal,* or *Spokane Business Journal,* which provide information on local businesses and issues as well as lists of different types of businesses and resources.

Trade Magazines:

If you want to research specific industries, the magazines published by and for those industries usually have annual statistical reports and forecasts.

GOVERNMENT INDUSTRIAL REPORTS

INDUSTRY CLASSIFICATION SYSTEMS: SIC, NAICS, and NAPCS

The U.S. *Standard Industrial Classification* (SIC) system was developed in 1930 by the federal government to enable statisticians to more easily measure industrial activity. SIC emphasizes manufacturing, but it doesn't provide good coverage for the growing service and high-tech industries.

The *North American Industry Classification System* (NAICS)—pronounced "nakes"—was developed in 1997 by the three North American Free Trade Agreement countries—United States, Canada, and Mexico—to meet the changing economy and to bring these nations into a single system. It establishes a new set of industry numbers and expands the current four-digit SIC system to six digits. NAICS is intended to provide comparable statistics across the three countries. It also provides for increased comparability with the International Standard Industrial Classification System developed and maintained by the United Nations.

Under NAICS, economic units that use like processes to produce goods or services are grouped together. NAICS includes some 350 newly recognized industries, such as the high-tech industries of fiber optic cable manufacturing, satellite communications, and the reproduction of computer software. Many of the newly recognized industries also reflect changes in the way business is done, such as bed-and-breakfast inns, environmental consulting, and warehouse clubs. The NAICS system was revised in 2002, and revisions are planned every five years. NAICS is being phased in by statistical agencies and is expected to fully replace SIC by 2005.

In 1999, the three NAFTA countries launched a joint multiphase initiative to develop a new, comprehensive, demand-oriented product classification system to complement the supply- or industry-of-origin–based NAICS classification. The new system will be known as the *North American Product Classification System* (NAPCS). The initial efforts are directed at identifying and defining products and services of industries in four NAICS sectors: Information, Finance, Professional, Scientific, and Technical Services; Administrative and Support; Waste Management; and Remediation Services.

For more information on NAICS, visit *www.census.gov/epcd/naics*. For a bridge from SIC to NAIC, visit *www.census.gov/epcd/www/naicstab.htm#download*.

Overall Industry Analysis

U.S. Industrial Outlook, published annually by U.S. Department of Commerce, International Trade Division, is a primary source for analyzing current and forecast trends for U.S. industries by four-digit SIC code. In addition to statistical data on value of shipments and employment, there are excellent narratives on industry trends, competitive factors, material on regulation, technological advances and vulnerability of its industry to restructuring. This information may be found at the website: *www.ita.doc.gov/industry/otea/usio/usio95.html*.

LOCAL AND REGIONAL NEWSPAPERS

Local and regional newspapers provide a wealth of information on a company's public life, including changes in management or markets; the strengths and weaknesses of product(s); legal, labor, and compliance issues; presence in the community; partnerships; remarks by leaders; gripes from customers, and more. Often, a company CEO or president will write an opinion-editorial piece which can help identify business needs.

TAX AND ECONOMIC DEVELOPMENT RECORDS

If a company is in financial trouble, one of the first things to slide is local tax payment. Since those records are public documents, check on the tax status of local firms at the city assessor's office.

Economic development organizations often keep detailed files on major local employers that can yield information on how these businesses relate to the commu-

as well as current leases on industrial buildings.

INDUSTRY COMPARISONS

Robert Morris Associates (RMA) Annual Statement Studies

RMA provides composite financial data on manufacturing, wholesaling, retailing, service, and contracting businesses with assets less than $250 million. A comparison of this composite financial data to a particular company will offer an indication of the health of that company relative to similar companies. Financial data compares information from balance sheet, income statement, and statement of cash flow. Companies are listed by their size and SIC code. Data is used by 80 percent of the commercial lenders in loan decisions.

Online News Services

A quick way to review industry issues and press releases is through one of the Internet news network services which broadcast national and international news, stock information, industry updates, weather from around the globe, scores, and other news from sources such as CNN, CNNfn, *Time*, *People*, and *Money* Magazines, Reuters, PR Newswire, and BusinessWire.

Value Line Data Base Service

This source also offers information on industry changes, primarily as a means to support financial outlooks for individual companies.

Standard & Poors Compustat Services, Inc.

A good source for predictions of emerging industries, which offers both hard copy and electronic forms of its analyses. A recent report identified wireless communications, multimedia systems, recycling,

biotechnology, and flatpanel display electronics as emerging industries with high-growth potential. Similar kinds of reports, especially for smaller businesses, can be found in *Inc.*, *Money*, *Entrepreneur*, and various investor publications.

State Labor Market Information

The Department of Labor, Bureau of Labor Statistics, contracts with each state to collect labor market information. In addition to labor market information about firms and occupational wage data, special reports on industry and regional employment trends are often published. Many states have this information on the Internet. Washington's Labor Market and Economic Analysis Branch's Internet site is: *www.wa.gov/esd/lmea*.

Other Sources

Several of the magazines listed above publish annual rankings of company and industry sector performance. Look at which companies are performing at the top of the charts, identifying their industries by SIC codes, then examining the overall industry characteristics to find other outstanding performers.

Many other sources can be used to analyze markets and target companies. The ones listed above are only a small sample, but they offer a place to start. Fortunately, the Internet has opened up major electronic sources for gathering information. There are hundreds of database sources worldwide. By relating the target selection back to the community analysis, it is important to identify the *reasons* why those companies should consider remaining or expanding in your community.

EARLY WARNING SIGNS

"ONE IF BY LAND AND TWO IF BY SEA..."

Lights in a Boston belfry tower triggered one of the more notable early warning systems in American history. And it spurred Paul Revere to ride through the night alerting the countryside that the British were on the move.

Today, early warning is still important in signaling critical movement. It operates as a major component of business retention and expansion programs (BREs) to identify companies in danger of closing, relocating, expanding out of the area, or laying off workers. Advance knowledge of these red-flag problems is crucial for giving the community an opportunity to work with a company on its decision or to plan strategies to counter the negative impacts that inevitably follow closure or relocation of a business.

More importantly, understanding early warning indicators, whether identified as immediate danger signs or as long-term patterns, can buy a community necessary time to develop alternatives to plant closures and job loss.

SPOTTING AT-RISK BUSINESSES

In theory, an early warning system flags at-risk companies based on information gathered from research on industries and businesses, surveys, and during business visitations or follow-ups (Chapters 4,

6, and 7). But in many cases, closings, relocations, layoffs, and out-of-area expansions are planned events that can be anticipated by monitoring key long- and short-term indicators.

IT'S NOT A DONE DEAL UNTIL THE INK IS DRY

The information needed by the BRE team to help keep companies from relocating and expanding outside the area hits the front steps every day. Local and regional newspapers and business journals routinely carry economic development stories that can reveal a lot about companies potentially on the move:

- What they produce, where their markets are, and current employment levels.
- The names of CEOs and top managers to contact.
- What type of new facility, services, and infrastructure they will require for relocation or expansion.
- Whether new workers will need to be hired and trained.
- Which communities are trying to recruit them.

Also consider using community and labor leaders as part of the program's early warning system.

Use both formal and informal networks to stay informed about local business.

EARLY WARNING TOOLS

A number of approaches can be used for identifying red flags. The local BRE program may want to try one or a combination of the following early warning tools:

- Flyer to businesses (see sample in Attachment 5-1).
- Short mail survey (see Chapter 6).
- Long survey — business visitation by BRE program staff or visitation team (see Chapter 7).

- Partners' (private sector, unions, employees, newspaper, etc.) communication on early warning signs. It is important to provide training to this group on what to observe so they can be the community's eyes and ears.
- Dun & Bradstreet Early Alert System — lists subsidiaries and branches with out-of-state corporate offices. These branches can be more at-risk as a result of acts by the parent corporation. The D&B system indicates a company's actual and historical payment performance as reported to Dun & Bradstreet.
- Worker Adjustment and Retraining Notification (WARN) — This federally legislated directive requires businesses that employ 100 or more full-time employees to give a 60-day notice of a plant closure or mass layoff to state and local offices (see Attachment 5-2). Unfortunately, few workers receive this notice, and 90 days usually is not sufficient time for turnaround intervention.
- Observation by BRE staff, community leaders and task force/committee members.

The following questions can provide additional insight into a company and its future. It is important not to jump to conclusions but to follow up with the firm to get accurate information.

EARLY WARNING SIGNS

- Sales and employment downturns
- Overall business climate
- Business climate complaints
- Rezoning initiatives
- Aging owners in family-owned businesses
- Conglomerate ownership; multisite operations

- Duplicate capacity
- Disinvestment
- Management myopia
- Management instability
- Unusual bargaining positions
- Expanding employment or sales

ROUND UP THE USUAL SUSPECTS —

Sales and Employment Downturns

Declining sales and reduced employment are probably the most obvious signals that a company is in trouble. They also indicate that time is a critical factor in mounting a rescue or salvage operation. When is the cutoff for doing any good? By the time a company issues the 60-day advance notice of closing required by the federal government, it is probably too late to act. An action plan needs to be in motion well before that point to yield results.

- Has a decline in sales paralleled a general industry decline, or does it reflect a separate trend?

- Is market share being steadily eroded?

- Are key client relationships breaking down?

- Has management consistently misread the market and competitive environment?

- Has the company experienced steady or drastic decline in employment?

- Is an increasing amount of work being outsourced?

- Is excessive overtime replacing the hiring of new staff?

- Has employee or management turnover increased significantly?

TRACK THE GENERAL BUSINESS —

Overall Business Climate

An active awareness of the overall business climate is crucial for charting the health of companies in the community, especially if the majority are members of cyclical industries. Increases in the cost of debt and erratic prime lending rates can spell trouble for large and small businesses alike. Changes in markets, booming technological advances, and restrictive government regulation can leave companies on the defensive and unable to withstand increased competition.

- Does the company's business cycle coincide with that of its industry?

- Are employment levels consistent with the rest of the industry?

- Are sales increasing or declining in line with the rest of the industry?

- Is the industry itself growing or declining?

- Is the company able to stay ahead of technological advances in its industry?

- Is the company positioned to respond to changes in its marketplace?

- Is the company gaining or losing market share?

- Are the life cycles of the company's main products coming to an end?

- Is the company experiencing increased competition in its traditional marketplace?

- Is the company competitive in expanded global markets?

- Are the company's primary competitors relocating to a common region?

GAUGE THE GROUSING LEVEL —

Business Climate Complaints

One of the first indicators that a company is in trouble, considering pulling up stakes, or planning an out-of-area expansion is management's expressed dissatisfaction with the local business environment. Such complaints may reflect genuine problems that need to be addressed by the community, or they may be diversionary tactics to shift the blame for poor business results away from management. Public issues such as high taxes and workers' compensation rates, restrictive building code requirements, high operating costs, and a poorly trained workforce typically draw fire from businesses.

- Does the company/community have access to a well-trained labor force?

- Does it have ties and proximity to suppliers, contractors, and its major markets?

- Does it have easy access to materials and transportation and a pool of experienced managers?

- Has the company engaged the services of a site consultant?

- Has the company sought public sector incentives to maintain or expand its business in the community?

- What incentives is the community willing or able to offer to retain the company?

- Are worker training grants available?

THERE GOES THE NEIGHBORHOOD —

Rezoning Initiatives

For many urban areas, initiatives to redevelop traditional industrial sites are two-edged swords. Rezoning and upscaling of manufacturing areas along rivers, lakes, and other coastlines may have city leaders pointing with pride, but such action can also cause displacement of local firms and their workforces. The quandary facing BRE programs is how to accommodate the creeping gentrification* of these areas, while keeping local businesses and jobs in the city.

---

*The process of rebuilding deteriorating areas by middle-class or affluent people which often causes displacement of earlier, typically poorer, residents and manufacturing firms.

Good communication is critical to this process. Targeted companies, their management and employees, local labor unions, and other businesses in the area need to be a part of negotiations. Early identification of this trend will help your team achieve consensus and craft workable solutions.

- Is the land around the plant being sold and converted to nonindustrial use?

- Are neighboring industrial businesses selling their land and moving out?

- Is land value in the area rising?

- Are property taxes going up?

- Has a public hearing to debate rezoning been scheduled?

- Are public sector initiatives in place to locate suitable alternative space for the plant in the community?

THE ISSUE OF OWNERSHIP —

Family-owned Businesses

The ownership of a company can have prime implications for its continuing viability as an operational business. Family-owned firms appear to be particularly vulnerable to a variety of long-term problems that may lead to closure or sell-off. Only about 25 percent of family-owned businesses survive a third generation of family ownership without a significant shift to outside ownership or investment. Additionally, the current top management may include family members with varying degrees of business ability, experience, and willingness to address real problems within the company.

A 1997 survey found that nearly one-third of Washington state's family-owned businesses expected to change hands by 2002. Success or failure of any significant leadership changes will impact the health of the economy.

- Has the company built a record of success under the current or founding management?

- Is there a succession plan in place with a well-qualified family member ready to assume the top management slot? (The survey found that 25 percent of the firms had no succession plan.)

- Is there evidence that managers are leaving the company because they perceive limited advancement opportunities?

- If no family member is prepared to lead the business, will the company consider addressing the succession issue with an employee stock ownership plan (ESOP), management buyout, or combination approach? (See Chapter 8 for more information on ESOPs.)

Conglomerate Ownership, Multisite Operations

A plant owned by a publicly traded corporation diversified along geographical and product lines should merit special attention from your early warning action committee. Such organizations tend to have minimal loyalty to any one site and frequently channel resources into business segments with potentially high growth rates and profitability. Typically, multisite operations experience high rates of management turnover and tend to emphasize achievement of short-term profitability targets over longer-term growth strategies. Today there is increasing pressure on such organizations to maximize shareholder return.

(*Note: A listing of branches and subsidiaries in your community may be purchased from Dun & Bradstreet.*)

- Has the conglomerate diversified into several industries, or is its business focus narrower?

- Are individual plants positioned in the conglomerate as branches or divisions?

- Has local management been fairly stable?

- Does the local plant maintain a positive cash flow?

- Is the plant contributing to the profitability of the conglomerate?

- Are the core industries pursued by the conglomerate considered to be cyclical?

- Is the home office of the conglomerate outside the state? Outside the country?

- If the plant is unionized, how does conglomerate management deal with the union on issues of contract renewal and partnership?

- Does management view the plant as an asset that needs to demonstrate targeted level of profit?

- Is there a trend to locate this type of plant in a certain region or country?

DUPLICATE CAPACITY CAN SPELL TROUBLE

If a company does business at more than one location, a management option to cut costs and increase profitability is to consolidate operations or to move production between plants. The pattern of job movement begins with relocation of the least-skilled positions and proceeds until high-skill and administrative jobs are absorbed into the new location, and the old facility is either closed or sold. A prime indicator that changes are imminent is the movement of accounting functions to a new site. Additionally, the consolidation of accounts receivable and payable under a new organization is a strong warning sign.

- Have changes in production capacity been observed at the local plant?

- Are other facilities being developed to take the local plant's place?

- Has the company acquired the operation of a competitor which might duplicate production of the local plant?

- Has movement of jobs from the local plant been noted?

THE DISINVESTMENT SPIRAL

When a company ceases to invest a reasonable share of its profits into plant modernization and maintenance, it could be signaling its intention to downsize or close the facility in the future. Lack of investment could also indicate that the parent company is "milking" the local facility to improve its cash flow, to fund acquisition or diversification initiatives, or to pay out high dividends to company shareholders. Whatever the reason, disinvestment tends to create a self-perpetuating downward spiral that frequently results in closure and job loss.

- Has the company's spending for maintenance, repairs or modernization declined lately?

- Did the decline coincide with changes in ownership or in key management positions?

- Is the company's debt-to-equity ratio high, yielding fewer funds for plant investment?

- Has the company sold equipment or transferred it to other facilities?

- Has the company asked for wage and benefit concessions from its workforce?

- Does the exterior of the plant and grounds indicate a lack of maintenance?

- Is the plant's equipment so old that production is inefficient or of lower quality than that of domestic and global competitors?

A CASE OF MANAGEMENT MYOPIA —

General Management

A company at risk often can be identified by the length of its vision. The replacement of long-term planning strategies by short-term tactics, the lack of clearly defined business goals and blocked internal communication channels can signal that a business is headed for sale or closure. Failure to reinvest in plant facilities and in adequate research and development initiatives indicates that interest in production efficiencies and product innovation is limited.

- Has the company taken recent steps to diversify its product base?

- Is there evidence of failure to act on worker ideas?

- Has quality control dropped off?

- Have company relations with local organized labor deteriorated?

- Are sales becoming dependent on a smaller pool of customers?

- Is there evidence of nepotism and cronyism in hiring?

- Have company executives abandoned the basic tenants of good management, such as planning, organization, evaluation, and communication?

WHO'S ON FIRST?

Management Instability/Changes

One way to determine whether a company is in trouble is to take a hard look at management. Is management acting as if it plans to be here a year from now? Two years from now? If the answer is no, changes may not be far away. Heavy management turnover is also a prime indicator that a company's days as a going concern are numbered.

- Are managers increasingly isolating themselves from other employees?

- Has communication between management and rank and file broken down?

- Is there evidence of indecisiveness and delays in taking appropriate action?

- Have current managers been abusive to employees and outsiders?

- Has the company ceased to participate in community activities?
- Has the company noticeably increased security in and around the plant?
- Have managers put their homes up for sale? Are they renting living quarters?
- Are incoming managers known for implementing downsizing strategies and layoffs?
- Have new management families taken steps to become part of the community? Have they bought homes or are they renting?
- Has unusual bargaining over severance packages been undertaken?
- Are regularly scheduled job evaluations and raises being routinely backlogged?

OTHER SIGNS —

Unusual Bargaining Positions

- Is the company dragging its feet in contract bargaining?
- Is the company negotiating for a shorter contract length, backloading the contract, or changing severance pay clauses?

Expanding Employment and Sales

- Has the company just negotiated a major deal?
- Is the company outgrowing their current facility?

THE FAT LADY IS SINGING —

Imminent Danger Signs

When these red flags begin to fly, it's a sure bet that a company is either ready to shut its doors or pack up and move. Eleventh-hour attempts by your early warning action committee should include clear and present alternatives to closure. At this point it's probably too late to sweeten the pot for a company bent on pulling up stakes and moving to a new location.

- Are workers being laid off from profitable product lines?
- Is equipment necessary to plant production being removed?
- Are suppliers demanding C.O.D. payment for materials?
- Are inventory levels spiraling downward?
- Are paychecks bouncing?
- Are unidentified persons touring the plant facility?
- Are equipment and property appraisers and auctioneers on site?

TIMING ISN'T EVERYTHING, BUT IT'S DARN CLOSE

Can BRE save every company from closing its doors or moving on? Unhappily, no. But the goal is to get in the game early enough so that all possible solutions are put forth and all viable alternatives are acted upon.

Program success can hinge on the ability to build and sustain a keen awareness of the local business environment and to make the right connections.

Management guru Tom Peters calls "connection power" one of the premier skills of the '90s. He may be right. Connections are at the core of everything from quantum mechanics to economics to business, retention and expansion programs.

Connecting with local businesses to determine which are at risk of closing, relocating, downsizing, or expanding out of the area will lead to those who can identify the real problems, and still others who can craft solutions.

Keeping information channels open, asking the right questions, and making the right connections will go a long way to stacking the deck in favor of a community's economic vitality.

CASE STUDY:

POTENTIAL
CORPORATE DIVESTITURE

A local Union Carbide facility was put at risk when its parent company, headquarters in Danbury, Connecticut, put it up for sale. The local facility was unprofitable, experiencing a decrease in sales, and was an unlikely fit with the rest of Union Carbide's chemical divisions. Union Carbide grows crystals that are used in Department of Defense programs, as well as aerospace applications. Its major customer is the federal government.

Local BRE staff read in the newspaper that Union Carbide was up for sale and notified the state BRE staff. State and local staff developed a strategy for contacting Union Carbide, and spent the next 24 months working with its plant manager and the city's major employer to retain 100 jobs. Initially, state staff worked with the plant manager to identify areas of the business that needed improvement. Union Carbide needed to increase sales and diversify its client base.

About 12 months into working with Union Carbide, the company became profitable. The corporate office invested capital into high-tech equipment, which helped increase productivity. Discussions were held about how the manager could purchase the company.

The role of the local BRE staff was multitasked: it included providing an entry for state staff to meet the president and manager, researching state and federal loan programs and what role these monies would play in the financing, and keeping the lines of communication open.

When the manager began writing his business plan to purchase the company, Union Carbide decided to keep the local facility open. As a result of BRE local and state assistance, the company's profitability improved, which in turn resulted in the headquarter's decision to keep the division.

HOW'S YOUR COMPANY FEELING TODAY?

Please check the appropriate boxes:

☐ We are experiencing some problems. Please contact us.

☐ We are doing fine. Thank you.

☐ We are interested in information about available financing programs.

☐ We would like more details on sales and B&O tax credits available for manufacturers.

☐ We are considering market expansion through export. Please let us know what help may be available.

☐ There are other problems/issues affecting our business that may be helped by outside attention.

Briefly describe: _____

_____

Please make any necessary changes to the label below:

SUMMARY OF THE
WORKER ADJUSTMENT AND RETRAINING
NOTIFICATION ACT (WARN)

KEY DEFINITIONS

Acceptable Notice — The mailing of notice to an employee's last known address or inclusion of notice in the employee's paycheck.

Affected Employers — "business enterprises" employing 100 or more workers, excluding part-time workers.

Employment Loss — Termination of employment for more than 6 months, or a reduction in hours of more than 50 percent during each month of the 6-month period.

Mass Layoff — A reduction in force, not the result of a plant closing, during a 30-day period which affects at least 33 percent of the workforce, but not less than 50 employees, or at least 500 employees (not including part-time employees).

Plant Closing — Permanent or temporary shutdown of a single site, a facility or operating unit within a single site that affects more than *50 employees over a 30-day period.*

ADVANCE NOTICE REQUIRED

An employer shall give 60-day notice of a plant closing or mass layoff to the following:

— Each representative of the affected employees, or each employee, if no representative exists.

— The state dislocated worker unit.

— The chief elected official of the area where the closing occurs.

Exceptions:

1. Less than 60-day notice can be given if:

    ▸ The employer was actively seeking capital or business which would have enabled the employer to avoid or postpone the shutdown, and the employer reasonably and in good faith believed that giving notice would have precluded the employer from obtaining the needed capital or business.

    ▸ The layoff or closing is caused by business circumstances that were not reasonably foreseen.

    ▸ The layoff or closing is caused by a natural disaster.

Under such circumstances the employer must give as much notice as practicable and shall provide a statement of the basis for reducing the notification period.

2. The Act does not apply if:

    ▶ The closing is of a temporary facility or is the result of the completion of a particular project, and the affected employees understand that their employment was limited to the duration of the project at the outset.

    ▶ The closing or layoff constitutes a strike or a lockout not intended to evade the requirements of the Act.

SALE OF BUSINESS

In the case of a business sale, the seller is responsible for providing notice of the sale. After the effective date of the sale, the purchaser is responsible for providing notice of any plant closing or mass layoff.

Exceptions:

A worker is not considered to have sustained an "employment loss" if the closing is the result of a relocation or consolidation of the business and the employer offered to transfer the employee.

PENALTIES AND FINES

Affecting Employees

An employer who violates the Act is liable for:
    ▶ Back pay for each day of violation that is the higher of the average pay for the last 3 years or the final rate of pay.
    ▶ Benefits, including the cost of medical expenses.

This liability is for a maximum of 60 days and can be reduced by:
    ▶ Any wages paid during the period of the violation.
    ▶ Voluntary, unconditional payments to the employee.
    ▶ Payments to a third party, such as premiums for health benefits.

Affecting Local Governments

    ▶ If a local government is not notified, the employer shall be subject to a civil penalty of up to $500 for each day of the violation.
    ▶ If the employer proves to the satisfaction of the court that the omission was in good faith, the court may reduce the penalties.

Enforcement

Employees or local governments may sue employers in any district court of the U.S. in any district where the violation occurred or where the employer does business.

CHAPTER 6

SURVEYS
TAKING THE PULSE OF LOCAL BUSINESS

When visiting the doctor, one of the first things that happens is that your pulse and blood pressure is taken, then the doctor gets into diagnosing specific problems.

Surveying is a good method of taking the community's pulse. This chapter provides both an introduction to surveying and a discussion on the use of the short survey as an early-warning tool for retention and expansion issues.

Maintaining a long-term, active awareness of the local business environment is a crucial element of the BRE mission. To build that awareness program staff need current business information about the companies that call the community home. They need direct, candid contacts with the management of those companies to get that information. They also need to establish credibility as a reliable resource.

"THERE ARE LIES, DAMNED LIES, AND STATISTICS"

Nineteenth century British Prime Minister Benjamin Disraeli was right: You just can't trust numbers. When it comes to surveying, the goal is to develop a database on companies. Forget statistics.

Focus on the specific information needed to identify problems and get to solutions.

There are three basic types of survey methodology: telephone, visitation/in person, and mail (or self-administered).

To determine the most appropriate surveying methodology, it is important to look at the desired outcomes. Attachment 6-1 looks at the advantages and disadvantages of the three methods. These surveys aren't meant to be academic exercises that seek data to support theories, create methodologies, or fill textbooks.

Each BRE survey is a strategic tool to help you build long-term relationships with the companies in your community. It can help you:
- understand their specific problems and challenges, and
- keep them healthy, happy, and local.

For a BRE program, the two primary survey methods are **mail** (self-administered), which is intended to provide early warning of troubled companies, and **in-person visitation**, which delves into identifying specific barriers and problems (see Chapter 7).

GETTING STRAIGHT ANSWERS CAN BE AN UPHILL PULL

Face it: No one in business likes to fill out surveys. It takes time. It takes effort. Giving out information could come back to bite later. And as managers approach all those questions and blank answer spaces, there's an inner voice that says, 'It's no one's business how we do business!'

You need a strategy to get companies to respond promptly, freely and candidly to your survey. Here are some questions businesses may want to know:

— *Who are these people and why do they want to know about my business?*

The initial BRE company survey will probably be mailed with a brief cover letter. Get right to the point of establishing credentials and credibility with management, while offering them compelling reasons why they should respond.

— *Why should I spend my valuable time answering these questions? What's in it for me and my company?*

The extent to which company respondents buy into the value of participating in the survey is the extent to which they'll take pen in hand. Here are the points to highlight the upside of participation and sweeten the pot for them:

- As representatives of the community, the BRE program understands the value of businesses like theirs and the need to help them respond to competitive challenges and opportunities.

- The BRE survey is a valuable tool in building open, unreserved channels of communication between business and the community.

- The BRE survey is just the beginning of a process that could offer alternatives and solutions to the challenges their company faces.

— *Who's going to see the completed survey? We cannot afford to have this kind of information on the street.*

The businesses need to understand and believe that responses will be kept absolutely confidential. *Absolutely.* Explain that information will be for BRE staff.

THE SHORT OF IT

The initial survey should be considered as an early warning indicator. It will probably be mailed to targeted businesses in the community and should be concise enough for a business manager to fill out in about five minutes.

The short survey is designed to accomplish three main objectives:

1. **To make initial contact with companies and establish the BRE program's credibility as a reliable resource for local businesses.**

2. **To demonstrate your community's concern for business and recognition of its value.**

3. **To uncover companies at risk of closing, moving, expanding out of the area, or downsizing, and to avoid or mitigate the impact of job loss in the community.**

Address the first two objectives in the cover letter and identify the benefits to responding companies. This is the foundation for further contact with these businesses. (See sample letter, Attachment 6-2.)

The third objective—to identify companies as risk of closing, moving or expanding out of the area, or downsizing—is critical program information. This is the direct and indirect focus of each survey question:

► Is this company considering expansion of its business?

► Is this company considering relocation of its business? Within the community? Elsewhere?

► Does this company anticipate increases or decreases in employment levels?

► What are the issues/problems/opportunities driving this company's decisions?

The short survey (see Attachment 6-4) leads respondents from brief, fact-based queries toward questions that spotlight opportunities and problems. Some of the questions may appear redundant or simplistic, but asking for specific information in different ways reveals consistency in responses and yields a more reliable overview.

TARGET YOUR EFFORTS

It is important to target survey efforts. Who is the BRE program focusing on? A key group to survey is any branches and subsidiaries of large companies, as they can be particularly vulnerable to closure or relocation.

It is also important for staff to follow up on all expectations that are generated by the surveys.

GETTING BACK THE SURVEYS

Mail surveys often have low response rates. Nowadays, a response rate of 30 percent is considered high by professional surveyors. Remember that with a response rate of 30 percent, approximately 70 percent of the surveyed businesses did not return a completed questionnaire. Are the businesses that returned the surveys different from those that failed to or chose not to return the surveys? This *non-returner bias* is important to consider when determining a survey's response rate.

Obtaining a high response rate from a mailed or self-administered survey is a little more difficult, mainly due to reliance on the respondent completing and returning the questionnaire. However, there are several ways to encourage participation:

1. Try to make the questionnaire as easy as possible to fill out.
   • Make sure type is clear and large enough to avoid strain in reading.
   • Be certain that instructions on how to complete the questionnaire are included on the questionnaire itself and are easy to understand.
   • Show an example of how to complete a question if necessary.

2. Include a cover letter explaining the purpose of the survey and reasons why a respondent should complete and return the questionnaire (Attachment 6-2).

3. Mail the packet with first class postage and include a self-addressed postage-paid return envelope with the questionnaire. This is one of the most valuable techniques to use in any mail survey.

4. Utilizing electronic media, send the short survey via e-mail or fax, so it is not just another piece of mail the business receives.

5. Send a reminder postcard (see Attachment 6-3) approximately one week after the questionnaire. This card can be sent alone or be in addition to a reminder telephone call.

WALKING THE WALK
BEFORE TALKING THE TALK

The short survey will also reveal valuable general information about targeted businesses and about the industries to which they belong. This can serve as a jump-off point for educating BRE staff or volunteer team who will make business visitations and conduct the long survey (see Chapter 7). A working knowledge of companies and their industries is crucial to getting the information you want and establishing the credibility you need to establish long-term relationships.

GAUGING SHORT
SURVEY RESULTS:

WHITE FLAG RESPONSE

There it is in black and white: No early warning indicators triggered by this company. No problems, no plans to move or expand to parts unknown, to shut down, sell out, re-engineer, downsize, rightsize, or change the locks on the doors.

> *If the first thought is to park this company's survey in the safe file, think again. There is no safe file, and there are no safe companies.*

A white flag response today is just that: today's response. As far as the business of business goes, tomorrow is permanent white water and change is the only constant. Put white flag survey responses in a "tickler" file. Revisit them systematically every six months or annually to keep communication channels open. Remember, you're building long-term relationships with these companies. If new challenges or opportunities arise, the goal is to be on their short list of resources to tap. It is also important to look for trends in survey responses over time.

Keep in mind that businesses often feel overwhelmed by the number of surveys sent to them. One Washington state BRE program developed a flyer as a way to revisit business issues without resurveying. They send it out every six months. (See Attachment 5-1.)

RED FLAG RESPONSE:
THE SKY IS FALLING,
CHICKEN LITTLE!

It is important to identify which questions represent red flags in retaining businesses and jobs. In the short survey (see Attachment 6-4), the following are possible early warning signs:

Questions 6a and b	*Decrease in jobs*
Question 8	*Areas of assistance; need to follow-up on*
Question 10	*Considering relocation*
Question 11	*Considering out-of-area relocation or expansion*

If one of more early warning signals sound as the result of a company's short-term survey response, the next step is to generate more detailed information. Red-flagged firms will require a second round of surveying by a personal meeting between company management and a BRE staff or visitation team member.

CRITICAL ISSUES
IN DESIGNING THE
SURVEY INSTRUMENT

Developing the appropriate survey tool for either the mail-out or visitation approach is very critical. The following excerpt is from a chapter in *Journey to Jobs*, "Retention in a Recruitment World: Existing Business Programs." © Blane, Canada Ltd. It discusses the shortfall of many survey tools currently being used.

Existing Business Programs

Eric P. Canada
© Blane, Canada Ltd.

Most economic development professionals begin with the process in mind. Focused on the "visit" process, the steps fall into place, action unfolds, reports roll in, results are tabulated, a report filled with pie charts, graphs, and quotable quotes is prepared. The end is celebrated. Only then, at the end of the process, does it become painfully clear that there probably will be no great saves (no companies on the verge of pulling out of the community are found). Leadership also recognizes the organization's role in helping companies expand is limited (usually limited to physical support and networking; valuable but not deal makers). And finally, after all of the effort of the contacts, not much new information was gained from the predominantly superficial interviews. Pie charts and bar graphs don't help leadership understand what will drive the community's economy forward. Is there more to consider than the process? Absolutely!

It is possible to make existing business programs pay the same kind of dividends experienced by the adrenaline rush of a successful business attraction program. It is all perception management. How we manage the perception of a community's business and political leadership will determine how the existing business program is viewed.

Brett Vassey, Business Services Manager, Department of Business Assistance, Commonwealth of Virginia, makes an important distinction in the difference between a successful program and a common program. Most economic development executive contact programs are built on the "business

service model." In the business service model, the organization is there to respond to the needs of a specific company. The most successful executive contact programs use a "community development model." In the community development model, the organization uses executive contact to provide direction and create leverage for substantive program and/or policy changes benefiting all companies, not just a single company.

The goal of an existing business program should be about gaining an understanding of the companies that will drive the community's economic engine in the future.

Often it is not necessary to go it alone on an executive contact program. There are many groups interested in local companies. For example, the North Dakota Department of Development & Finance, Small Business Development Council, and the Manufacturing Extension Program all collaborate on the existing business calls. Each contributes manpower to make the calls. Each of the partners derives beneficial information important to their individual programs.

At Blane, Canada Ltd., we believe the goal of an existing business program should be strategic information. To focus attention on this strategic information component, Blane, Canada Ltd. invented the portfolio assessment strategy for existing business programs. The portfolio management strategy is now in use in over 140 communities throughout the U.S.

To take an active role in managing the community's economic portfolio, it is essential to have better information about the companies in the community. This requires information similar to what an investor would look at to evalu-

ate the investment potential growth of a company's stock value.

Therefore, the portfolio assessment approach focuses on the collection of information that will allow the user to evaluate every company on critical factors such as:

- ▸ Value to the community
- ▸ Growth potential
- ▸ Technological adaptation and leadership
- ▸ Risk of downsizing and/or leaving
- ▸ Satisfaction with the community
- ▸ How should you change the process?

THE STRATEGIC INFORMATION TOOL

An essential step in building an executive contract program is to decide what will be discussed with area executives during the interview. Most economic development organizations prepare a set of questions to help organize the interview and explore important issues. The challenge here is not what question to ask, but rather, how to limit the appetite to ask the next question. There are always more interesting questions to ask than time available.

The challenge is deciding *why* to include a question. Let me explain. In 1996, Blane, Canada Ltd. gathered about 75 business retention survey forms from organizations around the country. Each organization had a proactive business retention program. Our findings (depicted in Figure 1) were startling: The vast majority of the time (53.2 percent) was being devoted to confirming easily obtained information (e.g., company name, contact, parent company, employment). This means that for an average 30-question survey, 16 questions were devoted to gathering information of absolutely no strategic value. Given this, it is clear that few if any were asking themselves why these questions were necessary.

If the answer to a question does not help determine the company's role in the community's portfolio, e.g., value, growth, risk, or satisfaction, why is it being included?

The other focus of the traditional survey instrument has been to identify problems. In our analysis, the typical survey instrument devoted 25 percent of the interview to identifying and/or documenting problems limiting business growth or thwarting the attraction of new companies. How many questions are required to identify/document problems—5, 10, 15, 20? Unbelievably, one survey analyzed posed 95 problem-related questions. Another posed 107.

Interestingly, quite a few of the problem questions were intended to document a known problem. When documenting a known problem, it is important to focus on the consequences of the problem. For example, in California, energy costs, availability, and reliability are issues because of the recent energy crisis. In this case, it is useless to ask if this is a problem; that is obvious for almost any significant company.

Therefore, an appropriate line of questioning could be: How has the energy crisis impacted the company? Can you provide examples? How has the company adjusted its business practices to minimize the negative consequences of the energy crisis? What are the long-term implications of these changes? This series of questions begins to explore the nature and consequence of the problem instead of just confirming what is already known: the problem exists.

SURVEY LENGTH

It is always important to respect the time of executives willing to meet. Consequently, early in the process of creating a survey, it becomes painfully clear that there are more questions than there will be time to ask them. To deal with this problem, we recommend that each question be required to do double or even triple duty. Take problem related questions for example. It is important for economic development leadership to identify any problems important to business executives. When framing a problem question as follows, "Are there any barriers to the company's expansion in the community?" The answer to this one question tells us three things:

- First, what is the risk of the respondent taking growth elsewhere.
- Second, what are the problems of doing business here.

- Third, the most important problems, those that could cause the company to take growth elsewhere, are identified.

Based on Blane, Canada Ltd.'s research and experience with on-site and telephone interviews, using a casual interview style, the average 30-question survey will require about 40 minutes for an on-site interview or 30 minutes for a telephone interview. The interviewer's skill and the interviewee's desire to elaborate will, of course, dramatically affect the length of time required to complete an interview. The other factors dictating how much time will be required during an interview is the form of the question. There are four basic question formats:

Simple (yes/no)

Compound (multiple choice)

Complex (multiple parts, e.g., arranged in order of importance)

Open-ended (solicits a comment)

Complex and open-ended questions generally take longer to ask and answer. Therefore, a survey tool with only complex and open-ended questions must include fewer questions in total to fit within the available time.

Tabulation and analysis is easiest when questions are simple or multiple choice. Complex and open-ended questions are more difficult to tabulate and analyze.

PORTFOLIO MANAGEMENT APPROACH

Think of the companies in a community as parts of an investment portfolio. The value of the portfolio is the sum total of the value of the individual companies. An investor is constantly asking about growth potential, value, diversity, balance, etc. Therefore, like an investor, community leadership should be asking, which are our most valuable companies? Which are our growth companies? Which are stable? Which companies are in decline? Now, given that knowledge (value, growth, risk), how should the community/economic development organization invest its resources (incentives, loans, grants, staff time, etc.) to maximize long-term value of the portfolio? Should the portfolio be conservatively or aggressively managed? Is the portfolio being neglected? What is the cost/ consequence of neglect?

Ultimately, the most important factor is moderation. Focusing on important questions, requiring questions that give insight into multiple issues and blending simple, compound, complex, and open-ended questions will produce the most interesting interview and most valuable information. Open-ended questions are very important, especially when combined with a simple or compound question, because they enrich the findings providing a context to aid understanding.

THE ASSISTANCE TRAP

The last dominant theme in the analysis of executive interview forms is the "assistance" question. More than 10 percent of the questions included in the surveys analyzed were directed at identifying forms of assistance that could be provided.

Everyone involved in economic development wants to help companies thrive in the community. However, most economic development organizations are pretty limited in what they can actually do directly to help local companies. Economic development organizations do not set law, do not manage government regulations, and do not have baskets full of money to distribute. Therefore, development organizations must rely on a partner, e.g., individuals in city, county, and/or state government, to address many of the concerns that face the businesses executives in our communities. In short, we must count on a third party to make the changes our clients desire.

To offer assistance that must be provided by a third party is a risky proposition. First, any offer will create an expectation on the part of the executive, an expectation of resolution. Expectations combined with an executive's imagination, almost always create a difficult combination to satisfy.

Second, when we ask if the company would like assistance with a specific activity, export financing for example, most often delivering the assistance probably requires a state employee to provide the assistance. If they cannot follow through on the request or if they fail to follow through, the person who made the offer is the one to let the company down. That person created the expectation. That person failed the executive.

Third, if follow-through is not provided, in the next meeting with that company executive, interactions will probably be awkward for everyone involved. The memory of the lack of follow-through will hang over the meeting. So, don't make any promises you cannot personally deliver.

If a large number of executive visits are being conducted at the same time, the individual or individuals responsible for managing the "follow-up" can easily be overwhelmed. When this happens, priorities must be set. Depending on the nature of the problems uncovered elsewhere and their priority, a response could be delayed for a long time.

For these reasons, Greater Louisville, Inc. staff members first performs an assessment based on a structured survey tool. With the assessment in hand and a better understanding of the company, they then return later to offer ways they may be able to help the company. This is an enlightened approach to dealing with the assistance trap.

SURVEY GAPS

Knowing community-related problems is important. Creating goodwill is valuable. Offering assistance is useful. But, in an environment of global competition these issues do not drive corporate decision-making. Therefore, our research documents that investing 88.4 percent of our information collection time on these issues (confirming company info, identifying problems, and offering assistance) is highly inappropriate. This is especially true in light of the information needed to decide how best to manage limited community resources.

The most disturbing finding from Blane, Canada Ltd.'s analysis of the traditional survey instruments was the information gaps. The research findings shown earlier in Figure 1 highlight three critical information gaps found:

▶ Only 5.2 percent of the questions (1.5 questions) gather company intelligence.

▶ Fewer than 0.6 percent of the questions (no questions) focus on gathering industry intelligence.

▶ The only predictive question (4.3 percent) sometimes asked is, "Do you plan to expand?"

Is it the assumption of economic development professionals that the industry (industry intelligence) and management practices (company intelligence) have no bearing on the future of the company's operation in the community? Ask any investor. This is, at best, a dangerous assumption.

A NEW CONCEPTUAL FRAMEWORK

In the book, *Economic Development: Marketing for Results!*, Blane, Canada Ltd. proposed a new conceptual framework for increasing the strategic value of information gathered through the business retention process because we believe development organizations must:

• Seek out and acquire information relevant to the decision–making process of companies;

• Create a process to transform unconnected pieces of information into relevant, accurate and useable strategic knowledge; and

• Focus information resources on helping identify marketing opportunities and predicting companies at risk.

Competitive or market intelligence is defined as "the selection, collection, interpretation, and distribution of publicly-held information that has strategic impor

FIGURE 1

ANALYSIS OF SURVEY QUESTIONS

Types of Questions	Percent	Average Number of Questions
▪ Confirmation questions	53.2	16.0
▪ Assistance questions	10.6	3.5
▪ Problem identification questions	25.3	8.0
▪ Predictive questions	4.3	1.0
▪ Industry intelligence questions	0.6	0.0
▪ Company intelligence questions	5.2	1.5
▪ Buyer/supplier linkage questions	1.1	0.0

SOURCE: Blane, Canada Ltd.

tance," according to authors Richard Combs and John Moorhead. Counter to the purpose of a traditional retention program, a competitive intelligence approach seeks to gather and organize predictive information as well as market intelligence. Predictive information provides value by helping the development executive anticipate changes impacting a community's economic base. Market intelligence seeks to document or quantify competitive advantages and weaknesses affecting retention and attraction.

Improved marketing results are the driving force behind the need for redesigning the executive contact survey tools. The proposed approach is not a radical new concept. It is supported by proven market research and competitive intelligence techniques used regularly in other industries. Today, more than 140 economic development organizations are using these principles as the foundation of their existing business program.

To achieve the maximum benefit from an existing business program, it should be viewed as a four-stage system:

1 — Compile employer information
2 — Conduct CEO interviews
3 — Compile and analyze the data
4 — Blend findings into the marketing plan

STAGE 1: COMPILE EMPLOYER INFORMATION

As pointed out earlier, more than 50 percent of a traditional business retention survey is devoted to collecting employer background information, e.g., company address, number of employees, union representation, senior executives, parent company, products, and SIC/NAICS codes. This information is widely available, easily known. Therefore, it should be collected through research or by phone from the company's executive assistant or human resource manager prior to conducting the CEO interview. There are two benefits to obtaining this background information in advance. First, during interviews with the CEO, interaction can be focused on questions that will provide more valuable information along with industry insights. Second, being prepared clearly demonstrates to the CEO that the organization has done its homework.

STAGE 2: CONDUCT CEO INTERVIEWS

The emphasis of the redesigned executive survey instrument should be on capturing strategic information: customer satisfaction, predictive information, and marketing research. Some predictive information and market research data cannot be easily captured in a written (mail-out) survey. Some of these questions do not lend them-

selves to multiple choice or short answers.

To maximize gathering of strategic information, a telephone or personal visit interview is recommended. Each interviewer should be prepared to probe for clarification by following up answers with questions. For example, "Would you give me an example?" "How does that work in your company?"

STAGE 3: COMPILE AND ANALYZE THE DATA

Company Level Analysis

Each survey form has value and provides insight as each describes one company's situation and one executive's view. This company level information must be analyzed separately. The first step of the analysis is to perform a "risk" assessment. Based on the company information gathered, a determination must be made regarding the following questions:

1. Is there any reason to believe that this company is at risk for downsizing, closure, or relocation?
2. Is there any assistance that can/should be provided to this company?
3. Is there any evidence the company is considering expansion locally or elsewhere?
4. Is this a high value company or a growth company?
5. Is the company committed to the community?

6. Regarding these findings, what steps, if any, should be taken by the organization?
7. Is there a marketing opportunity to be pursued?

This company screening should be completed immediately following the personal or telephone interview, and any necessary follow-up action should be scheduled as soon as possible. If the information needed to act is at the least bit confidential, it may be necessary to ask the executive permission to discuss details with prospective assistance providers.

After-visit follow-up requests run a wide range. From my own experience and comments of others, information requests comprise 50 to 80 percent of the company executives interviewed. These information requests cover the gamut from expansion assistance to the name of a contact or information on a training program.

The volume of information requests will, of course, vary depending on the "assistance offer" made during the interview and leave-behind materials taken into the meeting. The vast majority of information requests are easily filled using a post-visit letter. Even if no information was requested, a post-visit letter should be sent to every company executive, reinforcing the importance of the meeting and how the findings will be shared with participants and the community.

The post-visit letter can easily be prepared by the program administrator. To cover frequently asked questions, prewritten plug-in paragraphs simplify the response process.

For long-term follow-up requirements, it is necessary to record company information so that the needed follow-up can be tracked to completion.

Group Analysis

The real power of any executive contact program designed as a market research tool is gained from the aggregate result of numerous surveys. By comparing the answer given by each executive to each question, it is possible to identify trends among groups or clusters of companies. The clusters used for analysis can be made up of companies grouped by size, industry, location, market, or other shared characteristics. The goal of cluster analysis is to find recurring comments that identify opportunities or suggest potential problems. The condition of the community's product, community services, and attitudes toward the community, are of particular concern during cluster analysis. The search for competitive advantages also takes place in the cluster analysis.

The comments and insights provided by employers can help identify the community's real strengths and weaknesses. The purpose of the analysis is to identify groups of companies with the same or similar problems. Economic development organizations have identified and addressed many significant community issues in this manner.

The most frequent methods of evaluating findings include:

Totals, percents, and distributions: Frequently shown in tables, pie charts, and graphs
Key word frequency: Number of times a select word is used
Trends: Recurring themes entering the conversations
Quotable quotes: Individual comments that summarize the feelings of a broader group
One-Ups: Powerful, insightful comments that uncover an emerging issue
Problems: Appearance of recurring problems.

An analysis of groups of responses should be conducted regularly as new surveys are added to the information base. Results can then be compared to data from prior reviews to spot trends. This group or cluster analysis can be performed manually or electronically depending on the number of surveys involved and available resources.

BC Hydro in Burnaby, British Columbia, Canada, prefers to design their Business Care Program around statistically valid survey analysis. Validating the information statistically reduces the burden of defending the information, especially when it is negative. It also avoids the concern of representing some executive's personal pet peeve as a concern of the business community.

Everything else being equal, statistical validity is probably the way to go. Unfortunately, everything else is seldom equal because statistical analysis increases cost and information constraints by putting more limitations on how questions can be asked. Finally, achieving statistical validity generally removes volunteer community involvement. The way volunteers keep meeting records makes most survey professional nervous about interpretation.

STAGE 4: BLEND FINDINGS INTO THE MARKETING PLAN

The Report

Reports, like the existing business programs themselves, are highly personalized to the community, organization, and program leader.

An official report is unnecessary for an executive contact program that operates at the company service level providing service to companies with identified needs. These follow-up interactions after the interview are specific to that company and the content of the conversation with the company. A prepared report will have little relevance to the details of that interaction.

If the organization's goal is to affect changes—within the organization or outside—then a report is critical. The report records and organizes the findings, conclusions, and recommendations so they can be shared with leadership and influencers. The report builds the case for action by providing the evidence to document why action is necessary.

Based on our current research on existing business program results and outcomes, there are at least four levels of reporting:

— Meeting summary, no compiled report

— Basic information, simple tabulation, totals, percents, and distributions, informal reporting

— Moderate information, trend and key word analysis, summary reporting and conclusions, quotable quotes, one-ups

— Highly sophisticated, statistical analysis, extensive reporting, long-term recommendations

An interesting final note on the report originates from a conversation with Jim Igarta, previously with American Electric Power in Texas and who has been involved in many executive business contact programs in many communities. "The quality and detail of the report matters little," Mr. Igarta noted. "What really matters is what leadership is willing to act on." In other words, slick, colorful, and expensive reports won't change the outcome if there isn't substance in the information supported by leadership's willingness to act.

Connecting with Marketing

With the findings in hand, the final step in the executive contact information system proposed is to decide how the new information affects marketing.

- *What are the implications for future marketing activities?*
- *Are local companies at risk?*
- *Do local plant managers need community information packaged specifically for off-site decision-makers?*
- *Is more internal marketing needed with local executives?*

> ## SAMPLE REPORT OUTLINE
>
> 1 **Acknowledgments**
> 2 **Title Page, Table of Contents, Date, Sponsor**
> 3 **Summary of the report**
> 4 **Introduction**
>   **Purpose of the interview**
>   **Relevance to the community**
> 5 **Summary of findings**
> 6 **Recommendations to local organizations**
> 7 **Plans for implementation**
> 8 **Responsibility for implementation**
> 9 **Appendix**
>   **Tabulation of results**
>   **Methodology**
>   **Members of the committee**
>   **Procedure for selecting and interviewing businesses**
>   **Data tabulation and analysis procedures**

- *How should the organization respond to changing attitudes about doing business in the community?*
- *Are there supplier opportunities for business attraction to be researched or pursued?*
- *Can area executives open doors through their affiliations to help with business attraction?*

Any conclusions drawn from the analysis of the interviews must then be systematically blended into the current marketing plan.

STAGE 5: EVALUATION, EVALUATION, EVALUATION

Every phase of the process and results should be evaluated. Feedback, follow-up, and tracking are extremely important. Initially, all of the results are short-term. The short-term evaluation focuses on the process and the company specific actions taken.

- *Were the planned number of contacts made?*
- *When executives had questions, were they addressed?*
- *Were company information needs followed up and completed?*

- *Were any significant issues identified?*
- *What can be done to improve the process?*
- *What worked, what didn't work?*
- *What should we do differently next time?*

One short-term change that should be avoided is changing the interview questions dramatically or too frequently. It is important to have continuity. Not every trend is evident in one round of executive contacts. The better executive contact programs have stable question sets. It is far better to invest a great deal of time before beginning to make sure the questions are right than to start over every year.

Granted, there are always new organizational or community issues emerging that the organization needs to investigate. There are two options for doing this while maintaining continuity in the interview tool.

Option one is to conduct a special mail or telephone survey on the special issues as they arise. An organization could conduct two or three special-issue surveys during a year. A special survey will gather the required information without rewriting the executive contact survey tool.

Option two is to segment the survey into two parts. One section consisting of the core questions. These core questions do not change, no matter what. A second section is devoted to special issues. This section changes as needed to allow collection of information on important periodic issues.

Long-term evaluation focuses on the big-picture items that impact groups of companies and improve the community or the community's business climate. By their nature, such changes will take a year or longer to accomplish. Consequently, long-term evaluation requires tracking over time to determine what actions have been taken and what changes have resulted. In one case we were involved in, it became clear that companies needed room to grow. Yet there was a lack of industrial land in the community. As a result, the development organization set about building two new business parks, one in the community and another in the county. To achieve this, the organization had to secure political buy-in, raise millions of dollars, deal with reluctant land owners, and overcome challenging topographical issues. It took nearly four years to complete the task. At the end of four years, the community had more than 600 acres of prime industrial and business park space to support the growth of existing companies and attraction of new companies.

Based on our research, economic development organizations have a good record of producing good short-term and long-term results with executive contact programs. Not everyone goes about it the same way, but they end up getting to the same place anyway.

One component of the evaluation process that is sometimes overlooked is the need to report back and keep stakeholders informed. Feedback is very important to connect the results with the

starting point, the executive contact program. Frequently, economic development professionals get so involved the process, they forget to take credit for accomplishments. Many executives use their newsletter or newsletters of strategic partners to get the word out. These channels are fine, but limited. It is important to engage the media. For various reasons, this important vehicle is frequently underutilized.

CONCLUSION

The ability to gather strategic information should become a top priority for every economic development organization.

Today's business retention methodology and tools are ill-equipped to address the needs of the development organization wanting to build its local economy. Goodwill is no longer the issue. Continued reliance on the traditional business retention approach for information collection in today's competitive environment leaves development organizations vulnerable and open to criticism. Business retention programs should play a greater role in providing company, industry, and marketing information needed to build the foundation for solid marketing strategies.

Internal information resources will create opportunities and anticipate changes that impact businesses within a community. Plus, most importantly, better information at the company level makes it possible for the organization to manage the community's economic portfolio by directing resources—policy, time, and money—toward companies with the highest value and greatest growth potential. Portfolio management based on strategic information management creates a more efficient and effective approach than the traditional approach of reacting to events and demands.

There is tremendous potential for increasing the strategic value of a business retention program with-

out an appreciable cost increase. To capture the potential of this shift, development professionals must challenge traditional methods. They must increase experimentation to build better retention interview tools. To capture the potential of this shift, development professionals must challenge traditional methods. They must increase experimentation to build better retention interview tools.

REFERENCES

Canada, Eric P., *Economic Development: Marketing for Results!* Chicago Spectrum Press and Blane, Canada Ltd., 1995.
Combs, Richard E. and John D. Moorhead. *The Competitive Intelligence Handbook,* The Scarecrow Press, Inc., 1992.

ABOUT THE AUTHOR
Eric P. Canada is a principal of Blane, Canada Ltd., in Wheaton, Illinois, a consulting firm specializing in economic development marketing. He is the author of *Economic Development: Marketing for Results!* and *Marketer's Planning Guide,* and developer of a business retention computer software system. Eric has taught numerous economic development courses.
Eric P. Canada, Blane, Canada Ltd.
1506 Cadet, Suite 100
Wheaton, IL 60187
630-462-9222 630-462-9210 fax
ecanada@blanecanada.com
www.blanecanada.com

SURVEY METHODOLOGY
ADVANTAGES AND DISADVANTAGES

In-Person Surveying *(average 30 to 60 minutes per interview)*

Advantages:

▸ Personal contact with business
▸ Better understanding of local business issues
▸ First-hand view of facility
▸ Observations of any nonverbal responses
▸ More flexible and versatile than mail surveys due to the ability to probe certain responses
▸ Decreased likelihood of missed or skipped questions
▸ Faster than mail surveys

Disadvantages:

▸ More expensive than mail surveys
▸ More time-consuming than a telephone survey
▸ Possible geographic bias
▸ Time constraints

Telephone Surveying *(ideally, limit the interview to 10 to 15 minutes, 30 minutes maximum)*

Advantages:

▸ Easy to draw a random or non-random sample due to the high percentage of businesses with telephones
▸ Costs less than in-person surveys
▸ Ability to ask follow-up questions
▸ Fast turnaround
▸ Adaptable to a wide range of subjects

Disadvantages:

▸ Difficult to show exhibits
▸ Respondent's attention span decreases without visual exhibits.
▸ Dependent upon common language and hearing ability
▸ Length of the interview is constrained due to the respondent's limited attention span.
▸ Repeated scales or questions cause respondents to lose interest, and long questions increase the likelihood of the respondent misunderstanding the question.

Mail Surveying *(including traditional, fax, and e-mail)*

Advantages:

▸ Least expensive method of interviewing
▸ Less interviewer bias
▸ Can access hard-to-reach people such as farmers or frequent travelers
▸ Can attach exhibits
▸ E-mail and fax appear higher priority than business mail

Disadvantages:

▸ Low response rates (i.e., the number of people who return a completed survey compared with the number of total surveys mailed)
▸ No interviewer control
▸ Slow, due to increased reliance on respondent to complete the survey in a timely manner

SAMPLE COVER LETTER

[Date]

[Name]
[Company]
[Address]
[City, State, Zip]

Dear _____ Manufacturer [president or manager]:

The _____ Economic Development Council (EDC) is working to create a viable economic climate through its Business Retention and Expansion Program. The EDC is currently seeking a better understanding of manufacturing firms in our county. To help us do that, we are asking you to fill out the enclosed survey.

This survey will help us identify specific assistance that your company may need and identify countywide business issues. The survey should take no more than ten minutes to complete. Return postage is provided.

Your feedback is important to us. All your answers will be kept confidential.

If you have any questions about the survey or the EDC, please feel free to call me at ( ) *###-####*.

Thank you for your assistance,

[Your name]
[Title]

Note: The cover letter should explain who you are, why you are conducting the survey, why it is important for the respondent to complete the survey, and how the survey will benefit the respondent. Include added information regarding how long it will take to complete the survey or any incentive as needed to encourage participation in the survey.

EXAMPLE OF POSTCARD

[INCLUDE PROGRAM LOGO IF POSSIBLE]

Date

Recently we contacted you and asked you to complete the Business Retention and Expansion Survey. In order to better serve you, we need to understand what issues are important to you.

If you have already completed the questionnaire and sent it back, please accept our thanks. If you have not yet had an opportunity to answer those questions, please do so at your earliest convenience. **Your opinions are very important to us.** If you need another copy of the questionnaire, please call (INCLUDE PHONE NUMBER) and we will be happy to send one.

Thank you for your help.

[Date]

ECONOMIC DEVELOPMENT BUSINESS SURVEY
(short version)

Company Name: _____

Address: _____

Your Name: _____

Position with Company: _____ Phone Number: _____

Is this the company headquarters? $\square_1$ Yes $\square_2$ No

If no, location of company headquarters: _____

Parent company name (if different): _____

1. **Please indicate your company's primary product or service category** (CHECK ONLY ONE):

   $\square_1$ Food $\square_6$ Chemical $\square_{11}$ Electronics $\square_{16}$ Telecommunications
   $\square_2$ Textiles/Apparel $\square_7$ Petro/Rubber $\square_{12}$ Transportation $\square_{17}$ Other (SPECIFY)
   $\square_3$ Wood $\square_8$ Stone/Clay $\square_{13}$ Instruments
   $\square_4$ Furniture $\square_9$ Machinery $\square_{14}$ Environmental _____
   $\square_5$ Paper/Printing $\square_{10}$ Metals $\square_{15}$ Biotechnology _____

2. **How many years has your business been in operation at this location?**

   $\square_1$ 2 years or less $\square_3$ 6 to 10 years
   $\square_2$ 3 to 5 years $\square_4$ More than 10 years

3. **What percentage of your product is sold in the following areas?** (MUST TOTAL 100%)

   Local (100-mile radius) _____ %
   Regional _____ %
   National _____ %
   International _____ %
   100%

4. **Please estimate your company's total gross revenues for last year:**

   $\square_1$ Under $1 million $\square_3$ $6 to 15 million $\square_5$ $51 to 150 million
   $\square_2$ $1 to 5 million $\square_4$ $16 to 50 million $\square_6$ More than $150 million

5. **How many employees does your company have at this location?**

   $\square_1$ 1 to 5 $\square_2$ 6 to 20 $\square_3$ 21 to 50
   $\square_4$ 51 to 100 $\square_5$ 101 to 200 $\square_6$ More than 200

6a. What are your anticipated changes in the next 12 months?

☐$_1$ increase by _____ jobs.   ☐$_2$ Decrease by _____ jobs.   ☐$_0$ No change

6b. If you anticipate employment decreases, please indicate reasons.

☐$_1$ Decline in sales   ☐$_6$ Changes of ownership
☐$_2$ Foreign competition   ☐$_7$ Change in technology
☐$_3$ Change in labor skills needed   ☐$_8$ Regulatory compliance
☐$_4$ Increase production costs ☐$_9$ Decline of supplier links
☐$_5$ Lack of capital   ☐$_{10}$ Other (SPECIFY) _____

7. If primary company owner(s) is over age 50, has an in-house successor been identified?

☐$_1$ Yes   ☐$_2$ No   ☐$_3$ Unknown

8. Please indicate those areas in which you feel you could use assistance:
(PLEASE CHECK ALL THAT APPLY)

☐$_1$ Finance   ☐$_9$ Marketing
☐$_2$ Personnel   ☐$_{10}$ Export/import
☐$_3$ Energy costs   ☐$_{11}$ Equipment
☐$_4$ Accounting control   ☐$_{12}$ Job skill training
☐$_5$ Working capital   ☐$_{13}$ Business succession planning
☐$_6$ Regulatory   ☐$_{14}$ Employee ownership
☐$_7$ Business planning   ☐$_{15}$ Other (SPECIFY) _____
☐$_8$ Inventory

9. List the specific jobs for which you are having difficulty filling:

_____   _____   _____

_____   _____   _____

10. Are you considering relocating/expanding your business in the next two years?

☐$_1$ Yes, relocating   ☐$_3$ No
☐$_2$ Yes, expanding   ☐$_4$ Uncertain

11. If you are considering relocation or expansion, where are you looking?

☐$_1$ Within city   ☐$_4$ Outside Washington
☐$_2$ Within county   ☐$_5$ Outside United States
☐$_3$ Other Washington State location

THANK YOU for helping to complete our survey. Please return to:

[your address]

CHAPTER 7

BUSINESS VISITATIONS
LETTING BUSINESS KNOW YOU CARE

Communities can't do it all! They need to prioritize.

A visitation program is a planning process to set priorities and is key element of an effective BRE program. Not only does it cap off the information gathering activities and define the problems to be addressed, it establishes working relationships with targeted industries in the community. Open, unreserved communication channels between these companies and the BRE program will inevitably extend to other elements within the community as active economic and community development problem solving begins and other resources are tapped.

While everybody's talking, nobody's walking away from the community and away from the business of business.

It is important to remember that the average response rate for mail surveys is 20 to 30 percent. That means that *70 to 80% of the businesses do not return a mail survey.* Surveys are often not returned by those companies that have the greatest need for program services. *Visitation programs average an 80 to 90% response rate.* The main objectives of the visitation (visitation questionnaire/survey) are:

▶ To build a foundation of trust between the BRE program and company management and demonstrate a pro-business attitude.

▶ To further demonstrate the community's commitment to maintain a positive business environment.

▶ To identify and acknowledge specific problems that may be hampering company efficiency, productivity and profitability.

▶ To work together to assist businesses in problem solving to uncover alternatives to relocation, out-of-area expansion, closing or layoffs.

▶ To build understanding among local leaders of the economic realities of your community.

An effective business visitation program is at the center of the action.

Visitations may be conducted by:
1. volunteers/task force
2. BRE staff, or
3. combination approach which uses both program staff and volunteers.

Visitations have been done successfully in all size communities—from a rural county with a population of 20,000 to large cities such as Oakland and Detroit. The city of Detroit focuses its visitation program on specific industrial neighborhoods. In order to have a significant database to identify community strategies, visitation programs have found it effective to survey between 30 and 100 companies.

USING VOLUNTEERS

The volunteer model can have both short- and long-term benefits. Short-term benefits of the model include:

- Development of a high degree of cooperation between public and private development agencies and leaders, as economic development leaders can recognize shared interest.
- Creation of a forum in which sensitive information on the needs or complaints of businesses can be addressed effectively, yet confidentially.

The long-term impacts include:

- Improved understanding of a community's economic outlook.
- Development of a comprehensive strategic plan for encouraging local economic development.
- Development of informal channels of communication among local development-related organizations to facilitate flow of information.

A volunteer task force approach is long-term. The survey and assessment process may take between 3 and 12 months. Follow-up on community priorities identified through surveying may take a year or longer, depending on the tasks undertaken by the community. Attachment 7-1 provides a sample visitation timeline.

The volunteer approach—used in 26 states—has four major components:

1. recruitment and training of volunteers for visits to companies,

2. follow-up on company red flags,
3. analysis of data and report on trends noted through survey and development of community strategies, and
4. holding community meetings and implementing strategies/recommendations

The volunteer model uses three volunteer groups from the community:

Leadership Team
(4- to 5-person executive committee)

Tasks include recruiting task force members and visitation volunteers, and establishing the logistics/ action plan for the visitations. The leadership team should be made up of representatives of the community. Specific roles of team members may include visitation coordinator, meetings coordinator, business resource/red flags coordinator, media coordinator, and overall program coordinator.

Task Force

Group of 10 to 25 community leaders, such as representatives from:
- business
- education
- economic development
- government agencies

Their roles include recruiting additional volunteers, going on some of the visits to companies, helping with the immediate follow-up, reviewing research, and making decisions on recommendations aimed at improving the business climate. The task force might be an organization board, if it is broadly representative of the community; however, most boards do not include all of the four groups identified above. (Job description for task force members is found in Attachment 2-7.)

Task force members review the responses from companies, develop and conduct a data analysis of overall survey results, and engage in a strategic planning effort based on trends discovered in the surveys.

Volunteer Interviewers

(approximately 15 to 25, depending on number and kinds of companies targeted)

Volunteers to visit the firms may be:
- business leaders
- elected officials (city and county)
- education officials or teachers (as part of school-to-work programs)
- community leaders
- development professionals (utilities, railroads, regional development organizations)
- local association leaders
- youth enrolled in entrepreneurial classes, school-to-work programs, or college business classes

Volunteers usually visit two to four businesses. The interview usually lasts about an hour. Volunteers are usually asked to make all of their visits within a two- to three-week period. After their visits, volunteers return the completed survey to the coordinator. (See Attachment 2-6, sample volunteer interviewer job description; Attachment 7-2, volunteer recruitment letter; and page 82, "Volunteer Responsibilities During the Visit.")

VOLUNTEER TRAINING

Task Force

Early in the process, conduct an orientation meeting, which all volunteers, leadership team, and task force members *must* attend. Explain the purpose, objectives, structure, and time frame of the program, as well as the specific responsibilities of the task force members and volunteers. Discuss the strategies for economic development, develop criteria for identifying and selecting recommendations, and write strategies and recommendations. Task force members should conduct at least one practice visit. (Attachment 7-3, Initial Tast Force Meeting.)

Volunteers

Volunteer interviewers will participate in a 2- to 2½–hour training program (see Attachment 7-4, sample agenda), to receive training on how to approach firms and fill out the survey instrument, and practice visits. Training is usually held at least twice to accommodate the volunteers' schedules. Because it is crucial to have trained volunteers, many programs consider this training mandatory.

Before conducting the training, prepare a volunteer packet which includes:
- general information on BRE program and visitation program
- copy of letter sent to company (Attachment 7-7)
- extra copies of surveys
- guidelines for volunteers (see page 82)
- name, address, telephone number, and contact name for each firm to be visited by the volunteer
- list of volunteer teams and task force members
- scheduling postcard
- preaddressed, stamped envelope for returning survey

EVALUATION OF SUCCESSFUL BRE VISITATION PROGRAMS

Scott Loveride and Thomas R. Smith, in their article "Factors Related to Success in Business Retention and Expansion Programs," in *Journal of Community Development Society* (vol. 23, no. 2), found that the more successful BRE programs used their task force for developing recommendations to improve the business climate—e.g., creating a tangible product (which becomes an action agenda for the community) and getting community leaders involved in looking at the needs and issues of the businesses in the community. The programs were less likely to use their task force for follow-up activities with companies or to provide immediate follow-up on survey issues.

The University of Minnesota surveyed firms and visitation coordinators in six states on the four objectives common to BRE visitation programs. Their findings are discussed below.

Program Objective #1:
Demonstration of a Pro-Business Attitude

Through visits to businesses, and by developing a community action plan to address concerns raised by local businesses, a successful program shows firms that the community views them as a valuable asset. This can help overcome the reluctance by businesses to share their problems with local leaders, ultimately shortening the time between emergence of a program and its resolution. Both coordinators and businesses surveyed gave the program the highest scores in achieving this objective.

Program Objective #2:
Help Firms Use State Development Programs

State development programs are constantly changing, and it is difficult for business managers to keep updating their information. Furthermore, most firms use these programs infrequently, reducing their incentive to learn about the programs. The BRE visitation program attempts to overcome this difficulty by asking firms whether they could use information on state business assistance programs during the volunteer visit to the firm. Firms are provided information as part of program follow-up activities. Coordinators gave this objective their lowest average ranking, while firms rated it third of the four objectives.

Program Objective #3:
Assist Firms in Solving Local Problems

Political support for the program is built by addressing the immediate concerns of firms whenever possible. Moving a light pole to better illuminate a firm's entrance, as well as getting a city to improve its water purification facilities, would be categorized as solving local problems. Thus, a local problem solved by the program might relate to a specific firm (i.e., the light pole) or many firms (i.e., poor water quality). Success on this objective leads to greater business efficiency, which in turn translates into higher profits, greater market share, or both. Increased market share or profits increases the likelihood that the firm will remain in business or expand. Coordinators rated this objective third highest of the four objectives, while firms surveyed rated it last.

Program Objective #4:
Provide Data for Economic Development

A key objective of the visitation program is to help local leaders develop a picture of the needs and conditions of the local economy and enable them to formulate better strategic plans for community development. The information used in their planning comes from responses to the survey administered by the volunteer visitors, and it is supplemented with industrial outlooks pertinent to the local economy supplied by the state sponsor. Both coordinators and firms rated this as the second most successful objective.

The overall goal of BRE is to help communities strengthen their strategic planning capacities for economic development by providing means for community self-examination and improved communications between business and other groups. Since measurement of achievement of this goal is difficult, an evaluation of BRE must develop proxies for program success. The six-state survey of local BRE coordinators showed that programs experiencing success in job saving or creation interviewed more firms and spent more time on immediate follow-up with individual firms than did less successful programs.

Coordinators play a very influential role in determining how the program performs on various objectives through their time allocation. Among other things, the survey results show that:

1. Carefully developed training programs involving larger numbers of volunteer visitors lead to better immediate and long-term results;

2. Coordinators who spend more time on immediate follow-up to the problems of individual firms are more likely to have programs that work;

3. The most effective programs get local leaders actively involved on the task force both in working on a firm's immediate concerns and in developing final recommendations;

4. Coordinators who spend less time developing recommendations have programs that work better; this may be related to the level of assistance provided by state sponsors in analyzing results and report writing; and

5. Firms that reported that the program worked to solve local problems were smaller and younger than other firms.

PROFESSIONAL STAFF-BASED VISITATIONS

In a professional staff-based business visitation program, the visits can be made alone or as a team. A representative from another organization, such as the Chamber of Commerce, JTPA agency, vocational education school, or other appropriate agencies, may accompany the lead professional staffperson. Target the chief executive officer of the company for the visit, to inform them of the retention and expansion services available to the company. During the visit, explain local, county, state, and federal programs that provide financial and management assistance, job training assistance, and other technical help. Discuss any items of concern noted on the questionnaire, as well as the company's future direction and potential obstacles to its growth. Stress the commitment of the community to its existing businesses. Staff should address any problems and concerns noted by the company in at least two stages: short-range (within two weeks) and long-range (within two to three months). Program staff may want to establish a tickler file to follow up on some of the longer-term issues. In some metropolitan programs, the professional staff acts as ombudsperson and point of referral for the resolution of key issues of concern.

PREPARING FOR THE VISIT:

LINEUP FOR BUSINESS VISITS

Armed with feedback from the community information gathering network and the results of due diligence efforts (Chapter 4), it is time to plan business visitation sessions.

The first step is to prioritize the list of targeted companies. Theoretically, businesses in immediate danger of closing or pulling up stakes would be at the top of that list. But here's where the principle of economic triage applies. A company that's ready to

PROS AND CONS OF STAFF-BASED VISITATION PROGRAMS

Pros

1. Ongoing program—the pulse of the business community is under continual monitoring.

2. The program is future directed; programmatic. The results of business concerns and opportunities take the form of new or revised programs.

3. No worries that interviewers are doubling as salesmen during the interview or that they are competitors.

4. Staff treats all information with the confidentiality needed.

5. Information given to company executives is thorough and accurate. Promises are not made that the community cannot them keep.

6. No need for massive training of volunteer staff.

SOURCE: Northern Indiana Pubic Service Company's
           A Business Retention Guide.

Cons

1. The interview process and the database developed from it are cumulative rather than an overall snapshot of the community economy at a given point in time. This can make it harder to identify needed community strategies.

2. Volunteer approach broadens the communities understanding of local economic development issues.

3. Work load falls entirely on the staff, most often reducing the total number of firms that can be visited during a given time period.

4. The effort generally does not capture the imagination of the media; therefore, the visitation effort is often overlooked and the community does not realize the process is an ongoing concerted effort.

5. Analysis of the data collected is not as statistically correct given the time span of its collection.

6. It is the highest cost option.

board up the windows and doors or leave town is probably beyond any range of options and alternatives your team could offer. You may want to mount a salvage operation in these cases, but save visits for companies that can still be turned around.

If you are not surveying all firms in an industry or community, make sure the firms designated to be surveyed are representative of the community and include your primary sector and largest employers.

THE DYNAMICS OF THE SURVEY

The visitation questionnaire or survey (Attachment 7-5) is designed to be completed during the course of a visitation session with a company. It serves to initiate a face-to-face meeting with one or more top com

pany managers and to establish relationships leading to unreserved exchanges of information and active problem solving.

The structure of the survey is geared to move respondents from general, automatic response questions to those which outline the direction of the organization, any cut of its current management and workforce, its operational and competitive situation, and—most important—its future challenges and opportunities (Attachment 7-6).

Each section of the survey poses linked questions, not only to elicit facts but also to yield perceptions and opinions as well. Reserve write-in space for respondents to address specific problems. **It can point to what really ails a business, and put your team on a fast track to solutions and alternatives.**

A number of states and local communities have developed survey instruments. Rather than spending a great deal of staff/task force time in survey development, use an existing tool, and use the complete survey instrument. If you select questions from different surveys, you may lose some of the continuity that is developed in linked questions of a survey.

GETTING IN THE DOOR...

Send your letter to the targeted company a few weeks prior to the meeting. Introduce the BRE program, and explain the purpose of the visit and the community's interest in developing a business climate that will support and nurture their growth and profitability. Take the letter to the business and identify who will be on your visitation team. The letter for the volunteer approach should also identify your BRE team as community representatives who recognize the contribution of progressive companies like theirs. It may help to enclose a copy of the long survey so that company representatives can familiarize themselves with the information prior to the meeting. (Attachment 7-5.)

Several days after the letter is sent, follow up with a telephone call to set a time and date for the visit and to thank them for their willingness to participate. If you are using staff instead of a volunteer approach, you may want to mail batches of 15 to 20 letters to allow you sufficient time to follow up with phone calls and make appointments within a week of sending the letters.

When you set up a business visitation, request a tour of the facility to supplement the assessment of the company's condition and intentions.

Using press releases may generate visibility of the visitations and help open the door with businesses. In the press release, explain that BRE is surveying local companies to find ways to help build a better business environment and a better community. (See Attachments 7-8, 7-9, and 7-10.)

The City of Oakland distinguished their survey from other survey instruments that crossed the desks of businesses and developed a carefully planned marketing strategy. This included personalized mailings, press releases to the local media, and personalized letters from the mayor. They found that their personalized approach paid large dividends in getting businesses to participate.

COORDINATING THE DOG AND PONY SHOW

Business visitations are generally conducted by a two-person team. One member may ask the questions while the other records answers, although this setup may vary to reflect the issues addressed during the meeting and the professional background of each team member.

Before the visit, the volunteer or staff should: 1) participate in volunteer training, 2) review the questionnaire, and 3) review the industry outlook summary for that particular industry.

OPENING THE GATES

Phoenix staff found a way to trick the CEO gatekeepers/protectors. After a couple of attempts to schedule an appointment, staff write a personal handwritten note on 4-by-6-inch stock. The gist of the card is "We have been unsuccessful in reaching you to schedule a ____-minute appointment to discuss tax credits . . . that might benefit your company."

Ninety percent of the handwritten notes garnered a call from the CEO. It may be that the gatekeeper thought it was a personal note and did not screen it, or thought it was an invitation.

THE VISITATION:

BUILDING TRUST REQUIRES CONFIDENTIALITY

Which business executives today would speak candidly about their company's financial competitive and management problems if they thought for a minute the information might find its way around town or beyond?

As a BRE staff or visitation team, confidentiality is essential. Some programs that use a task force to review surveys assign ID numbers to each company, and the first page of the survey with the company's name is removed before information is shared with the task force (Attachment 7-11).

Trust is one area where one cannot afford mistakes. Trust between the team and companies takes time to establish, and the credibility and success of the program depend upon building and nurturing trust.

DON'T MISS A THING

Review the early warning questions discussed in Chapter 5. Keep your eyes and ears open. The collecting of information on the company starts at the parking lot. For example:

- Are the buildings and grounds being appropriately maintained?
- Are there signs of equipment or furniture being moved?
- Is there evidence of intensive sprucing up that may signal that the facility is up for sale?

BE PROFESSIONAL, ALERT, AND EFFICIENT

After pleasantries have been exchanged, get down to the business of completing the long survey form. This exercise will drive the meeting, but allow opportunities for company representatives to express opinions and ask questions outside the survey format. Remember: Time is money for a businessperson.

LET THEM KNOW YOU CARE

Managers are more likely to deal with a visitation team on a peer level if members demonstrate a working knowledge of the company's industry and its business. This level of interest and preparedness encourages managers to cut to the chase of detailing problems and opportunities, and it builds the team's credibility. Do your homework before you arrive by collecting industry data and compiling the general information. Ask for confirmation of that information; it's not as if you know nothing about the business.

> One veteran business visitation team member places a thick folder labeled with the targeted company's name in front of him at the start of a visitation. The clear implication is that much is already known about the company and that no skeletons remain in the closet.

DON'T JUST LISTEN TO WHAT IS SAID; ABSORB WHAT IS COMMUNICATED

No matter what is known about the company and its dealings, don't attempt to prejudge the meeting. Assume you will learn new things and get some unexpected answers.

Business visitations with at-risk companies deal with thorny issues and problems. It's not unusual for company representatives to openly express anger and frustration during a meeting or to simmer below the surface. Be sensitive to what's being said and what's not being said. Nonverbal communication that can reflect disunity among company representatives or signal undisclosed external problems.

VOLUNTEER RESPONSIBILITIES DURING THE VISIT

▶ Emphasize that the survey is confidential and that the answers are voluntary (they can skip any question they are uncomfortable with);

▶ Use a pen, not a pencil, when recording responses;

▶ Write legibly, and circle rather than check answers;

▶ Read the question as is and don't paraphrase;

▶ Pursue conversation and ask tangent questions;

▶ Do not suggest answers to problems identified during the visit;

▶ Do not take offense to the company's comments, opinions, beliefs, or criticisms;

▶ Do not promise solutions, only that the company's concerns will be addressed;

▶ Follow the questions on the survey carefully; and

▶ Thank the company representative and, if applicable, invite them to the community meeting where the results of the program will be discussed.

GET THEM TALKING AND KEEP THEM TALKING

The survey will give a focus to the interview, but encourage managers to digress into their own stories about the company and its issues. For example:

— Is government regulation taking too big a bite from their resources?

— Have they been battling with county officials for months to get better access to their facility?

— Are they thinking of relocating elsewhere because they believe the community is indifferent to its issues?

— Is the local workforce falling behind in technical training?

The purpose of the visitation is to get to the core issues that are driving decisions to close, relocate, expand out of the area, or downsize.

DON'T OVERREACT TO ANSWERS

Asking the right questions may hit a corporate sore spot. An angry manager may demonstrate their frustration over a city official's unwillingness or inability to deal with a problem that's vexing the company. Acknowledge the manager's strong feel-ings, but resist the urge to join in pounding the table. *Taking sides at this point can get in the way of uncovering solutions later.*

DON'T PROMISE ANYTHING AT THE MEETING

Another key urge to resist during a visitation session is to make promises. Leave it to a follow-up meeting. Why take an unnecessary risk? Don't be misled that the easiest solution gets to the core issue. Get the solution set in cement before ordering a drum roll.

> *Making a commitment to a company and failing to deliver destroys credibility. And the word will get around.*

AFTERWARDS

Send a thank-you note to each company representative who participated in the business visitation, stressing the company's importance to the community.

Within two weeks, send a follow-up letter or do a follow-up visit with the company to discuss the problems and opportunities brought up at the visitation meeting.

Outline the issues to be addressed by the BRE program on behalf of the company.

Add any information gathered to your cumulative database. *With permission of the company,* determine which information may be useful to other agencies in the development of their programs. For example, information on training and educational needs may be shared with the local colleges, universities, and training providers; and base information and market demand for raw materials and supplies could be useful to the marketing agents for the area and the state. Obviously, information will be shared within your economic development office and used to develop future economic development directions to provide specific help when needed.

Washington state's Survey Program Checklist (Attachment 7-12) is a good reminder of the steps in the process.

REVIEWING SURVEYS FOR BUSINESS "RED FLAGS"

The follow-up surveys can either be done by a task force member or BRE professional staff. Examples of possible red flags in the sample visitation survey are identified at the end of Attachment 7-6. A follow-up worksheet is a good tool for tracking action taken (Attachment 7-13).

OVER-DELIVER WITH FOLLOW-UP

Build follow-up momentum and establish the program's effectiveness by solving the company's easiest problem first. One fast success can go a long way toward convincing company managers that the time invested was well spent.

Don't be shy about letting the company know of the actions taken on its behalf:

▸ Send brief updates to the designated company contact to keep communications channels open.

▸ Send supplemental information on issues that were discussed at business visitation sessions.

> *Responding to survey questions is an investment of time, effort, and trust by a company's management. They have a right to expect a return on that investment.*

MAKE SURE YOU'RE SEEING BOTH THE FOREST AND THE TREES

Remember to address the individual needs and issues identified in the business surveys and visitation, as well as update the community's strategic BRE plan. Are there patterns seen in the issues businesses are facing? Does the community have specific barriers for certain types of industry?

COMMUNITY STRATEGIES

DEVELOPING RECOMMENDATIONS

Use a task force or committee to develop community strategies from the responses of the surveys. Once formed, these collations can continue to provide feedback and support for economic development.

Three models have been used successfully in developing and writing strategies and recommendations:

1. The facilitator drafts a report on the survey findings and suggests several strategies which could be considered in business retention and expansion.

2. The research staff at a university or other outside group drafts the survey findings and sends them out in advance. No strategies are suggested. In these two models, the facilitator leads the task force members through the process of developing strategies and

recommendations. The second model, however, requires the task force to take on more of the responsibility for developing the strategies and recommendations.

3. A team of resource/technical assistance people reviews a summary of survey information and drafts recommendations which are prioritized and discussed by the task force.

PRIORITIZING RECOMMENDATIONS

Task force members are divided into small groups to discuss recommendations/strategies for addressing business issues. Each group nominates a strategy and provides a brief explanation as to why this as an obvious conclusion/issue. The process should be repeated with any additional recommendations from each group. The nominated items should be recorded.

Once all the nominations have been recorded, encourage the group to discuss the conclusions and issues more fully. Groups that have been together several times before usually handle the discussion much better than the ones that are meeting for the first time.

After discussion, the group members may decide to combine similar items before voting on the top three to five priorities. Some programs simplify the voting procedure by giving each individual sticky dots to vote for their highest priorities. Any strategy with less than three dots is dropped.

In order to assure that there is follow-up on strategies have task force or community members identify the one they will work on. If no one will commit to work on a strategy, consider dropping it.

NOTHING WAS EVER WON WITH 100 PERCENT OF THE VOTE

When using the task force approach, remember that consensus building is never easy. When dealing with public policy issues as thorny as business closures, job loss, and dwindling tax revenues, decisions won't please everyone. The team represents diverse elements of the community and members will approach problem solving from different angles. Those differences can yield creative and spontaneous solutions to the tough problems ahead. Seek instead broad-based compromise that work and that everyone can live with.

SUMMARIZING THE SURVEY RESULTS

Local leaders or BRE staff are encouraged to develop a written report on survey results and strategic planning areas.

Sample Outline for Final Report on Visitations

- Introduction
- Economic Development Trends and Outlooks
- Survey Results and Follow-up Strategies
- Accomplishments (demonstrate that the program is interested in action)
- Tables
- Type(s) of information provided to firms (direct and referral)
- Types of assistance provided
- Recommendations

COMMUNITY MEETING

A community meeting is typically held to share the recommendations with a broader range of concerned citizens. At this meeting, the BRE survey findings, strategies, and recommendations are presented. This provides an opportunity for members of the community to learn more about their business environment and understand the economic development initiatives being implemented. (See Attachment 7-14, suggested agenda.)

OTHER SURVEY RESOURCES

This chapter provides a very brief overview of the visitation model. It is strongly recommended that communities use staff who are trained in this process to help coach them.

For assistance on implementing the visitation approach, contact state staff to identify if there is state technical assistance available for these processes. Business Retention and Expansion International, a nonprofit professional organization, has established a "consultant" certification. You can find your nearest "consultant," as well as information on training to become a consultant, at www.brei.org.

A set of booklets that focus on the BRE visitation approach can be purchased from the Northeast Regional Center for Rural Development, (814) 863-4656.

VISITATION TIMELINE

Activity/By Whom   **By When**

Introduce Program / Sponsoring Organization . . . . January–March

- — *Gain public and private support*
- — *Individual meetings and community discussions/workshop*

Hire a Program Coordinator / Sponsoring Organization . . . . March

Establish a Task Force / Program Coordinator . . . . April

First Task Force Meeting (3 hours) . . . . April

- — *Program overview*
- — *Task force role and responsibilities*
- — *Begin delineating program scope*
- — *Develop detailed workplan*
- — *Establish task force committees*
- — *Elect a task force chair*
- — *Schedule next task force meeting*

Program Coordinator . . . . May–June

- — *Begin to develop program materials*
- — *Collect business lists and data on local business sectors for developing program scope*

Second Task Force Meeting (3 hours) . . . . June

- — *Complete program scope*
- — *Begin designing survey instrument*
- — *Develop interviewer recruitment plan*
- — *Design response network*
- — *Develop publicity campaign*

Program Coordinator . . . . July–August

- — *Complete survey instrument*
  Establish computer system for input
- — *Volunteer interviewers*
  Recruit interviewers
  Schedule interviewer training session
- — *Develop response network*

Activity/By Whom   <u>By When</u>

Third Task Force Meeting (3 hours) . . . . August

- — *Finalize survey instrument*
    Check status of interviewer element
    Review status of response network
    Assign interviews to task force members

Business Outreach and Visitations / . . . . August–November
Program Coordinator and Interviewers

- — *Mail out Mayor's letter*
- — *Arrange company visits*
- — *Supervise interviewers*
- — *Conduct interviews*

Response Network / Program Coordinator . . . . Ongoing

- — *Develop system for processing immediate problems revealed by survey*
- — *Invest time in working with response network*

Ongoing Program Development and Final Report / Task Force . . . . December

- — *Input survey data into computer/tabulate*
- — *Hold focus group with interviewers*
- — *Draft report of results*

Fourth Task Force Meeting (3 hours) . . . . December

- — *Review draft report and survey tabulations*
- — *Begin discussion of on-going economic development needs
    revealed in survey data analysis*

Post-Survey / Program Coordinator . . . . January

- — *Finalize report*
- — *Circulate results via press releases, presentations to City Council, etc.*

Fifth and Subsequent Task Force Meetings . . . . 1–2 years

- — *Begin designing economic development programs, such as:*
    Revolving loan fund, small business assistance center,
    manufacturers roundtable, business incubator, job training/
    first source hiring program and facility location service.

<u>SOURCE</u>: *California Business Retention and Expansion Program Manual*

SAMPLE LETTER FOR RECRUITING VOLUNTEERS

[Date]
[Volunteer Name]
[Volunteer Organization]
[Volunteer Address]
[City, State, Zip]

Dear [Name of Volunteer],

Thank you for agreeing to participate in the _____ [County/Community] Business Retention and Expansion (BRE) Program. As a volunteer, you are a critical element in this project, which is sponsored by [local sponsor].

The overall purpose of the BRE program is to assist our existing business and industry. To do this, we have asked local leaders like yourself to visit several firms with a survey to gather information about their needs, concerns, and opinions of _____ [County/Community] as a place to do business. This information will help us improve our local business climate to better meet the needs of both our existing and future businesses.

To tell you more about the program and your role in it, we are holding two training sessions for all volunteers. The training sessions will cover all essential information regarding the BRE program. Volunteers must attend one of these training sessions to visit firms. You need to attend only one of these two and one-half–hour sessions. You may select either of the following sessions:

1. [Place, date, time of Session One]
2. [Place, date, time of Session Two]

Please complete and return the enclosed response card to confirm your participation. If you are at all unsure about participating, please attend one of these sessions anyway. You can make your decision after the meeting.

We greatly appreciate your cooperation in this [County/Community] effort. Your participation as a volunteer is critical to the success of our future business climate.

If you have questions about the program, please call me at [phone number].

Sincerely,

[Coordinator Name]
BRE Coordinator

SOURCE: *Business Retention and Expansion in the Western U.S.: People and Planning Can Make a Difference*, U.S. West Foundation Grant/Utah State University.

SUGGESTED AGENDA FOR
INITIAL TASK FORCE MEETING

Mayor's Welcome and Introduction

Orientation of Any City's Business Retention and Expansion Program

> What is a Business Retention and Expansion Program?
> Review key elements
> What needs to be accomplished?

Roles and Responsibilities

> Program Coordinator
> Sponsoring organization
> Task force structure:
>> *Chair*
>> *Executive committees*
>> *Subcommittees*

Program Scope

> Discussion of sectors and number of businesses to survey

Establish Objectives and Tasks

> **Survey:** Review business survey for local applicability

> **Interviewers:** Identify potential interviewers and time frame for training

> **Response:** Discuss response network for survey respondents' problems and opportunities (red flags) and analysis of interview responses (computer time, written report, printing, and distribution)

> **Promotion:** Discuss publicity (newspaper, radio, television, and timing)

Summary

> Review tasks and action items
> Set time, place and agenda for any subcommittee meetings
> Set time, place and agenda for the next task force meeting

Adjourn

SOURCE: *California Business Retention and Expansion Program Manual*

SAMPLE AGENDA
FOR
INTERVIEWER TRAINING SESSION

Introductions
Acknowledge visitors, such as mayor and chamber of commerce representatives

Discuss Business Retention and Expansion Program
Background
Other municipalities' programs
Objectives and process

Video covering visitation approach*

Question and Answer time [with experienced visitation coordinator]

Distribute Visitation Packet

Discuss business survey
Review survey question-by-question
Confidentiality of information obtained
Maintenance of interview information (at some location other than City Hall)

Discuss the importance of the interviewers' role in the program

Conduct role play exercises

Discuss unusual circumstances that might be encountered
Interruptions
Hostile responses

SOURCE: *California Business Retention and Expansion Program Manual*

---

* *Business Retention and Expansion International and several state programs have videos which can be good training tools to give overview of how visitation approach has worked in other communities and the interview process.*

[Date]

ECONOMIC DEVELOPMENT
BUSINESS SURVEY (long version)

Company Name: _____

Address: _____

Your Name: _____

Position with Company: _____ Phone Number: _____

Is this the company headquarters? $\square_1$ Yes $\square_2$ No

If no, location of company headquarters: _____

Parent company name (if different): _____

A.1 **Please indicate your company's primary product or service category:**
(CHECK ONLY ONE)

$\square_1$ Food	$\square_7$ Petro/Rubber	$\square_{13}$ Instruments
$\square_2$ Textiles/Apparel	$\square_8$ Stone/Clay	$\square_{14}$ Environmental
$\square_3$ Wood	$\square_9$ Machinery	$\square_{15}$ Biotechnology
$\square_4$ Furniture	$\square_{10}$ Metals	$\square_{16}$ Telecommunications
$\square_5$ Paper/Printing	$\square_{11}$ Electronics	$\square_{17}$ Other *(SPECIFY)*
$\square_6$ Chemical	$\square_{12}$ Transportation	_____

A.2 **How many years has your business been in operation at this location?**

$\square_1$ 2 years or less $\square_3$ 6 to 10 years
$\square_2$ 3 to 5 years $\square_4$ More than 10 years

A.3 **What percentage of your product is sold in the following areas?**
(MUST TOTAL 100%)

Local (100-mile radius) _____ %
Regional _____ %
National _____ %
International _____ %
100%

A.4 **Please estimate your company's total gross revenues for last year:**

$\square_1$ Under $1 million $\square_4$ $16 to 50 million
$\square_2$ $1 to 5 million $\square_5$ $51 to 150 million
$\square_3$ $6 to 15 million $\square_6$ More than $150 million

_____ *KEEPING BUSINESS HEALTHY, HAPPY, AND LOCAL*

B. COMPANY DESCRIPTION AND HISTORY

B.1 **How many locations does your company have?** *(PLEASE CHECK THE APPROPRIATE BOX)*

☐₁ 1   ☐₂ 2   ☐₃ 3 to 5   ☐₄ 6 to 10   ☐₅ 11+

B.2 **If more than 1, how many are in this county?** *(PLEASE CHECK THE APPROPRIATE BOX)*

☐₁ 1   ☐₂ 2   ☐₃ 3 to 5   ☐₄ 6 to 10   ☐₅ 11+

B.3 **What is the corporate structure of local firm?**

☐₁ Sole Proprietorship   ☐₄ Corporation (public)
☐₂ Corporation (closely held)   ☐₅ Other *(SPECIFY)*
☐₃ Partnership
                                  _____

B.4 **Are you currently trying to expand into new markets or products?**

☐₁ New markets   ☐₂ New products   ☐₃ Neither

If yes, a. Where _____

   b. What _____

   c. Does this represent a significant change from current product line?

      ☐₁ Yes   ☐₂ No

   d. What resources are you working with to help expand?

      ☐₁ Other private firms   ☐₄ Public programs
      ☐₂ Industry associations   ☐₅ State export assistance
      ☐₃ Universities or colleges   ☐₆ Other *(SPECIFY)* _____

B.5 **To what type of customer do you sell your product?**
(ESTIMATE PERCENTAGE SOLD TO EACH TYPE BELOW. MUST TOTAL 100%.)

_____ % Manufacturing firms
_____ % Building contractors
_____ % Wholesalers
_____ % Retailers
_____ % Direct to consumers
_____ % Institutional/public
_____ % Other *(PLEASE DESCRIBE)* _____
  100%

C. EMPLOYMENT AND LABOR

C.1 Please estimate how many employees your local firm:

Has today: ☐₁ 1 to 5 ☐₃ 21 to 50 ☐₅ 101 to 200
☐₂ 6 to 20 ☐₄ 51 to 100 ☐₆ More than 200

Had 1 year ago: ☐₁ 1 to 5 ☐₃ 21 to 50 ☐₅ 101 to 200
☐₂ 6 to 20 ☐₄ 51 to 100 ☐₆ More than 200

Had 5 years ago: ☐₁ 1 to 5 ☐₃ 21 to 50 ☐₅ 101 to 200
☐₂ 6 to 20 ☐₄ 51 to 100 ☐₆ More than 200

Will have in 1 year: ☐₁ 1 to 5 ☐₃ 21 to 50 ☐₅ 101 to 200
☐₂ 6 to 20 ☐₄ 51 to 100 ☐₆ More than 200 ☐₇ N/A

Will have in 5 years: ☐₁ 1 to 5 ☐₃ 21 to 50 ☐₅ 101 to 200
☐₂ 6 to 20 ☐₄ 51 to 100 ☐₆ More than 200 ☐₇ N/A

C.2 If you anticipate employment decreases, please indicate reasons.

☐₁ Decline in sales ☐₆ Changes of ownership
☐₂ Foreign competition ☐₇ Change in technology
☐₃ Change in labor skills needed ☐₈ Regulatory compliance
☐₄ Increase production costs ☐₉ Decline of supplier links
☐₅ Lack of capital ☐₁₀ Other *(SPECIFY)* _____

C.3 How many shifts does your company operate?

☐₁ one ☐₂ two ☐₃ three

C.4 If you had more orders, do you currently have the capacity to produce more?

☐₁ Yes ☐₂ No

C.5 Do you employ part-time workers? ☐₁ Yes ☐₂ No

C.6 Do you employ seasonal workers? ☐₁ Yes ☐₂ No

C.7 Does employment at your firm require specialized training/retraining?

☐₁ Yes ☐₂ No

C.8 How are your workers trained? *(CHECK ALL THAT APPLY)*

☐₁ On the job ☐₃ Trade school ☐₅ Community college
☐₂ Vocational school ☐₄ University ☐₆ Union/Apprenticeship program
☐₇ Other *(SPECIFY)* _____

C.9 How significant a problem is employee turnover? *(PLEASE CHECK ONE)*

$\square_4$ Very $\quad$ $\square_3$ Somewhat $\quad$ $\square_2$ Not very $\quad$ $\square_1$ Not at all

C.10 How much trouble do you have replacing skilled employees? *(PLEASE CHECK ONE)*

$\square_5$ Quite a lot $\quad$ $\square_4$ Some $\quad$ $\square_3$ Little $\quad$ $\square_2$ Very little $\quad$ $\square_1$ None

C.11 How do you hire workers? *(CHECK ALL THAT APPLY)*

$\square_1$ Private employment service $\quad$ $\square_5$ Department of Employment Security
$\square_2$ Place sign in front $\quad$ $\square_6$ Private Industry Council
$\square_3$ Vocational school $\quad$ $\square_7$ Union hall
$\square_4$ Newspaper $\quad$ $\square_8$ Word of mouth
$\quad$ $\square_9$ Other *(SPECIFY)* _____

C.12 Are there specific jobs you are having difficulty in filling? *(SPECIFY)*

_____ $\quad$ _____

C.13 What percentage of your employees are unionized?

$\square_1$ 0 to 10% $\quad$ $\square_2$ 11 to 20% $\quad$ $\square_3$ 21 to 50% $\quad$ $\square_4$ 51+% $\quad$ $\square_5$ None

C.14 What percentage of your time is spent on complying with federal, state and local regulation?

$\square_1$ 0 to 5% $\quad$ $\square_2$ 6 to 10% $\quad$ $\square_3$ 11 to 20% $\quad$ $\square_4$ 21 to 30% $\quad$ $\square_5$ 31+%

D. TRENDS AND OUTLOOKS

D.1 What has been your average annual growth in the last five years?

$\square_1$ Decline $\quad$ $\square_3$ Up and down $\quad$ $\square_5$ + 6 to 10% $\quad$ $\square_7$ + 21 to 50%
$\square_2$ None $\quad$ $\square_4$ + 1 to 5% $\quad$ $\square_6$ + 11 to 20% $\quad$ $\square_8$ 51% +

D.2 How serious a problem is cash flow in your company?

$\square_4$ Very $\quad$ $\square_3$ Somewhat $\quad$ $\square_2$ Not very $\quad$ $\square_1$ Not at all

D.3 Is your business seasonal? $\quad$ $\square_1$ Yes $\quad$ $\square_2$ No

If yes, please specify _____

D.4 Is your company suffering from an economic impact or trend?
$\square_1$ Yes $\quad$ $\square_2$ No

If yes, please specify _____

D.5a Do you anticipate any problems with your financing needs?
☐₁ Yes   ☐₂ No

(If no, then skip to D.6. If yes, answer D.5b and D.5c; please explain:)

_____

D.5b What kind of financial help might you need? *(CHECK ALL THAT APPLY)*

☐₁ Short-term loans   ☐₃ Long-term loans   ☐₅ Other *(SPECIFY)* _____
☐₂ Low-interest loans ☐₄ Loan guarantees   _____

D.5c What type of capital do you need? *(CHECK ALL THAT APPLY)*

☐₁ Working   ☐₃ Equipment   ☐₅ Other *(SPECIFY)* _____
☐₂ Investment   ☐₄ Land   _____

D.6 How important are the following factors to the financial condition of your company?

	₄ Very	₃ Somewhat	₂ Not very	₁ Not at all
Material costs	☐	☐	☐	☐
Labor costs	☐	☐	☐	☐
Interest rates	☐	☐	☐	☐
Selling costs	☐	☐	☐	☐
Transportation costs	☐	☐	☐	☐
Regulatory compliance	☐	☐	☐	☐
Energy costs	☐	☐	☐	☐
State and local taxes	☐	☐	☐	☐
Training/Retraining	☐	☐	☐	☐
Land, construction costs	☐	☐	☐	☐
Other *(SPECIFY)*	☐	☐	☐	☐

D.7 How important are the following factors to your current operation?

	₄ Very	₃ Somewhat	₂ Not very	₁ Not at all
Foreign imports	☐	☐	☐	☐
Domestic competition	☐	☐	☐	☐
Changing markets	☐	☐	☐	☐
Outdated machinery	☐	☐	☐	☐
Insufficient space	☐	☐	☐	☐
Transportation problems	☐	☐	☐	☐
Labor productivity	☐	☐	☐	☐
Labor availability	☐	☐	☐	☐
Inadequate supplier network	☐	☐	☐	☐

D.8a **Within the next two years, how likely are you to be involved in the following:**

	4 Very	3 Somewhat	2 Not very	1 Not at all
Reduction of workforce	☐	☐	☐	☐
Acquisition of other companies	☐	☐	☐	☐
Merger with other companies	☐	☐	☐	☐
Acquisition of your company	☐	☐	☐	☐
Expansion in domestic markets	☐	☐	☐	☐
Expansion into (of) foreign markets	☐	☐	☐	☐
Relocation to another state	☐	☐	☐	☐
Expansion of existing facility	☐	☐	☐	☐
Downsizing of existing facility	☐	☐	☐	☐
Purchasing equipment to increase production	☐	☐	☐	☐
Retirement of major owner/ stockholder	☐	☐	☐	☐
Site closure by company HQ	☐	☐	☐	☐
Employee ownership	☐	☐	☐	☐

D.8b **If you are considering relocation or expansion, where are you looking?**

☐₁ Within city   ☐₄ Outside Washington
☐₂ Within county   ☐₅ Outside United States
☐₃ Other Washington state location

D.9a **What is your overall opinion of the county as a place to do business?**
(CHECK ONE)

☐₁ Excellent   ☐₂ Good   ☐₃ Fair   ☐₄ Poor

D.9b **What is your overall opinion of state as a place to do business?** *(CHECK ONE)*

☐₁ Excellent   ☐₂ Good   ☐₃ Fair   ☐₄ Poor

D.9c **Why did you say that?** _____

_____

E. LOCAL GOVERNMENT SERVICES

E.1 **Economic Development Initiatives — What economic development programs are you aware of?** *(Please put an X in front of the programs you are aware of and those you have used in the past two years.)*

Aware	Used	
☐	☐	Industrial Revenue Bonds/Umbrella Bond Program
☐	☐	Small Business Administration financing
		Department of Community, Trade and Economic Development:
☐	☐	Community Finance Program
☐	☐	Business Assistance Center
☐	☐	Community Development Loan Fund
☐	☐	Local revolving loan fund
☐	☐	Local Economic Development Council
☐	☐	Small Business Development Center
☐	☐	Export Assistance Center
☐	☐	Center for International Trade in Forest Products
☐	☐	International Marketing Program for Agricultural Commodities & Trade

(Use additional sheet for comments about any of the above programs.

Specify program.)

E.2 **Adequacy of Local Government Services — How satisfied are you with the following?**

	4 Very	3 Somewhat	2 Not very	1 Not at all
Overall local govt. services	☐	☐	☐	☐
Water supply	☐	☐	☐	☐
Waste water treatment	☐	☐	☐	☐
Police services	☐	☐	☐	☐
Streets and roads	☐	☐	☐	☐
Fire protection	☐	☐	☐	☐
Planning department	☐	☐	☐	☐
Permitting process	☐	☐	☐	☐
Schools (K-12)	☐	☐	☐	☐
Community college/university	☐	☐	☐	☐
Vocational/technical institutes	☐	☐	☐	☐
Child care	☐	☐	☐	☐
Social services	☐	☐	☐	☐

(Use additional sheet for comments about any of the above programs.

Specify program.)

E.3 Please indicate those areas in which you feel you could use assistance.
(CHECK ALL THAT APPLY)

$\square_1$ Finance $\square_6$ Regulatory $\square_{11}$ Equipment
$\square_2$ Personnel $\square_7$ Business planning $\square_{12}$ Job skill training
$\square_3$ Energy costs $\square_8$ Inventory $\square_{13}$ Business succession
$\square_4$ Accounting control $\square_9$ Marketing   planning
$\square_5$ Working capital $\square_{10}$ Export/import $\square_{14}$ Employee ownership
                                                 $\square_{15}$ Other *(SPECIFY)*

_____

E.4 If primary company owner(s) is over 50, has an in-house successor been identified?

$\square_1$ Yes $\square_2$ No $\square_3$ Unknown

THANK YOU for helping to complete our survey. Please return to:

[your address]

EXPLANATION OF SURVEY

SECTION A — Addresses basic information about the company, including its primary product or service category, years of operation at its location, market area and annual revenue range. *This section also identifies the respondent by his or her position in the organization. YOU HAVE MUCH OF THIS INFORMATION ALREADY. FILL IN THIS PART OF THE SURVEY AND CONFIRM THE INFORMATION.*

SECTION B — Develops a snapshot of the company, including information describing its corporate structure, whether it does business at more than one site, and the nature of its products and markets. *Early warning signals should be tripped by responses pertaining to ownership. A maturing family-owned business could indicate inexperienced management and vulnerability to sell off. A multi-unit firm with an out-of-town headquarters is often more likely to move than a locally owned operation.*

— Reveals where the company sells its products, whether it is engaged in active research and development, and how its distribution channels work. *Difficulties or opportunities in any of these areas can and should be viewed as early warning indicators of possible expansion, relocation, or downsizing.*

SECTION C — Deals with workforce issues and reveals whether training is a priority of company management, whether relations with labor unions have been constructive, and whether the company is equipped to meet competition in new and expanding markets. *Red flag triggers point to a workforce that lacks information-based skills, inadequate training programs, high employee turnover, and constant friction between management and union leadership.*

SECTION D — Reveals financial trends within the company that could lead to closure, out-of-area expansion, relocation, or layoffs. *Much of this information will already be known by the visitation team conducting the long survey, but these questions often prompt the respondent to speak candidly about the company's problems and identify elements in the business environment and in local government that impact how it operates. This series can herald early warning of dissatisfaction with the businesses environment and intentions to relocate or downsize.*

SECTION E — Tests levels of company awareness, involvement and satisfaction with local government and the community. *This section can serve not only as a tool for your BRE team but as a heads-up for area elected and appointed officials as well. Relationships between local government and business will not always be smooth. But as long as open communication is maintained, each other's interests are understood and respected, and companies feel that their contribution to the community is valued, there remains a foundation for future discussion and negotiation.*

EARLY WARNING SIGNS ON SAMPLE LONG SURVEY

The following are possible early warning signs to watch for on the long survey:

Question:	Early Warning Sign:
C.1	Decrease in employees
C.7	Require specialized training and have decline in employment
C.9	Turnover is very or somewhat significant. Need to work with training institutions identified in C.7.
D.1	Decline in annual growth
D.2.	Cash flow is very or somewhat serious
D.3.	Seasonal unemployment become recession
D.4.	Yes
D.5a.	Yes
D.8a.	Answered "very" or "somewhat likely" for:

- — Reduction in workforce (1)*
- — Merger (3)
- — Acquisition of your company (4)
- — Relocation (7)
- — Downsizing (9)
- — Retirement of major owner/stockholder (11)

Question:	Early Warning Sign:
D.9a.	Answered "fair" or "poor"
E.3.	Identified technical assistance needs

* ( ) = *order of question*

SAMPLE MAYOR'S LETTER

Office of the Major

Date

Ms. Jane Doe, President
General Manufacturing Group
123 Main Street
XYZ City, CA 90000

Dear Ms. Doe:

The economic well-being of our city comes from existing firms in our industrial and manufacturing sector. Because of its importance to our community, positive steps are being taken to identify and meet the needs of these firms.

To support this effort, an in-depth survey of industrial and manufacturing firms is being conducted under the sponsorship of the Mayor's Office in cooperation with the City Manager's Office, the Chamber of Commerce, and the Manufacturers Association. The survey consists of interviews between business leaders and representatives of one of the participating organizations.

The survey will help keep us abreast of your company's plans and determine if you are satisfied with this community as a place to do business; and, in turn, we would like you to know about services to businesses available through this office.

I respectfully invite you to participate in this important survey. Shortly, one of our interviewers will contact you for an appointment. Your candid responses to the survey questions, which will be held in strict confidence, are vital if you and we are to benefit from this business outreach program. The interview should require approximately an hour of your time. You will be provided with a summary report when an analysis of the results is completed.

We are committed to fostering a vibrant economy here in the City of XYC. Your participation will help us continue these important efforts.

Sincerely,

JOHN SMITH
Mayor

Establish schedule and appropriate timing (no more than two weeks prior to follow-up contact by interviewer) for mailing of mayor's letters. Assign each interviewer two to five initial firms to contact.

SOURCE: *California Business Retention and Expansion Program Manual*

Press Release

FOR IMMEDIATE RELEASE
[DATE]

CONTACT: [BRE spokesperson]
[Telephone, fax numbers]

LOCAL BUSINESS VISITATION TEAMS RECEIVE TRAINING

[Community, state] — [Number] local volunteers attended training sessions this week as part of a new economic development program to help retain local businesses and keep them growing in this community.

The sessions were conducted by [organization], which also is the sponsor of the Business Retention and Expansion (BRE) program.

[Insert quote from sponsoring organization spokesperson expressing enthusiasm for the program and how the training will help volunteers with their task.]

The BRE program is designed to stimulate economic growth by helping local businesses identify and solve problems that affect productivity, profitability and competitiveness. Volunteers will seek to uncover problems by surveying local companies. Recent training sessions prepared volunteer teams for upcoming business interviews.

[Insert quote from a volunteer about what he/she learned from the training sessions and how the community will benefit from the BRE program."]

[Coordinator] emphasized that the information gathered through interviews and surveys will be strictly confidential. It will be used by BRE staff and Task Force members to seek solutions to problems identified during the business visits.

[Insert quote from coordinator about his/her expectations for the program in terms of its benefit to the community.]

SOURCE: *Business Retention and Expansion in the Western U.S.: People and Planning Can Make a Difference*, U.S. West Foundation Grant/Utah State University

Press Release

FOR IMMEDIATE RELEASE
[DATE]

CONTACT: [BRE spokesperson]
[Telephone, fax numbers]

VOLUNTEER TEAMS BEGIN LOCAL BUSINESS INTERVIEWS

[Name of community] — Businesses will have an opportunity to voice their opinions on the local business environment through a newly established economic development program geared to help retain business and jobs in this community.

Trained volunteer teams began this week to conduct interviews with more than (number) local firms to identify needs and concerns and to determine how the business climate can be improved.

[Insert quote from the program coordinator stressing the importance of the interviews and the value of the contribution being made by volunteers teams.]

[Name], sponsor of the Business Retention and Expansion program (BRE), will assist staff and task force members in reviewing the information gathered during interviews and seeking solutions to problems identified through surveys and face-to-face meetings.

[Insert quote praising local businesses for participating in the interviews and their support of the program.]

SOURCE: *Business Retention and Expansion in the Western U.S.: People and Planning Can Make a Difference, U.S. West Foundation Grant/Utah State University*

Press Release

FOR IMMEDIATE RELEASE
[DATE]

CONTACT: [BRE spokesperson]
[Telephone, fax numbers]

MAJORITY OF LOCAL COMPANIES FAVOR [NAME] BUSINESS CLIMATE

[**Community, State**] — More than _____ percent of local companies consider [**community**] an excellent or a good place to do business according to results of an extensive survey by the Business Retention and Expansion (BRE) program.

Results were announced at BRE community meeting _____ night, attended by more than [**number**], according to Program Coordinator [**name**].

[**Insert quote from coordinator reporting how significant the results are and confirming their value in solving business problems in the community.**]

Several concerns identified through interviews with local companies will be addressed by the BRE program. Surveys showed that:

- Two of every five businesses in [community] want Highway Route__ widened.

- Nearly 30 percent of local companies are dissatisfied with medical care in [**community**]

    [**Continue list**]

BRE Coordinator [**name**] said the program's task force would be reviewing interview responses next month and would begin meeting with local officials to seek solutions.

SOURCE: *Business Retention and Expansion in the Western US: People and Planning Can Make a Difference*, U.S. West Foundation Grant/Utah State University

SAMPLE
VISITATION SURVEY COVER PAGE

Check responses or fill in the blanks as appropriate. Feel free to write additional information in the margins.

In order to maximize the results of this business retention and expansion effort, it is vitally important to explain the following general facts about the program to the person interviewed.

The program is sponsored by_____.

The following local organizations have endorsed the program: _____

_____

The survey is a cooperative effort involving many volunteers drawn from other local businesses, local government institutions, and community organizations.

There are three objectives for this project:

1. To identify specific problems of individual businesses that might be addressed locally.

2. To identify the common problems, needs, and wants of the existing local business so the community can do all it can to help local businesses prosper.

3. To learn the future plans of local companies with respect to expansion, relocation, and/or closure.

Confidentiality: Individual responses to this survey are confidential and will not be released. They will be summarized with the responses from other companies in a final report of the overall results.

Copies of the report will be provided to all companies interviewed. *(optional)*

Sample BRE Survey Cover Sheet (for task force use)

Company ID: _____

Company: _____

Address: _____

_____

Name and title of person to be interviewed: _____

Names of volunteer visitors: _____

_____

Date of visit: _____

SOURCE: *Business Retention and Expansion in the Western U.S.: People and Planning Can Make a Difference,* U.S. West Foundation Grant/Utah State University

BUSINESS SURVEY
PROGRAM CHECKLIST

✓	LEADERSHIP TEAM — EXECUTIVE COMMITTEE
	Membership: 3 to 5 members, or existing advisory group (roles: coordination, media, red flags)
	Identify *businesses* to be surveyed: • Number (minimum of 50 recommended) and locations (countywide or county and specific city focuses) for interviews. • Kinds of businesses (in addition to manufacturers, who else are the significant businesses?).
	Staffing for project: Identify Coordinator job duties, support staff role and compensation. Possibly identify co-sponsors to help fund.
	Work with coordinator to develop *project timeline*.
	Identify *volunteers recruitment plan:* Need 2 people per visit—normally do two visits each. Consider asking volunteers to recruit friend, or use school-to-work or college students as notetakers. _All_ should attend volunteer training.
	Identify *task force members:* Representatives from 5 sectors: business, economic development, government, education, and community leadership—no more than 50 percent from any one sector.
	Review and design *survey:* Caution: Don't make survey too long. Make sure questions and answers are on the same page and that you complete the reference to your county.
✓	COORDINATOR
	Develop publicity/media plan: Issue a *press release* on your project. (Note: Someone else on leadership team may take lead for this.)
	Business contact list—addresses and phone numbers.
	Recruit volunteers.

BUSINESS SURVEY PROGRAM CHECKLIST (continued)

✓	**COORDINATOR** (continued):
	Send *letter* to businesses from an elected official—city or county. Include background survey; on-site survey optional.
	City or county Business Proclamation of Appreciation (optional).
	Follow-up call to businesses to explain project.
✓	## VOLUNTEER TRAINING
	Set up a minimum of two volunteer *training sessions* (2 hours each).
	Equipment needed: • Overhead or LCD projector • Speakerphone • BR&E tape • VCR
	Notify volunteers, leadership team, and task force about training (letter or e-mail).
	Arrange for experienced visitation coordinator to be available (by phone or in person) for training to answer questions on process.
	Prepare training packet for volunteers (see resource guide for contents).
	Create visitor teams and match with businesses. The interviewer is lead person on team.
	Work on *agenda* and assign tasks (see sample).
	One week after training: Schedule appointments with businesses (can be done by either the coordinator or volunteers. If volunteers have not returned card for scheduling the visit, call or e-mail volunteers to *verify* that they have their *appointment scheduled*.
✓	## SURVEY DATA
	Send *thank you letters or cards* to businesses as surveys are returned (optional).
	Review surveys for "red flag" issues—identify businesses that need individualized technical assistance.
	Refer to appropriate technical assistance provider or EDC staff person for follow-up.
	Enter data on survey on database.
	Call volunteers who haven't returned surveys.

BUSINESS SURVEY PROGRAM CHECKLIST (continued)

✓	TASK FORCE
	Set up meeting on findings (retreat or 3½ hours minimum). Purpose: 1) prioritize community issues; and 2) establish work groups for major issues. Pick task force and work group chairs.
	Follow up on work groups: Should meet twice between first and second task force meetings to develop work plan (see sample worksheet, Attachment 7-13).
	Hold *second* full *task force meeting* to discuss individual work group plans.
	Finalize report on findings and action plan.
	Meet with task force members every two to three months to hear reports on the progress of work group's plans.

✓	COMMENCEMENT/COMMUNITY MEETING
	Plan event for *reporting back to businesses and community* on survey findings and plan (see sample agenda, Attachment 7-14). (Optional)
	Contact media for coverage on report findings and action plan.
	Send *copies of final report* with action plan to county and city government officials, task force, and businesses, if requested.

BRE TASK FORCE
FOLLOW-UP WORKSHEET

Company ID # _____

Community/County _____

Date of Visit ___/___/___

Today's Date ___/___/___

SURVEY QUESTIONS NEEDING FOLLOW-UP	NATURE OF CONCERN/PROBLEM	RECOMMENDED FOLLOW-UP	FOLLOW-UP PERSON	FOLLOW-UP DATE

SOURCE: *Business Retention and Expansion in the Western U.S.: People and Planning Can Make a Difference,* U.S. West Foundation Grant/Utah State University.

KEEPING BUSINESS HEALTHY, HAPPY, AND LOCAL

COMMUNITY MEETING
AGENDA

The following meeting format was developed from a number of past BRE program meetings and seems to be the most effective method of presenting the findings. Changes may need to be made based on the community situation. A sample agenda is as follows:

Introductions (Coordinator)

Sponsoring organizations
Endorsing organizations
Assistant Coordinator and Task Force members
Volunteers
Participating firms
BRE Consultant
Dignitaries

Dinner

Hosting meal is optional, but it should be held at this point, if included.

Review of Program History

BRE staff could conduct this portion of the program.

Testimonials

This portion of the program should consist of statements by business representatives and/or program accomplishments by the staff.

Presentation of Recommendations

Survey findings
Strategies and recommendations (35 to 45 minutes maximum) (Coordinator and Task Force)
Implementation
Closing remarks/adjournment

SOURCE: *Business Retention and Expansion in the Western U.S.: People and Planning Can Make a Difference*, U.S. West Foundation Grant/Utah State University.

CHAPTER 8

BUSINESS RETENTION/EXPANSION STRATEGIES

HOW TO GET RESULTS

American educator David Russell believed that the "hardest thing to learn in life is which bridge to cross and which bridge to burn." Understanding the main objective of an effort is crucial.

The main objective of a BRE program is to preserve *businesses*—to keep them healthy, happy, and *here*. Local businesses create family-wage jobs, contribute to a stable tax base, and support a growing local economy.

The Chinese word for crisis is made up of two characters: Danger and Opportunity. What may initially seem like the danger of losing an at-risk firm or a company expansion in another area could become an opportunity to make a difference.

With the right local partnerships, leadership, early warning system, visitations and community buy-in and open, unreserved communication, a BRE program can save some local businesses from going down the tubes or down the road and help local businesses expand. It's an investment of time, funds, and resources that can bring the community great future returns.

IDENTIFYING YOUR TECHNICAL ASSISTANCE PARTNERS

No one knows all the answers or needs to do it alone. It is important to identify and utilize the local and state business assistance network that can assist companies in the community. Identify resource-

people before beginning to work with businesses. Feel free to change and/or expand the list in Attachment 8-1.

To insure survival of the fittest and expansion of local companies, identify the resources available at the local, state, and federal levels to help businesses in trouble or expanding and to bring the right public- and private-sector partners together at the right time to negotiate the right deals.

GOVERNMENT RESOURCES

Government assistance programs that can benefit small- to mid-sized companies are typically divided into five categories:

Loans, made directly to a business or applied as a guarantee to a bank loan;

Grants, usually made to accomplish a specific business-related purpose, such as research and development of a new product or process;

Contract awards, made for products or services provided by a company to local, state, or federal governments;

Credits or exemptions, generally tax incentives awarded to businesses that create new jobs or contribute to economic growth in a community or region;

Technical assistance (TA), generally targeted for industry-specific groups.

FEDERAL

A number of federal programs work with small businesses. Federal assistance generally is focused on technical assistance and financing issues. Funding and technical assistance available to businesses at the federal level are under the auspices of the:

U.S. Small Business Administration (SBA)

Created in 1953 as an independent agency of the federal government to aid, counsel, assist, and protect the interests of small business concerns (companies under 500 employees or $3.5 million). Composed of various finance and investment programs:

- *Innovation Assessment (IAC)* — Specialized service of SBDC which provides an evaluation of the commercial viability of an invention, innovation, or idea. Access to the IAC is through an SBDC counselor. For a small fee, the innovator can obtain an assessment of the concept, product, or service from a panel of experts.

- *Loan Guarantee Program (SBA)* — Helps small businesses obtain needed credit by giving the government's guaranty to loans made by commercial lenders. The lender makes the loan, and the SBA can guarantee 75 percent of the loan amount up to $750,000 and for loans of $100,000 or less, the guaranty rate is 80 percent of any loss in case of default. Access to this program may be provided by state, local and bank staff.

- *Service Corps of Retired Executives (SCORE)* Program sponsored by the SBA that matches volunteers with small businesses that need expert advice. Volunteers, whose collective experience spans the full range of American enterprise, share their management and technical expertise with present and prospective owners/managers of small businesses. For Alaska, Idaho, Oregon, and Washington, call the SCORE office at (206) 553-7320.

- *Small Business Development Centers (SBDC)* — Cooperative effort of state universities and colleges, other universities, community colleges, private sector organizations, the state, and the SBA to provide business management and technical assistance, training, and research to small business owners and managers to improve profitability and stimulate economic growth. In Washington, call (509) 358-7890, or visit *www.sbdc.wsu.edu.*

- *Small Business Innovation Research Program (SBIR)* — Under the SBIR Program, small businesses propose innovative ideas in competition for three levels of awards to meet specific R&D needs of the federal participating agencies (Phase I and Phase II) and can result in commercialization of the effort (Phase III). Contact the U.S. SBA Office of Technology (202) 205-6450 for more information.

- *Small Business Investment Corporation (SBIC)* — The SBA licenses private venture-capital firms and small business investment companies, and supplements their capital with U.S. Government-guaranteed debentures or participating securities. SBICs make equity investments and long-term loans to small businesses. The SBIC Program is operated directly from the SBA's Washington, D.C., office, (202) 205-6515.

- *Surety Bond Program Guaranty Program* — By law, prime contractors to the federal government must post surety bonds on federal construction projects valued at $100,000 or more. Many states, counties, municipalities, private sector projects and subcontracts also require surety bonds. People in California, Idaho, Alaska, Oregon, Arizona, Nevada, and Washington may call (206) 553-7065 for information.

For more information on SBA programs, check out *www.sba.gov/*.

In addition to funding provided to state technology/R&D and agricultural programs, federal technical assistance includes:

Manufacturing Extension Partnerships (MEP) — The U.S. Department of Commerce's National Institute of Standards and Technology has partnered with state and local organizations to deliver services that address the critical and unique needs for smaller manufacturers. Every state is served by a MEP. In Washington, the program is called Washington Manufacturing Services, (425) 438-1146; *www.wamfg.org*.

CASE STUDY

A local bicycle company had seen employment levels fluctuate from 5 to as many as 125 employees over the past several years. It had ongoing problems with correctly forecasting sales by product line or market area. Difficulties with maintaining inventory levels of fast moving parts was also common. The company generally did not devote money to new product development, even though it is in an industry where style and technology are important.

With BRE program staff's help, the company took the following steps to correct these problems:

- Applied for—and was approved by—the Federal Trade Adjustment Assistance Program, administered by the Northwest Trade Adjustment Assistance Center (TAAC). This allowed the company to gain technical assistance in developing a system for tracking orders and linking inventory needs to sales changes. TAAC also provided resources to help with new technology development. The company, which had some new product work underway for the past few years, was now able to devote resources to finishing this effort.

- With the support of the local BRE staff, became involved in local trade assistance efforts and was approved as a Foreign Trade Zone site. Both of these activities help to strengthen the company in their overseas sales and production efficiency. These efforts involved cross-linkage with both state and federal programs to assist in recovery.

As the company improved its efficiency and sales effort, it also was able to deal with its cash flow problems. A major international firm purchased the company. The companies have compatible lines and strong marketing capability. Product expansion is underway, and plans are being developed to allow for employment growth. The acquiring firm also worked with BRE staff in reviewing salary and benefit programs for the local company and has made some definite improvements. Plans are now in place for a very successful expansion.

Procurement Technical Assistance Centers (PTAC) — These statewide centers, funded in part by the Department of Defense, assist businesses and individuals in contracting with local, state, and federal government agencies. A PTA center assists in: placing business names on bidders lists, accessing the *Commerce Business Daily* (electronic bulletin boards for placing quotes, and lists of government purchasing agencies, bidding, and proposal procedures), and acting as ombudsperson for any issues that may arise. In Washington, contact (425) 743-4567 for information on PTAC sites. For information in other areas, visit *www. snoedc.org.*

Trade Adjustment Assistance Centers (TAAC) — These regional centers, funded as part of the Trade Act, are a valuable resource to work with at-risk businesses. To be considered for TAAC services, a firm must be certified by the U.S. Department of Labor to meet all three of the following criteria: 1) decline in gross sales of at least $1,000; 2) 5 percent or greater decline in employment; and, 3) at least part of the decline is due to competition from imports in the domestic market. The TAAC works with certified companies to identify the strengths and weaknesses and can jointly fund, with the company, projects to focus on specific problems such as marketing or diversification. They also have America Competitiveness Grants to help U.S. manufacturers maintain competitiveness in the global economy and to keep jobs in America. These grants can be used to:

- ▸ design new products
- ▸ develop new markets
- ▸ improve production process
- ▸ install total quality systems

Contact the TAAC serving Washington, Oregon, and California, (206) 622-2730.

STATE

While states may have different agency names, there are some basic services offered by all states.

Business Retention and Expansion Program — The Department of Community, Trade and Economic Development (or its counterpart in other states) has staff that work with economic development organizations and strategic firms to assist in the retention and expansion of manufacturing processing companies. For information on Washington state's program, contact Ginger Rich, (206) 256-6112.

Community and Technical Colleges — The colleges are good sources for customized training for the companies. They also provide workshops on basic business and management skills.

One-Stop Centers — The unemployment and job search functions in most states are being incorporated into one-stop centers. The centers, which are in the initial planning and implementation phase, will give clients access to multiple state agency programs and services. While the priorities for services provided at each center may vary with location, most centers will provide help to job seekers and employers seeking workers.

PRIVATE SECTOR

Private sector partners can be used as an initial technical assistance resource. Chapter 3 discusses some of the roles that local accountants, attorneys and other private sector partners play. Attachment 8-2 is a Sample Fee-For-Service Agreement that was developed by one local BRE program. Outside TA providers should be screened prior to using them. As your agents, they can either help create or destroy the confidence and trust that a business has in the BRE program.

FEDERAL AND STATE ASSISTANCE/PROGRAMS

	Counseling	New Products	Technical Assistance	Business Financing/ Loan Assistance	Workforce Issues	SBIR
FEDERAL: SBA	X		X	X	X	X
SBIC				X		
SBDC	X		X	X	*	
IAC		X				
MEP (WMS)	X	X	X		X	
SCORE	X		X			
TAAC		X	X	X		
PTAC	X		X			
STATE: BRE	X		X	X		
ONE-STOP CENTERS					X	
COMM. COLLEGES			X		X	

* depends on local staff

DELIVERY OF TECHNICAL ASSISTANCE

HOLD HARMLESS

Unfortunately, we are a litigious society. There is always the concern that a business who fails could turn around and sue the BRE program or staff for "poor business advice." A recent jury trial in Washington state required a Small Business Development Center to pay $70,000 or half of the damages for a company who did not feel the technical assistance provider properly informed him how factoring worked as a finance option. Attachment 8-3 is a sample hold harmless agreement developed by one local program contractor.

CONFIDENTIALITY: DON'T LEAVE HOME WITHOUT IT

A key objective of any early warning action initiative is to gather critical information about local companies to determine which should be considered at risk. Gaining a company's confidence and getting them to provide financial information for analysis is no small challenge. That's why the credibility of the program and its success depend largely on preserving confidentiality and on keeping a tight lid on all information gathered about local businesses.

Establishing trust is a long-term proposition, and it's built company by company, contact by contact, day by day.

BUSINESS RETENTION

Business retention should be a primary objective. The cost of losing businesses, either through closure or relocation out of the area, can impoverish the overall physical and financial health of your community. For example:

— Decline in personal income can undermine the bottom lines of local retail and service businesses.

— Loss of local property tax revenues will limit funds necessary to maintain education systems, fire and police protection, and other services.

— Reduction in federal and state income and sales tax revenues can increase pressure to raise other taxes to ease deficits.

— Heightened demand for social services, including unemployment compensation, health care assistance, food distribution programs, welfare and others, can stretch the fabric of community life.

— A dip in public funding can increase pressure on charitable and volunteer social agencies to meet community needs.

— Higher rates of stress-related problems among idle workers can lead to alcohol and drug abuse, domestic violence, and higher crime rates.

GETTING TO THE ROOT OF THE PROBLEM

The process of working with and saving a company really starts with a basic question: *What is the problem?* A good business expansion and retention program can sort out fact from fiction to answer this question. This is where good *early warning* research proves to be crucial.

Since each case has its own unique set of circumstances and participants, it is very important to establish an effective process that sifts through the facts of each case. Because there are too many twists and

turns in the process of saving or retaining a company, it is vital that the most appropriate data be collected. The professional must be aware of this data and how it does or does not apply to the current retention effort.

A basic retention process needs the following elements to be successful:

1) a trained professional,

2) a willing client (management) who will admit there is a problem once it has been identified, and

3) a desire on management's part to work on solving the problem.

It is important to get all the facts related to the case by obtaining data from the company or from outside sources. This information consists of:

1) a completed business, retention and expansion survey,

2) up-to-date business plan with projections over no less than two to three years,

3) previous three years financial statements (accountant preparation preferred), and

4) previous three years' tax returns.

All the information has to be analyzed to identify the specific problem(s) of that company. (Additionally, items 2, 3, and 4 are needed if the company is seeking financial help.)

Most troubled businesses say they need more cash and require a loan. Is cash really the problem? A company may not need a loan. Instead, the company may have excess inventory, slow collection on accounts receivables, too much debt, or not enough equity. Solving these problems for a smaller company may solve the cash problem. These and many other real problems will surface once the analysis is made. From this data, a recognized problem will emerge, which management will then agree to act on and solve.

For the large facility/publicly traded company, the problem may be more com-

RESTRUCTURING
OF FINANCES

Local BRE staff was contacted by the owner of a wholesaler of roasted coffee and gifts to assist the company. The loan from their bank had been called because of lack of payment, and the company was losing a significant amount of money. The company was at risk of bankruptcy and laying off five full-time employees, and, during peak season, ten employees.

After analysis of the company's financials, the following problems were observed: 1) There was no understanding on how to keep and use monthly financial reports, 2) the product pricing was too low to sustain the business, 3) the owners had no understanding of cash flow and payment schedules.

With assistance from a business professor at the state university and a local Incubator Board member, the company was assisted in the following ways:

1. Putting together the previous years' financials and training the owner on how to look at the information.

2. Putting together an 18-month cash flow statement and setting up a budget for the business.

3. Reviewing the price structure and increasing prices (prices are still below competition).

4. Assisting the owner in a marketing plan.

5. Going to the owner's bank and convincing the lender that the company was viable. The bank extended the one-year term loan that had been called to a two-year term loan.

6. Going over the production process and helping the company establish a concept of modules of capacity for the production line, so they can plan on increased production at lower costs.

The company has grown at a sustainable rate of between 20 and 30 percent per month over the last year, and the owner is now comfortable with understanding budget requirements and financially managing the company.

plex and have no relevance to that of a smaller company. Is the problem related to poor plant performance, raw materials, product life cycles, or closure of a plant? Could the plant be sold to a new investor/owner? All these facts need to be identified.

Assessment Tools

There are a number of assessment tools that can help staff begin working to identify specific problems or issues. Again be sure to review any surveys returned by the company. Don't re-ask the same questions. Conducting a due diligence review on a company will help determine whether a company will remain viable. Attachment 8-4 is a list of information to be reviewed during the due diligence process. One Washington program used the Five Basics Program for manufacturers as an assessment tool (Attachment 8-5).

Ten common ratios that are used in doing an analysis of a company's fiscal viability are found in Attachment 8-6. Financial institutions use these ratios to look at solvency, profitability, and management of assets. They can help the BRE staff and company identify problem areas. Robert Morris Associate's (RMA) *Annual Statement Studies* is also used by financial institutions to compare a firm's performance with other businesses in their industry.

The National Institute of Science and Technology has also developed several excellent assessment tools. Check with the local Manufacturing Extension Partnership Center to find out more about these tools or explore the possibility of MEP staff assisting with the assessment process.

Secondary Assessments and Counseling

Often, during a one-on-one visitation, there will be a need to go into more detail, so a secondary, detailed assessment of the company's process and management will need to be done. Many types of survey/audit templates are available to help the BRE professional with this assessment; the Malcolm Baldridge Quality Assessment and the American Society for Quality Control (ASQC) audit systems are two examples.

The majority of firms who have gone through the Malcolm Baldridge or a state's quality assessment have found it a good learning experience. An important point to note: When the secondary assessment is complete, be sure to list and explain all reasons behind the strengths and weaknesses found in the audit. Unless you are an expert in business and quality assurance, *never* prescribe (suggest) how to manage the business better. Comments should be on whether the business does or does not meet the criteria set in the template.

Business Plan

A business plan is used to: 1) identify the company's strategic plan, 2) document a company's short- and long-term goals, and 3) serve as a tool in seeking financing. Attachment 8-7 provides an overview of the elements of a plan.

At times, a businessperson may fail to see the necessity of preparing a plan. BRE staff need to explain the benefits it provides to the business. Planning is the key to business success, and the business plan is a blueprint or road map for a company. This is *not* something that BRE staff can develop for the company. Without a plan, any technical assistance by BRE is only a bandage. In the Washington state program, if a business was unwilling to develop a plan, program staff will not give the business any further assistance.

Management Seminars

In addition to technical assistance given to specific companies many programs conduct a series of management seminars. Held in cooperation with local government, the chamber of commerce, and perhaps one or more of the local colleges and universities, the seminar could be developed as a quick once-over of management techniques and responsibilities, or could be developed as a continuing series, building on the knowledge shared in the prior seminar. Subjects could be devised in joint planning with the co-sponsors but might include:

- ▸ **Development of a business plan**
- ▸ **Simplified accounting for managers**
- ▸ **Human relations for managers**
- ▸ **Discrimination: the law**
- ▸ Projecting **capital improvement** needs and devising financial mechanisms
- ▸ **Workforce training** (with a local Private Industry Council and Job Service Employer Committee)
- ▸ **Programs** available at the **local, state, and national level** (co-host with trade or professional organizations)
- ▸ **Technical issues,** i.e., ISO 9000 and Total Quality Management.

ENVIRONMENTAL ISSUES

Companies face an increasing number of environmental issues that need to addressed. A critical role BRE staff can play is to serve as a facilitator in meetings between business and environmental regulatory staff. Misunderstandings can occur as a result of miscommunication between these two groups. BRE staff can help assure that both parties are hearing what is being said and help expedite the decision processes.

Brownfields are defined as properties that are abandoned or under used because of environmental contamination from past industrial or commercial practices. Often the perceived potential liability associated with the contaminated property hinders business development or expansion on the property. While there are cleanup issues associated with these properties, they are usually in desirable locations, have existing infrastructure and cost less to purchase.

Additionally, companies may be eligible for state and federal benefits or incentives to help in cleanup activities. By helping existing businesses become involved in development of these brownfields you can help both the business and the community.

For information on federal brownfield initiatives, check *www.epa.gov/swerosps/bf/pilots*.

The Department of Ecology, Department of Community, Trade and Economic Development, and EPA are developing a homepage of all federal and state brownfield resources. Visit *www.ecy.wa.gov*.

ENVIRONMENTAL CASE STUDY

A local processing plant faced changing environmental and land issues that had a significant impact on whether or not they would continue operations at their current site. The company employed 90 full-time and 400 seasonal employees. Company financials included $3.1 million in payroll, $2 million in average new capital, and $1.5 million in research and maintenance.

Local program staff worked with the company on the following issues: waste water treatment (including secondary uses), looking for suitable land for treatment and training (quality control, occupational skills, and health and safety).

FINAL SOLUTIONS:

1. Lease was extended.
2. Company purchased additional land for waste water disposal.
3. Company purchased new equipment to reduce waste water.
4. A training curriculum was designed for the company.

ASSISTANCE FROM BRE:

— Staff met with land owner and helped negotiate an extension on the lease.

— Staff met with city staff and discussed possible alternatives for the company's waste water problem, including the city treatment facility.

— Research on waste water treatment systems.

— Staff worked with community college and the company to develop a training curriculum to upgrade current employee skills.

— Staff helped to identify tax benefits and financing options for the new equipment.

CONVERSION TO NEW PRODUCTS

Conversion to new products can be beneficial for both expanding and troubled companies. If a business is closing because a main product line has declined in its markets, the BRE program may want to generate opportunities to convert the facility to production of new products for which an active market exists. Here are some factors that should be addressed prior to embarking on a conversion project:

▸ Assist in research to determine whether a new product line could be supported by an adequate customer base, suppliers and current distribution channels.

▸ Assessment of costs to refit existing facilities or build new ones and to buy new or refitted equipment.

▸ Inventory of current management and workforce skills to determine level of retraining or new hiring necessary to convert to production of new products.

▸ Identification of possible resources for the conversion from federal and state economic development agencies.

▸ Potential buy-in and support from local community—including commitments to reschedule taxes, fund grants, and speed regulatory processes—for further conversion efforts.

Your state's Manufacturing Extension Partnership staff is a good source for help with new products or technologies.

IDENTIFY NONTRADITIONAL FINANCING OPTIONS —

THE BOTTOM LINE ISSUE

The main reason many companies run out of steam is because they've run out of money or close to it. The local BRE program should be a source of both public and private funding information for hometown companies.

Attachment 8-9 is a list of questions most frequently asked by bankers in the loan process. However, traditional bank financing may not be an option available to all firms. It is important to be familiar with other alternative forms of financing. Tapping the right solution at the right place at the right time is critical. Companies may uses resources such as equity, cash flow, inventory, and expected profits as collateral for funding. Possible lending institutional ($) and nontraditional (♦) financing might include:

$ *Accounts Payable Financing* — Terming out suppliers on a long-term basis; that is, reaching an agreement to keep current on payments going forward and to establish a payment plan (for example, a two-year note) on previous accounts payable.

$ *Accounts Receivable and Inventory Financing* — This is borrowing against a company's current assets (A/R, inventory) on a month-to-month revolving loan basis.

$/♦ *Application Only/Unsecured Credit Line* — Nonfinancial needs funding based on credit scoring. This is provided by large banks and non-banks such as COSTCO—up to $50,000 without financials.

♦ *Barter* — Exchange of surplus assets is a growing resource in this electronic age. It works especially well with time-sensitive inventories and seasonal markets or markets undergoing rapid changes. Barter brokers or trade exchanges can help firms find new customers, gain market share, and dispose of surpluses.

$ *Credit Enhancements* — Assets of recognized value (such as Certificates of Deposit, insurance, stock, appraised collections of coins, etc.) that can be "rented" or borrowed to support a loan or other debt obligation. This strengthens the company's asset base and can result in increased borrowing power or help guarantee future payment to a major supplier. This can be particularly beneficial for a company experiencing rapid expansion.

♦ *Employee Stock Option Plan* — An ESOP can provide businesses both tax breaks and an additional source of capital. Besides being a financing tool, recent studies of employee-owned firms that use participative management techniques found productivity growth that was 50 percent higher than their competitors. These companies also had annual sales growth rates 6 percent above the competition. (See pages 122-123 for more information on ESOPs.)

$/ ♦ *Equipment and Real Estate Financing* — Obtaining a loan on the lendable value of machinery, equipment, and real estate which a company has.

♦ *Factoring* — A company can obtain quick cash by selling their accounts receivable at a discount. The factoring firm does not make loans but buys the receivables and then collects directly from the customer when the invoices are due.

$ *Flooring* — A form of inventory financing to get intermediary credit until inventory is sold. Typically used on high cost inventories such as machines and vehicles.

♦ *Hard Money Lending* — Collateral-based, high-risk lending. Generally 40 to 50 percent secured by real estate or marketable assets. Usually short- to medium-term. Bad credit history and other normal underwriting criteria not a concern.

♦ *Lease Financing* — A company can secure needed items (such as office space, vehicles, office equipment, heavy machinery, furniture, and phones) with a minimum initial outlay of cash. The two basic type of lease entities are "captive" lessors (generally a corporation that leases its own product directly to the company) and "third party" lessors (company which engages in leasing but does not manufacture or represent a specific product).

$/ ♦ *Mezzanine Financing* — Long-term subordinated debt (i.e., this note is junior to existing secured and unsecured borrowing). Expected investor return on investment is 20 to 40 percent.

♦ *Partnerships* — Partnerships can provide funding and shared knowledge and costs are shared for such items as research and development, marketing analysis and advertising expenditures. The two basic partnership categories are: 1) *joint venture* or "working" partnership, where both parties are active participants, and 2) *limited partnership* or "silent" partnership, in which one party maintains complete control and liability.

$/ ♦ *Purchase Order Financing* — Obtaining capital on a short-term basis to handle seasonal needs or a large increase in sales on the basis of a company's firm purchase orders.

♦ *Revolving Loan Funds or Micro-Enterprise Loan Funds* — Many local and regional economic development organization have established these funds for the companies that need a small amount of capital. Most of these loans are less than $50,000 each.

♦ *Venture Capital* — Money invested in a high risk enterprise which has an expectation of substantial profits (normal investor goal is a 40 to 300 percent return on investment). This kind of funding may be an option for a new invention or patented process a firm wishes to investigate.

Angel Capital Electronic Network (ACE-*Net*), a program sponsored by the Small Business Administration's Office of Advocacy, has a listing service for providing information to angel investors on promising small businesses seeking to raise $250,000 to $5 million in equity financing. *https://ace-net.sr.unh.edu./pub/*.

FAMILY-OWNED BUSINESSES

Family-owned firms can be particularly vulnerable to long-term problems with succession planning that may lead to closure or sell-off. The median life span for family-owned businesses is 25 years. By the third generation of ownership, the likelihood of a family-owned business remaining closely held without an influx of outside investment is approximately 25 percent. Additionally, the current top management may include family members with varying degrees of business ability, experience and willingness to address real problems within the company. It is also not uncommon for these businesses to have competent management but primary corporate decisions being made by absentee family members.

If the current business leadership is more than 50 years old, having a succession plan in place with a well-qualified family member (or members of the current management team) ready to assume the top management slot is very important. The succession plan is typically a separate document from the business plan, or it may be part of a buy-sell agreement.

Family succession counseling is provided by some institutions of higher education. In Washington and Oregon, they include: **Big Bend Community College** (which specializes in farm-related businesses), (509) 762-6289, and **Oregon State University**, (541) 737-6017 (the preeminent authority in the Pacific Northwest).

If no family member is prepared to lead the business or no manager is designated, the company may wish to consider addressing the succession issue with an employee stock ownership plan (ESOP). An ESOP can be a vehicle to cash out noninvolved family members, leaving involved family members (or management) at the helm. (See pages 122-123.)

BANKRUPT OR FINANCIALLY TROUBLED COMPANIES

Staff may work with situations in which a significant employer has financial difficulties and needs to do a major turnaround. The program can provide guidance and technical assistance in the restructuring of a company's financing, finding new equity, and in numerous cases finding new owners.

Cultivating numerous nontraditional financing sources (see pages 119-120) has often helped bail out a financially troubled company.

Client cases involving bankruptcy have increased substantially over the last several years. Many economic development officials avoid these types of cases, because they don't really know how to help a company that has filed a Chapter 11 or 7. (Bankruptcy is discussed in more detail in Chapter 12.) With training on bankruptcy, many facilities can be saved from the auctioneer's gavel. The BRE staff may be able to find new owners/investors to purchase facilities that otherwise would have been sold and dismantled for their liquidation value. The local program or state staff can help locate numerous investors who may be looking for such opportunities. A recapitalized facility can become a productive entity in a community again.

FINDING A NEW BUYER

Remember, the objective of the BRE program, when faced with closure of a local company, is to preserve business and jobs for your community. That may require changing the sign over the door.

Finding a new buyer for a closing company can be a real challenge. Companies can have local, regional, national, or international roots and include entrepreneurs, a group of employees or managers from the existing company, another corporation in the same or a related business, outside investor groups and others. Obviously, a local buyer who is known and respected within the community and with long-term plans for the business, could offer the best solution.

Questions to ask:

- *What is the financial situation of the prospective buyer?*
- *Will the sale be heavily leveraged?*
- *Will the buyer have sufficient cash to manage the sale without selling company assets?*
- *What is the buyer's labor relations history?*

EMPLOYEE OWNERSHIP

What are the typical reasons for looking at employee ownership?

- To create a market for shares of stock held by current stockholder.
- To create an alternative to sale of the company to outsiders or to a public offering.
- Present owner(s) plans to retire in next ten years and wishes to transfer the business to key management and employees on a tax-favored basis.
- To cash out minority shareholders who are not active in the business—for example, noninvolved family members/siblings of company officers—on a tax-favored basis.
- Acquiring an existing subsidiary or division from a company that is divesting—or financing the acquisition of a company or business on a tax-preferred basis.
- Refinancing debt at more favorable rates with pre-tax dollars.
- Increasing cash flow by creating tax deductions with stock contributions.
- Increasing employee motivation and productivity through ownership participation.
- Financing the purchase of assets on a tax-preferred basis.
- Rewarding employees who have helped the business become successful.

What tax breaks are there for employee-owned companies?

Capital gains rollover: A business owner selling stock to the employees through an Employee Stock Ownership Plan (ESOP) or a cooperative can postpone capital gains taxes for years; with proper planning the owner may never pay capital gains taxes.

Principal deduction: Loans made for business purposes through an ESOP qualify for a tax deduction of the loan principal (as well as the interest). The bottom line impact is like taking the loan out interest free.

Dividend deduction: Both ESOPs and cooperatives qualify for special single tax treatment on dividends paid to stock of employee owners.

How large does a company have to be to use these benefits? Do the employees have to own the whole company?

ESOPs rarely make economic sense if the company does not have approximately $90,000 to $100,000 in before-tax earnings to "shield" from taxation. The typical ESOP firm has more than 15 employees (although there are examples of ESOP firms with 6 employees). For an owner to gain the capital gains rollover, the ESOP must end up with at least 30 percent of the company's stock ownership. The principal deduction is available at any percentage of ESOP ownership. ▷

- *Does the buyer have a reputation for investment and/or disinvestment?*
- *Can the buyer point to success in the industry to which the closing company belongs?*
- *Is the buyer willing to share the cost of retraining laid-off workers?*
- *Will the buyer demonstrate a long-term commitment to the company and the community?*

BUSINESS EXPANSION

It is important for BRE staff to identify businesses considering expansion and ensure that these businesses are aware of any opportunities within the community and to provide technical and other assistance to facilitate this expansion. In many cases, the community may be competing with another community's recruitment

What about cooperatives?

Cooperatives are cheaper to set up than ESOPs but have fewer tax benefits. They can range in size from 3 employees to 600. A cooperative typically requires majority ownership by the employees and that a majority of the employees of the business be involved. Like ESOPs, cooperatives offer the capital gains rollover and a deduction for dividend.

What types of firms should *not* look at employee ownership?

Both national and Washington state studies show that employee-owned firms which actively involve their employees in improving their business market, products, and/or services are likely to significantly outperform their competitors in both revenues and job growth. However, the "nonparticipative" employee-owned firms in these studies tended to perform slightly below their competitors. Staff working with ESOPs have found that if the management team that will be in place after the transaction is not comfortable with trying employee participation, employee ownership is probably not a good choice.

Other negative indicators for employee ownership include: highly cyclical businesses that require large cash reserves to weather the low end of the cycle, companies with a young or very transient employee base (unless the plan is to use ownership together with short-term incentives), and firms that are industries which are unlikely to continue longer than ten years.

What type of assistance is there for looking at employee ownership cases?

Washington's BRE Program provides:

- Up-to-date information on employee ownership structures, statutes, and uses.
- Technical assistance for evaluating cases, finding necessary feasibility resources, reworking financials, connections to state financing resources, and preliminary structuring assistance.
- A referral list of regional and national employee ownership consultants, lawyers, accountants, valuators, and lenders. Linkage to other employee owned firms both in the region and nationally.
- Custom presentations on the uses and structures of employee ownership.

SOURCE: Jim Keogh, Washington State BRE Program, (360) 725-4041

For more information, contact:

The ESOP Association,
www.the-esop-emplowner.org/

Foundation for Enterprise Development (F.E.D.),
www.fed.org.

The National Center for Employee Ownership,
www.nceo.org/index.html

---

effort. You may want to complete a site selection checklist for expansion cases (Attachment 8-8). This will help identify the areas to provide assistance and help present the community's competitive position.

Questions to ask of businesses considering expansion:

- *Have they outgrown their current location?*
- *Are they expanding with the same product, or is the new facility going to make a different product?*

CONSIDERING EXPANSION?

Rick Davis, CEO of CCG Venture Partners LLC, a Houston firm that specializes in helping single-location businesses expand to multiple markets, suggests a five-point test to ask firms considering expansion:

1. ***Do you have the desire to make the effort, take the risk, and own a business that you don't personally operate?*** Owning and operating a business is very different from owning a business that someone else operates for you.

2. ***Is your business performing well financially?*** If your first location isn't doing well, chances are a second one won't, either.

3. ***Do you have the know-how to own a business that you don't operate?*** This requires an entirely different set of skills.

4. ***Is your existing business running smoothly?*** Consider how much time your business requires; be sure that you can realistically take time and energy away from it to focus on a second location.

5. ***Do you have the money?*** Opening a second location takes initial capital as well as operating funds. Davis recommends having sufficient cash resources to get you through a worst-case scenario.

<u>SOURCE:</u> *Entrepreneur,* September 1997.

BRE staff needs to assist the company in collecting its due diligence information and decide whether the possibility exists for a good fit between expansion and community. In most cases the companies have no interest in relocating. They just need help with their expansion needs.

Some expansion issues that may take facilitation on the part of the BRE staff are:

Infrastructure development — Many communities have the land but don't have the infrastructure to provide for a company's expansion. These companies know how to build a product but have no idea how to develop water, sewer, road, and utility capabilities. Facilitating the effort to provide infrastructure needs can become necessary.

Permit processing — Many communities have a maze of permit processing requirements which can cause a company to become lost in the shuffle. Facilitation of these issues becomes absolutely necessary to allow the company to expand.

Environmental requirements — Many communities require environmental planning and testing before allowing expansion. Assistance in this area can help keep small issues from becoming large problems.

Financing needs (see pages 124-125).

Workforce training — When a company expands its operations, more than likely they will be hiring more employees. This, on top of their regular attrition rates, can cause a company major grief. Working with training partners as a coordinator to put together programs for advertising, interviewing, and training employees before they become a burden to the company can eliminate many normal hazards of workforce increases. (See Chapter 9.)

BE PREPARED

Find out ahead of time what state and local incentives can be offered to companies considering expansion (Chapter 11). Some communities or states may initially feel they have minimal incentives, while closer research will identify a cadre of expansion tools. For example, is there a state or local program to help train the new employees? What type of state tax exemptions are available for which industries? Are there special incentives for specific geographic areas in the state (i.e., rural or resource dependent programs or distressed regions due to high levels of unemployment)?

DO YOUR DUE DILIGENCE ON PROPOSED EXPANSION PLANS

Not all expansion plans are good for a community. Some business expansions may hurt rather than help the community. James Hettinger, Executive Director of Battle Creek Unlimited, in his chapter, "Is It a Deal or a Dog?" in *The Race to Recruit*, identified the following:

KEY ATTRIBUTES OF A RISKY DEALS

- ✔ **The company needs financing** or the project will not take place. Studies show that companies choosing to expand based upon a financing need are likely to be marginal companies.

- ✔ **Incentives should not be necessary for the transaction to ensue.** Incentives must be incidental to the project; they can never be the main reason for the transaction to take place. Studies show that companies choosing expansions based upon a need for incentives are likely to be marginal companies.

- ✔ **Management does not appear to know their business** and the circumstances in which it will grow. This may result in the **business organization failing to provide timely and qualitative responses** to questions and need for information. The implication here is that the more exhaustive the business has done its homework, the better the chances for a successful expansion.

- ✔ **The client does not respond in a timely manner** with adequate information. In such cases, the business does not have the information; does not want to provide it for whatever reason; or does not consider it important. In any case, you cannot forego the responsibility of assisting in the success of the project. This responsibility cannot be met if there is inadequate information.

- ✔ **The management style is inconsistent.** Local practitioners should closely observe management styles of the business and, if at all possible, attempt to learn something from the venture about employee relations. Compare observations with prevailing practices within the community. An inconsistent management style or one that disrupts labor peace in the community is definitely undesirable. With value added costs increasing, workforce considerations become much more important.

- ✔ **The business organization has a disproportionate impact on community infrastructure.** In order to maximize community resources and the appropriate use of the infrastructure, local practitioners need to assess the "fit" between the company and the community. Certain food processors, for example, may require extensive use of water or sewage treatment. Capacity of the community system to meet current and future needs will impact not only the company's ability to grow and expand, but, more generally, the community's ability to accommodate future growth on the part of current and future employees.

CHANGE OF OWNERSHIP
NORTHLAKE SHIPYARD, INC. /
UNITED MARINE PROPERTY

Washington state's Business Retention and Expansion Program (BRE) was asked to assist the current United Marine (UNIMAR) owners in finding new investors and/or a new owner group. The goal for the program was to save the existing workforce and preserve the shipyard site for continued ship repair and ship construction work in the Puget Sound area.

Background

Since 1950 there has been an operating shipbuilding and repairs site at the north end of Lake Union in Seattle. The operations involve steel repairs and hull painting. A Chapter 11 bankruptcy proceeding in 1988 resulted in a reorganization plan for the existing owner. Under that reorganization plan, 83 percent of the company's stock became owned by an Employee Stock Ownership Plan, with the remaining stock owned by various other parties, including Drexel, Burnham & Lambert, prior owners, and a group of unsecured creditors.

During the following years, the operation worked very hard to pay down the tremendous debt load. But this caused the company to experience a significant cash shortage in its operation. The company also experienced a significant downturn in the ship repair business due to the uncertain business climate in the fishing industry, pressure from foreign competition, and the general downturn in the economy.

By the early first quarter 1994, the company found its cash flow substantially reduced due to sales volume and an inability to provide the needed financial bonding capacity to bid on new work. With this chain of events, the company filed a Chapter 11 bankruptcy. BRE staff continued technical assistance with the prospective buyer in hopes of saving the assets from being auctioned. By July 1994, the company's bankruptcy was converted to a Chapter 7 (liquidation). The judge then approved to the sale of assets to the current owner/investors.

Program Assistance

During the period when BRE was involved with the management of the company, staff provided technical assistance covering a myriad of issues. Management needed counsel in the process of finding and evaluating the various investors who showed interest in the facility. The BRE department tried to locate domestic investors and utilized the network of State foreign offices to try to locate investors in Asia, Europe, and Canada. The due-diligence process with each investor took many months. The investors who ultimately purchased the facility were a local investment group with whom management had a prior business relationship. The local investment group had a number of its fishing boats repaired at the facility and felt that the facility needed to remain viable as a shipyard.

As the due-diligence process unfolded, there was some concern with prior contamination of underwater sediment at the site resulting from past operating practices. During the process of evaluation, concerns of the various governmental agencies seemed to outweigh the investors' needs. The investors became very concerned that their interests were not being addressed by the agencies.

So, prior to the consummation of the sale of the facility BJRP established an interagency team led by the Department of Ecology, with representatives from the Departments of Community, Trade and Economic Development, Department of Natural Resources, and the U.S. Environmental Protection Agency (EPA). The team worked together to identify prospective purchaser environmental issues. The agreement signed with the new owners established a cleanup fund, which is anticipated to accumulate $1.1 million over 15 years and is expected to fully fund future cleanup of the site.

Department of Ecology staff were instrumental in securing a consent degree to limit the liability on historic contamination. In addition to providing an environmental benefit, the consent decree allowed the shipyard to resume operations. This saved the existing job base, contributed to a working waterfront on Lake Union, and provided that one of only two shipyards in the Seattle area capable of large repair work required on military craft would remain open.

The state retention program also linked the prospective buyers with various financing tools that King County and the City of Seattle had available to the investor group. The investors at the time of the transaction decided not to pursue that course of action.

Outcome

This case is an excellent example of utilizing federal, state, and local government resources to help solve job retention issues. Since the purchase of the facility, the investors of the Northlake Shipyard, Inc. have decided to use the successful Portland (Oregon) shipyard model to run the facility. In this model, the facility is leased out to various industry users rather than operated as it had been before. The facility has also remodeled and modernized some of the interior spaces. Since remodeling the spaces, they have been rented to fifteen (15) other businesses, including retail/wholesale marine electronics and radar, naval architects, ship repair specialists, and a naval artist gallery. All the various businesses have employed more than 100 individuals. This is about two-thirds as many employees the shipyard had during its peak employment period several years ago.

Even with the changing character of the ship repair and construction business, the long-term viability of the facility under the new yard model seems assured. The changing economic times in the industry dictated a change in the traditional working model of the shipyard. The new owners of the yard are not locked into the old way of doing business. They have come up with a model that will take them well into the 21st century and keep an active and vital shipyard from the auctioneer's gavel.

KNOWING WHEN TO WALK AWAY
FROM A RETENTION CASE

— When a company does not have a *business plan* and is not willing to write one. As discussed on page 118, this is a critical planning tool. (See also Attachment 8-7.)

— When company *management will not provide* the necessary *information* or the information provided turns out to be incorrect.

— When it routinely takes two or three phone calls to get the company to *return calls* (the suggestion is that they are not taking your presence seriously).

— When a company is dealing with a *state or federal tax agency* on back taxes and cannot live with the negotiated deal or stay current with payments schedule.

— When part of a *team on a complex case*, be cautious about trying to fulfill an advisory capacity which requires technical specialists (such as a bankruptcy attorney).

— If the company does not or *cannot involve needed specialists.*

— When the problem is with *management* who won't make necessary changes (such as a owner who will not retire or an administrator with technical skills who doesn't have financial and planning skills and won't hire or rely on staff for those areas).

— Because of workload, BRE staff cannot work with all retention or expansion cases. A small two person company can take as much time as a "significant" company. Determine which companies identified to target by your BRE program.

— When a company is in a serious *negative net worth situation* and the owners seem unwilling or unable to bring in additional equity.

— When the financials show a *marginal company and a check of aging of receivables* shows significant money that is overdue by more than 90 days.

— When their banker, attorney, and/or CPA and provides a *consistently negative picture* regarding likelihood of recovery.

— When the financials show a strong level of inventory or work in process and a walk through the *factory shows little product.*

— When the management gives an optimistic story about how busy the firm is yet observations show *few employees* present and *little activity.*

— When, after authorization, conversations with potential new bank or investor indicate that their *story about possible financing is dramatically different than given by the firm.*

SOURCE: Bill Lotto, Director, Lewis County EDC

CLOSURES:
ECONOMIC DARWINISM AT WORK

The fact is, some businesses in the community *will* fail, shut their doors, or consider expansion in other communities. And not all businesses can or should be saved in their present form, under their current ownership, or with a new owner.

YOU CAN'T SAVE THEM ALL...

It's confirmed. No deals are on the table. A local business is closing and a major layoff of workers will occur in the community. A local partnership such as a labor-management committee can play an important role in making contact with federal and state agencies that can help the community adjust to the closure.

The State Dislocated Worker Unit (usually in Employment Security) or their equivalents can help:

- Identify available federal, state and local government and private resources to retrain workers and help them secure new employment.

- Empower the BRE Task Force, comprised of representatives from economic development agencies, local government, vocational education and training agencies, local labor, business, and other community organizations, to help identify new employment opportunities.

- Develop a process to refer workers unlikely to return to their previous jobs to employment and retraining resources.

The local One-Stop Center and/or Workforce Development Council can bring together local public and private sector resources, identify emerging personal, family and community problems, and find solutions, such as:

- Increased levels of need in social service programs, such as food and clothing banks, medical clinics and housing and securing supplemental funding.

- Assemble a team of mental health care professionals and counselors who will make their services available to individuals and families.

- Church organizations and other private assistance centers that offer help to individuals and families affected by layoffs.

ADDRESSING THE LONG-TERM CHALLENGES

Closure of a major local business or out-of-area expansion by a company can have a positive impact on a community by sparking new insights and guiding retention and recruitment efforts. Also remember that closed sites represent property with existing infrastructure and can provide an opportunity for another company to expand. This is a good time to pull out the plan that was developed during the program start-up (Chapter 2) and do an update based on lessons learned through surveys and visitations.

KEEP THOSE WARNING SYSTEMS ACTIVE

Remember to maintain the *early warning systems*. As the following article points out, today's healthy/profitable firm can easily become tomorrow's retention case.

EVEN PROFITABLE FIRMS FACE PITFALLS
Scott Clark*

Start-up companies face almost overwhelming odds against making it through the first three years. For the 20 percent that survive after three years, a precious few ever become very profitable.

Of those that make it, a large percentage still fail. Here are the ten most common reasons why profitable companies self-destruct:

- **Managerial apathy.** The chief executive becomes bored and restless with the duties of everyday management. It isn't fun anymore.
- **Failure to keep up with customer needs and technology improvements.** Do you keep track of your customers' changing needs? If a competitor offers better performance, more bells and whistles or lower price, your sales could evaporate overnight. Constant strategic planning is essential for continued success.
- **Increased cost of borrowed money.** When interest rates skyrocket, you could be forced to shrink your business, or convert some of your debt into equity. Make sure you consider this possibility in your planning process.
- **Lack of managerial ability.** Companies sometimes outgrow the CEO's ability. In this case, it's not the company or the market that's the problem, it's you. Have the courage to conduct an annual management assessment by your peers and subordinates.

- **Managerial cowardice.** Sometimes senior executives know certain steps need to be taken to streamline the business (for example, eliminating some jobs) but they lack the fortitude to take action, hoping things will improve magically. Instead, morale suffers because employees see the problem and sense management's unwillingness to act.
- **Lack of adequate cash for new product.** Companies rush to introduce an exciting new product line without recognizing (or perhaps choosing to ignore) the barriers to entry and the dollars involved to capture market share.
- **Sudden unforeseen real world developments.** Copper prices spiral, oil and plastics prices skyrocket, a patent challenge suddenly appears, or product liability insurance triples overnight. Usually you can't predict these events, so the best protection is to have some diversification within your business.
- **Management conflicts.** Healthy competition among the ranks of senior management is good for business, but bad blood is not. The CEO must resolve potentially damaging management conflicts before they get out of control.
- **Expansion beyond sources of capital.** This may sound like a great problem to have, but it has proven fatal to many successful companies. Planning for growth

and having adequate cash flow are absolutely critical. Visit your financiers long before you really need cash; otherwise you probably won't get it.
- **Dependence on a single product or customer.** It's not unusual for a small company to start out with a single product and/or a single customer, but unless you are a consummate gambler, you had better expand to include others.

In each of the above failings, the chief executives led their companies to self-destruction just as surely as if they had struck a fatal blow.

When your company arrives on Easy Street, your vigilance cannot stop. Make sure you periodically review all company operations, plan ahead, and anticipate those problems that could seriously affect your business. That's the best way to ensure survival.

---

* Scott Clark, a business consultant and author, is a nationally syndicated columnist.

For more business information, see Scott Clark's Home Page, *www.saclark.com*

LOCAL, STATE, REGIONAL, AND FEDERAL
ECONOMIC DEVELOPMENT RESOURCES

TOPIC	PROGRAM	CONTACT PERSON	PHONE
Enterprise Zones			
Environmental Issues			
Export/Foreign Markets			
Financing Problems: banks			
factoring co.			
public infrastructure			
revolving loan funds			
special state funds			
venture capital			
equipment leasing co.			
Labor/Workforce Training state			
local			
Management Seminars			
Manufacturing Extension Partnership			
Marketing Strategies			
Private Industry Council			
Recruiting Employees			
Small Business Development Center			
Tax Abatement			
Tax Issues			
Technological Innovations			
Trade Associations for key industries			

NOTE: Feel free to change and/or expand this list.

SAMPLE FEE-FOR-SERVICE AGREEMENT

_____ Economic Development Council
Business Retention and Expansion Program

REQUEST FOR SERVICE AGREEMENT

THIS AGREEMENT is made this _____ day of _____, 20___ by and between _____ ECONOMIC DEVELOPMENT COUNCIL (hereinafter "EDC") and _____ (hereinafter "Contractor").

Contractor hereby requests service from EDC's Business Retention and Expansion Program to assist Contractor in obtaining information about financial sources, methods of reducing costs of doing business, and accessing other sources of private and public sector assistance.

Contractor acknowledges that the first two hours of the assistance is to be provided through the Business Retention and Expansion Program and is free of charge. The Contractor has the option, but is not obligated, to retain the services of any professional persons ("Technical Assistance Providers") introduced as a result of this program.

The EDC Business Retention and Expansion Program attempts to keep information provided by participating companies confidential. However, non-company, specific information about participants may be included as part of required reports by the Business Retention and Expansion Program to its contracting agent, the Washington State Department of Trade and Economic Development.

In consideration of the requested services, Contractor or its agents, assigns, heirs, executors and administrators hereby release the EDC, its employees, officers, board members, assigns, heirs, administrators and executors from any every claim, demand, action, deed or right of whatever kind of nature, direct or indirect, arising out of services performed under this agreement. Contractor states that it has carefully read the foregoing release and knows the contents thereof, and signs the release as its own free act.

Contractor specifically assumes responsibility for all decisions made regarding the assistance provided under this program.

EDC has advised Technical Assistance Providers that they are not authorized to use the program as a basis for selling or recommending any services, equipment, or supplies in which Technical Assistance Providers have a direct or indirect financial interest.

The fee schedule hereunder shall be as follows:

0 to 2 hours —	no charge
3 to 6 hours —	30% of assigned Technical Assistance Providers' fee
7 to 10 hours —	70% of assigned Technical Assistance Providers' fee
11+ hours —	Contractor contracts for services with professional of Contractor's choice

SAMPLE FEE-FOR-SERVICE AGREEMENT (continued)

All the funds generated from the third through the tenth hour will be retained by the EDC and used to sustain the retention program.

The normal fee of Technical Assistance Providers shall be revealed by Technical Assistance Providers to the Contractor at the initial counseling session.

This agreement constitutes the entire understanding between the parties and may be modified by a written document signed by both parties.

_____ECONOMIC DEVELOPMENT COUNCIL

By _____

its _____

_____
[Contractor]

By _____

its _____

HOLD HARMLESS STATEMENT

Economic Development Council
Business Retention and Expansion Program

REQUEST FOR SERVICE AGREEMENT

I request service from the _____ County Business Retention and Expansion Program to assist our company in obtaining information about financial sources, ways of reducing costs of doing business and accessing other sources of private and public sector assistance. I understand that this assistance is free of charge and that I am free, but not obligated, to retain the services of any professionals introduced to me as a result of this program.

The _____ County Business Retention and Expansion Program makes every attempt to keep the information provided by participating companies confidential. However, information from participating companies may be included as part of the program's required reports to its contracting agency, and treated by them as a public record subject to disclosure.

In consideration of the requested services, I, my company, and any agents acting on the company's behalf hereby waive all rights to any and all claims arising from this service against the EDC and/or any of its employees, officers, board members, or independent contractors. I further understand that my company bears all responsibility for all decisions made regarding the assistance provided under this program now and in the future.

INDIVIDUAL REQUESTING SERVICE: _____

SIGNATURE: _____

TITLE: _____

DATE: _____

DUE DILIGENCE LIST

Following is a list of the types of information you may request when working with a company.

_____ 1. Breakdown of sales and profit (if available) by dollar volume, division or major product lines for the two or three most recent years.

_____ 2. List of company's major customers (5-10), including total sales to each during the past year.

_____ 3. List of company's major suppliers (about five), including total purchases from each during the past year.

_____ 4. List of the company's major competitors (best estimates) in each major product line with the rank and percent of the market for each company.

_____ 5. List of officers and key personnel (at least seven people), including the following data on each: name, position, age, time with company, formal training, total annual compensation, and number of company shares owned and controlled. List of outside directors and their principal affiliation.

_____ 6. Total number of employees broken down by office, sales production, etc.

_____ 7. List of the company's major facilities, including the following data on each: location, land area, building area, and age of building. If property is leased, indicate annual rental obligation, expiration date of lease, and renewal terms.

_____ 8. Outstanding short term bank loans at the end of each month and for the past two years.

_____ 9. Annual financial statements for each of the past five years. Copy of the most recent company prepared balance sheet and income statement in comparative form with the same period in the prior year.

_____ 10. Summary of accounts receivable and accounts payable aging as of the most recent balance sheet date and as of the same date in the prior year. Indicate total bad debt write-offs on accounts receivable for each of the past five years with notes on any unusual items.

_____ 11. List of all subsidiaries, (if any), including correct corporate name, state of incorporation, and percent of stock owned by parent.

_____ 12. Copies of sales brochures and other printed data describing the company and its products.

_____ 13. Projection of sales and profit (if available) by dollar volume, division or major problem lines for the next year.

_____ 14. Individual personal financial statements(s) on guarantors(s).

_____ 15. Detailed equipment list including vendor brochures on major items.

_____ 16. Other: _____

THE FIVE BASICS PROGRAM
Michael H. Tracy

Demystifying the manufacturing process into its component parts is an effective technique to be employed when managing an overall production operation.

The "Five Basics" Program is one approach for conducting an assessment of the fundamentals of manufacturing in an easy-to-understand manner.

The Five Basics Program is an 11-point system based on five key principles of manufacturing. The five basics can be used as an assessment tool as well as an operating instrument for a manufacturing business. Depending upon the level at which management will address, different areas are emphasized, beginning with the five basic principles of manufacturing. These five principles are:

People
Process
Schedule
Equipment
Facilities

Sit down with the company and ask them about their involvement in each area and sub-area. You may do this in a conversational manner regarding their answers for each area. For certain areas you may want to see documentation.

In addition to the first five principal areas, Part II has six additional areas to be incorporated depending upon the level of involvement by personnel managing the business. Part I is used for a quick audit, or within the business, at all levels of personnel. When engineering and upper management are involved, Part II becomes important. The six additional areas are:

Procedures
Budget
Cost
Quality
Quantity
Customer

Each of the 11 areas, when defined, are key to successfully operating a manufacturing concern.

Each of the above points has five key components within the definition. More can be added or eliminated, depending upon the situation. All employees and management personnel should be made aware of the five basics program and specifically trained in the areas for which they will be held accountable. When auditing, each point should be addressed, either with positive reinforcement or with suggested opportunities for improvement.

FIVE BASICS PROGRAM ASSESSMENT

Company:_____ Date:_____

PART I

People:
- ☐ hiring practices, including salary and hourly labor
- ☐ policies and procedures
- ☐ personnel assessment
- ☐ training programs
- ☐ team concept or vertical management

Process:
- ☐ yield management
- ☐ cycle time management
- ☐ productivity improvement programs
- ☐ product flow improvements
- ☐ statistical process control (SPC)

Schedule:
- ☐ on-time delivery
- ☐ short- and long-term scheduling
- ☐ material planning
- ☐ in-process inventory control
- ☐ JIT (just-in-time processing)

Equipment:
- ☐ maintenance
- ☐ down-time analysis
- ☐ cycle times
- ☐ process flow
- ☐ state-of-the-art

Facilities:
- ☐ cleanliness
- ☐ product flow
- ☐ use of space
- ☐ OSHA and safety issues
- ☐ future planning

PART II

Procedures:
- ☐ on-line written procedures
- ☐ document control
- ☐ personnel training
- ☐ design control
- ☐ vendor/supplier control

Budget:
- ☐ zero-based or P&L responsibility
- ☐ cost control
- ☐ short- and long-range budgets
- ☐ problem analysis
- ☐ cost center responsibility

Cost:
- ☐ overhead and G & A expenses
- ☐ cost improvements
- ☐ financial planning, including risk analysis
- ☐ money management issues
- ☐ R & D and future product costs

Quality:
- ☐ Total quality management (TQM) plans, continuous improvement
- ☐ reject analysis, including root cause definition
- ☐ SPC (statistical process control)
- ☐ personnel quality awareness
- ☐ corrective action plans and resolutions

Quantity:
- ☐ inventory control
- ☐ stockroom practices
- ☐ kitting issues
- ☐ yield management
- ☐ corrective action plans

Customer:
- ☐ marketing plans, including good business practices
- ☐ product awareness
- ☐ customer satisfaction and corrective action plans
- ☐ business long-range planning
- ☐ product integration

SOLVENCY AND LIQUIDITY RATIOS

Following are ratios used by bankers in assessing a company's financial viability and by BRE program staff's comparisons of a company with industry averages. The figures needed to calculate these ratios come from two accounting forms:

Balance sheet (BS) — Accounting form that lists total assets, liability and equity (net worth) on a particular date

Income statement (IS) — Accounting form that reports business revenues, expenses and resulting profit or loss for a particular period. Also called profit-and-loss statement or statement of income and expenses.

1. **Current Ratio: (BS + BS)**
   Liquidity (bill-paying ability)

   $$\frac{\text{Current Assets}}{\text{Current Liabilities}}$$

2. **Quick Ratio: (BS + BS)**
   "Acid Test," short term;
   shows how inventory-dependent a company is

   $$\frac{\text{Cash} + \text{Accounts Receivable}}{\text{Current Liabilities}}$$

SAFETY RATIOS:

3. **Debt to Net Worth (BS + BS)**
   Risk, Leverage

   $$\frac{\text{Total Liabilities}}{\text{Net Worth}}$$

PROFITABILITY RATIOS:

4. **Gross Profit Margin: (IS + IS)**
   effected: cost of
   inventory/price/labor/shrinkage (retail)

   $$\frac{\text{Gross Profit}}{\text{Sales}}$$

5. **Net Profit Margin: (IS + IS)**
   Expense control or volume

   $$\frac{\text{Net Profit Before Tax}}{\text{Sales}}$$

6. **Return on Assets: (IS + BS)**
   Efficiency

   $$\frac{\text{Net Profit Before Tax}}{\text{Total Assets}}$$

7. **Return on Net Worth: (IS + BS)**
   ROI or ROE
   Investment return

   $$\frac{\text{Net Profit Before Tax}}{\text{Net Worth}}$$

ASSET MANAGEMENT RATIOS:

8. **Inventory Turnover: (BS-BS)**

   $$\frac{\text{Cost of Goods Sold}}{\text{Inventory}}$$

9. **Days in Inventory: (worksheet)**
   Average turnover

   $$\frac{365}{\text{Inventory Turn Ratio}}$$

10. **Accounts Receivable Turnover: (IS + BS)**

    $$\frac{\text{Sales}}{\text{Accounts Receivable}}$$

DEVELOPING YOUR BUSINESS PLAN

A business plan is a blueprint for a business, today and as it grows. A thoroughly researched and well thought-out business plan will clarify goals, focus your energy, direct your work, and measure your progress.

Planning for a business is important. As a business plan is developed, there are general questions to ask. Even though not every question will apply, carefully consider each question.

Before beginning a business plan, determine if personal goals meet business goals and resources; if strengths are compatible with business goals.

The business plan does not need to be long, probably not more than ten pages, plus financial statements.

For further assistance in preparing a business plan, contact your local Small Business Development Center.

- **PLAN SUMMARY**

The Plan Summary is a one- or two-page summary describing the business to prospective lenders and investors. A well-developed plan will help convince lenders or investors to examine the business further. Even though a Plan Summary appears first in the business plan, it should be written last.

The Plan Summary should include:
1. A brief description of the company's history.
2. Description of products and services.
3. Production process.
4. Management.
5. Profit—break-even analysis.

- **PURPOSE OF THE BUSINESS**
1. Mission statement.
2. Description of the business.

- **PRODUCT AND SERVICE DEFINED**
1. The market that needs the product or service.
2. A complete description of the product or service.
3. The cost and profit of each product and service. Describe the break-even point.
4. The major sources of competition.
5. Proprietary features—should the product or service have a patent or trademark?
6. Opportunities to better develop the product or service.

- **MARKET ANALYSIS**
1. Market research—size of market and how long it has existed. Barriers to the business entry and growth.
2. Target market—who will buy the product or service?
3. Where most sales will occur.
4. Sales estimates.

- **MARKET STRATEGY**
1. Define product advantage—the difference between your product and service and competitors.
2. Evaluate the competition—the size of the competition, market maturity.
3. Pricing strategy—are the company's prices competitive?
4. Distribution channels
5. Promotion—how to get the word out about the company's product or service.

- **MANAGEMENT**
1. Identify organizational structure and key employees.
2. Provide a resume for each person.
3. Identify management skills.
4. Professional services.
5. Identify any technical or specialty services.

- **SCHEDULE OF EVENTS**
1. List critical dates.
2. Make short-term goals.
3. Project long-term goals.
4. Identify barriers or risks—solutions.

- **FINANCIAL INFORMATION**
1. Financial statement.
2. Start-up expenses.
3. Funding.
4. Equity—owner's investment.
5. Financing.
6. Expense sheet.
7. Monthly cash flow analysis
8. Sales forecast.
9. Income projection.
10. Operation expenses.
11. Methods of financial reporting you will use.
12. Break-even analysis.
13. Balance sheet—assets and liabilities.

EXPANSION SITE SELECTION CHECKLIST

PROJECT TITLE: _____   **PROJECT NUMBER:** _____

Please provide as much detail as possible. If you plan to phase in your operation, provide your initial requirements as well as your plans for expansion.

BUILDING:	Initially *(sq. ft.)*	Ultimately *(sq. ft.)*	Column Spacing *(ft.)*

Size —
Production area:	_____	_____	_____
Office area:	_____	_____	_____
Warehouse:	_____	_____	_____
Other: _____	_____	_____	_____

Approximate overall facility dimensions: _____

Clear ceiling heights (ft.): _____
Production area:	_____	_____	_____
Office area:	_____	_____	_____
Warehouse:	_____	_____	_____
Other: _____	_____	_____	_____

Floor thickness —
Production area:	_____	_____	_____
Other: _____	_____	_____	_____

Which areas of the building require heating and/or cooling and/or ventilation?
Production area:	_____	_____	_____
Office area:	_____	_____	_____
Warehouse:	_____	_____	_____
Other: _____	_____	_____	_____

Truck dock requirements: _____

Compressed air requirements: _____

Lighting level requirements:
- Production area: _____
- Office area: _____
- Warehouse: _____
- Other: _____ _____

Other building requirements: _____

LAND:

- Size and dimensions of property desired: _____
- Zoning requirements: _____
- Types of transportation access at site: _____
- Other needs: _____ _____

WATER:

Average discharge per month: _____

Percent of total discharge for manufacturing process: _____

Composition of waste discharge (i.e., chemicals, heavy metals, solvents): _____

_____

PROCESS EFFLUENT DISCHARGED INTO: _____

Air: _____

Water: _____

Solid waste (produced, both hazardous and nonhazardous): _____

Liquid waste (produced, both hazardous and nonhazardous): _____

ELECTRICITY:

Total installed kW:

Approximate load factor: _____

Approximate peak demand: _____

Average demand: _____

Service voltage needed: _____

Peak hour of operation during the day: _____

NATURAL GAS:

Estimated production process gas consumption/month: _____

Estimated total monthly gas consumption for all uses: _____

LABOR:

Provide a breakdown of your labor needs by job skill type. If possible, include labor wage rates and worker's compensation codes.

Job Skill Category	Number of Employees	Current Wage Rate	Worker's Compensation Code
_____	_____	_____	_____
_____	_____	_____	_____
_____	_____	_____	_____
_____	_____	_____	_____
_____	_____	_____	_____

Training needs: _____

_____

OPERATION SCHEDULE:

	Initially	Projected Ultimate
Days/week:	_____	_____
Hours/day:	_____	_____
Shifts/day:	_____	_____

TELECOMMUNICATIONS (i.e., video conferencing, remote computer connections to mainframe):

_____

TRANSPORTATION:

Rail service: _____

_____

Air service: _____

_____

Motor freight: *Inbound*   *Outbound*

FTL services number of trucks daily: _____   _____
LTL services number of trucks daily: _____   _____

What major market areas would a new facility in your region serve, and how many FTL and LTL truck shipments would be made to each of those major market areas?

Market Destination	*FTL/Year*	*LTL/Year*	*Lbs./Year*
_____	_____	_____	_____
_____	_____	_____	_____
_____	_____	_____	_____
_____	_____	_____	_____
_____	_____	_____	_____
_____	_____	_____	_____
_____	_____	_____	_____

PROPOSED GEOGRAPHICAL REGION(S) UNDER CONSIDERATION: _____

ESTIMATED COSTS OF PROJECT:

Building(s): _____
Land: _____
Production equipment: _____
Inventories: _____

SOURCES OF FINANCING FOR PROJECT: _____

_____

_____

TIMING OF PROJECT:

Location selection: _____

Projected date of occupancy for production/distribution purposes: _____

_____

THE QUESTIONS MOST FREQUENTLY ASKED BY BANKERS

1. What is the present name of the company?

2. Is the company a corporation, partnership, or sole proprietorship?

3. If the company is a corporation, please set forth the date and the state of incorporation.

4. Please furnish the names of the persons who formed the company.

5. Was the company originally organized as a corporation, partnership, or sole proprietorship?

6. Please furnish the names of the initial shareholders and/or providers of funds (debt and equity) of the company.

7. Please describe the nature of the company's business. Has the nature of the company's business changed or evolved since its inception? Is it intended to place future emphasis on different areas?

8. Does the company conduct business under names other than its own? If so, please set forth the names and places where they are used.

9. Does the company utilize any trademarks or trade names? If so, what are they?

10. What geographical area does the company serve? Are there any limitations on what markets can be reached, e.g., freight, duties, service, maintenance, patent licenses, tariffs, government regulation, etc.? Does the company intend to enlarge its present areas of distribution or service?

11. Please describe the major products or services of the company.

12. In which states and/or countries, other than its state of incorporation, is the company licensed or qualified to do business?

13. Please furnish a listing of leases.

14. Please describe the method or methods of distribution and sale. If any contractual arrangements are involved, please describe.

15. Please list and describe, to the degree relevant, all patents, technical information, trademarks, franchises, copyrights, patent and technical information, and licenses owned and/or used.

16. Please furnish a detailed three-year breakdown of sales, earnings, income, or losses of the company's major divisions, departments, and product categories. Give the percentage of total income or loss attributed to each.

17. Please furnish a detailed breakdown of major suppliers of raw materials, goods, etc. Give their names. Are other sources readily available or is the company dependent to any degree on any one supplier? What would result if the product or products of said supplier or suppliers were no longer readily procurable? Does the company have any long-term contracts with its suppliers?

18. If the company utilizes the services of subcontractor and/or processors of its products or components of subassemblies, please describe the work done and the availability of other subcontractors or processors. Does the company have any long-term contracts with such persons?

19. Who are your top four customers?

20. Please furnish names of the company's major competitors; describe the nature and area of their competition—is it direct or indirect? What is the company's approximate rank in the industry? Are there numerous competitors? What is the degree of competition? Can new companies readily enter the field? Do the company's competitors possess greater financial resources? Are they longer established and better recognized?

21. Please furnish a complete list of all officers and/or directors, plus the following data:

    a. Education
    b. Title and function—responsibilities
    c. Length of service with company
    d. Posts held and functions performed for company prior to present post
    e. Past business associations and posts held
    f. Special distinctions
    g. Other directorates or present business affiliations

22. Please furnish a copy of all stock option plans

23. Please state the total number of employees, full- and part-time, the major categories of employees and number within each. If the company is to any degree dependent on technology or other expertise, please give details, e.g., number of Ph.D.s, M.A.s, engineers, technicians, medical personnel, etc.

24. Are your employees represented by one or more unions?

25. Please furnish a general description of labor relations, past strikes, handling of grievances, etc. Has the company experienced any difficulties in obtaining qualified personnel? Has the company had any problems with respect to personnel turnover?

26. Please describe all acquisitions of other companies, assets, personnel, etc., made by the company, or any intended acquisitions.

27. Please describe any major dispositions of subsidiaries, divisions, assets, equipment, plants, etc., made by the company.

28. Has any officer, director, or major shareholder ever: (a) had any difficulties of any nature with the Securities and Exchange Commission, the National Association of Securities Dealers, or any state securities commission or agency, (b) been convicted of a felony, or (c) been under indictment, investigation, or threatened by the SEC, NASD, a state commission, or public agency with prosecution for violation of a state or federal statute? Has any such person ever been adjudicated a bankrupt? If the answer to any of the questions is in the affirmative, please describe the circumstances in detail.

29. Has the company made: (a) any private placements of its equity or debt securities, or (b) any public sale of its equity or debt securities? If so, please furnish complete details including copies of documents used in the placement and/or sale.

30. Are there any options to purchase stock or other securities or warrants outstanding other than employees' stock option plans? If so, please describe such plan.

31. Does the company have any long-term or short-term debt, secured or unsecured, or has the company guaranteed such debt on behalf of others? Please furnish copies of the documents creating the debt or guarantee, or describe the debt or guarantee.

32. Please furnish detailed statements for the last three years, if available.

33. Please furnish interim statements covering the period subsequent to the last audited financial statement.

34. Please furnish comparative figures of earning and net worth for three years.

35. Please furnish an explanation of any and all abnormal, non-recurring, or unusual items in earnings statements or balance sheets.

36. Please furnish a statement of cash flow if materially different from statement of net earnings.

37. Please furnish a statement as to any contingent or possible liabilities (pending suits) not shown on balance sheet. Please include guarantees, warranties, litigation, etc.

38. With respect to the company's inventories, please state: (a) major categories, (b) method used in valuation, last in first out (LIFO), first in first out (FIFO), other, and (c) control systems. If your "inventories" are distinctive in any fashion, e.g., film libraries, promotional displays, etc., please state how they are handled on your books.

39. What is the company's policy regarding depreciation, depletion, and amortization? Which items are capitalized and which expensed? Are there any deferred write-offs?

40. Are your company's methods of accounting similar to the rest of the industry? If not, please describe the differences and the reason for such differences.

41. Please state the status of federal and state tax examinations. What was your last examination, and are there any open questions?

42. Please describe all bank relationships and credit lines. Are factors involved?

43. Please describe any pending or threatened claims and litigation and the amount involved.

44. Please describe all insurance coverages, e.g., plant, equipment, properties, work interruption, key employees, other.

45. Please describe your company's projection of sales and earnings for the next three years, including explanations with respect to any increase or decrease.

46. Be knowledgeable with respect to all real estate owned by the company, including, without limitation, the following: (a) the improvements on the property, (b) the assessed valuation and amount of current real estate taxes, (c) any mortgages, including amount, rate of interest and due date, (d) any liens or encumbrances, and (e) the estimated present value.

47.   Be knowledgeable with respect to all real estate leased by the company, including, without limitation, the following: (a) the amount of space, (b) the rent-fixed and contingent, (c) the term of lease, (d) the renewal options, (e) the purchase options, (f) the minimum annual gross rentals, and (g) the minimum total gross rental obligation to expiration of all leases in force.

48.   Please list all equipment leased by the company if aggregate annual rentals exceed $5,000 or if the company is dependent on the equipment. If any other property is leased at a sizable aggregate annual rental, please furnish details of the lease, including without limitation on the terms, options to renew and/or purchase, etc.

49.   Please furnish copies of all brochures, catalogs, mailers, publicity releases, newspaper or magazine articles, literature, and the like distributed by the company or concerning the company, its products, personnel, or services.

50.   Please describe the company's research and development activities.

51.   Please give a complete description of any unusual contracts relating to the company, its business, products, or services.

52.   Please describe exactly how the net proceeds (after underwriting commission and all expenses) are to be used by the company.

53.   Please describe the company's plans for expansion or growth.

54.   Please set forth any information not previously disclosed in your answers that an investor would use in making a decision as to whether he or she should invest in the company.

CHAPTER 9

WORKFORCE
CRITICAL EMPLOYER RESOURCE

We live and work in a period of rapid change driven by economic, political, technological, and societal forces. Several major trends that will impact the future of work include:

- *Globalization* and increased interrelatedness of the world's economies.

- *Demographic shifts,* including the aging of the baby-boom generation, increased immigration, and more diversity of the workforce, with greater participation by women and minorities of both sexes.

- *New management practices* and forms of work organizations, such as total quality management and just-in-time inventory control systems.

- *More employment instability* and transiency due to corporate fluidity as well as job-hopping by individuals.

These changes have far-reaching implications for employers and workers, as well as for the system that prepares people for work and careers. In this chapter we examine existing systems and identify issues that need to be addressed in the next generation of workforce preparation.

Economic development can only succeed when qualified workers are available to fill the new positions. It does little good to create jobs if there are no people who can fill them, or to train people for jobs that no longer exist or will soon be obsolete.

Employer Workforce Needs

A recent Washington State Workforce Training and Education Coordinating Board survey* of approximately 4,000 businesses found:

- More than half (59%) of firms looking for workers reported difficulty finding qualified applicants.

- The scarcity of skilled workers affects all industries, particularly construction and manufacturing.

- The most serious shortage was of workers with postsecondary training.

---

* The complete report can be found at *www.wtb.wa. gov/employer-survey.pdf.*

- Among those reporting difficulty, 61 percent of firms said the scarcity of skilled workers lowers productivity, while two-thirds said it reduces output and sales and reduces the quality of their products and services.
- Among those reporting difficulty, nine out of ten employers had a hard time finding skilled workers with occupation-specific skills.
- Nearly half of all employers reported that skills required to adequately perform production or support jobs increased during the past three years.

Even with the changes in the economy, these same findings are mirrored by firms throughout the United States.

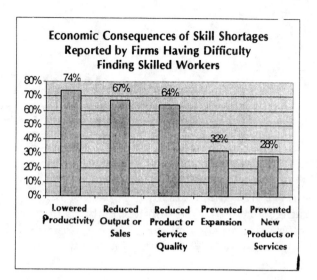

Economic Consequences of Skill Shortages Reported by Firms Having Difficulty Finding Skilled Workers

WHY IS WORKFORCE DEVELOPMENT IMPORTANT?

- **Increases Productivity** — The rate of worker productivity—the amount of work produced per unit time—has been steadily increasing in the United States. Workforce development is critical to continue that trend.

- **Enhances Ability to Compete** — A skilled workforce helps companies expand and remain competitive.

- **Fewer Entry-level Workers** — An expected decline in the number of young workers may lead to labor skill shortages in all professions.

- **Low-skill Jobs are Disappearing** — They are being replaced by jobs that require a higher level of technical skill, especially with computers.

- **Reduces Illiteracy** — More than one in five American adults can't read a newspaper, compute with fractions or decimals, or find a street section on a map. Skill-building will enhance the self-esteem of the workforce, which will increase productivity.

- **The Workforce is Aging** — Without effective training, older workers could become entrenched in old ways, unwilling or unable to learn the new methods and technology.

- **Opportunities for Women and Minorities** — Nearly 50 percent of the workforce is now women, and 65 percent of the entrants into the labor market will be women and minorities.

- **Aids in Retention of Workers** — A trained workforce will lead to steady jobs, which will encourage their families to stay in the community.

- **Increases Standard of Living** — Better job skills will lead to increased wages and upward mobility.

- **Reduces Gap Between the Haves and Have-nots** — Skill shortages contribute to economic disparities between people in many communities. Workforce development helps balance the scale.

FIRMS REPORTING DIFFICULTY FINDING QUALIFIED APPLICANTS WITH SPECIFIC SKILLS AND ABILITIES

Occupation-Specific Skill	91%
Problem-Solving or Critical Thinking Skills	90%
Positive Work Habits and Attitudes	85%
Communication Skills	83%
Teamwork Skills	80%
Adaptability to Change in Duties and Responsibilities	78%
Computer Skills	78%
Ability to Accept Supervision	70%
Math Skills	64%
Writing Skills	59%
Reading Skills	40%

The need for skilled workers is found in all sectors of the economy and in businesses of all sizes. Among the firms that report having difficulty, the most commonly cited problem is finding applicants who have the required occupation-specific skills. Forty-seven percent of all firms indicated that they had increased skill requirements for jobs. The largest increase in skill requirements was in high-technology (76%), service (56%), and manufacturing (48%). Firms also reported difficulty in finding applicants with positive work habits and with skills in problem-solving, communication, and teamwork.

Workforce Development System

In an age of global competition, the places that thrive will be those with the best educated, most innovative, and most productive people. Workforce development is intended to prepare people for jobs and to assure employers of a skilled workforce. Following are some of the resources that can help businesses and economic development organizations address workforce issues.

PUBLIC WORKFORCE PROGRAMS

Federal and state governments are actively involved in workforce development.* These programs provide an array of services, such as job training, employment services, work-related support services, adult education and literacy, vocational rehabilitation, and secondary and postsecondary education. Public programs that can assist business and economic development practitioners include:

- **Workforce Investment Act**
- **One-Stop Centers**
- **Trade Act**
- **Job Skill Program**
- **Apprenticeship**
- **Tax Credits**
- **Alternatives to Layoffs**
- **Welfare Reform**
- **School-to-Work Programs**
- **Running Start**

Workforce Investment Act (WIA):

Since the 1930s Depression, the federal government has been involved in workforce training. The current Workforce Investment Act was passed by Congress in 1998. The program goals are to increase the employment, retention, and earnings of participants, and to increase occupational skill attainment by participants. The program also works to improve the quality of the workforce, reduce welfare dependency, and enhance the productivity and competitiveness of the nation.

The WIA mandated the establishment of One-stop Centers (discusssed in the next section). It also directs the state and communities to provide, for the first time, information about the effectiveness of training programs.

Employers play a major role in this new Act through involvement on state and local development boards. (Employers are required

---

* *In Washington state, public funding of workforce programs is split: 27.8 percent federal, 72.2 percent state.*

WORKFORCE: CRITICAL EMPLOYER RESOURCE

to represent at least 51 percent of membership on local councils.) The WIA also established Workforce Development Councils (WDCs) that are responsible for providing workforce development planning and promoting coordination between education, training, and employment efforts in their communities. WIA also set a priority to link economic development and workforce planning. *Economic development staff need to become involved in planning workforce strategies for their community.* A listing of Washington state's 12 WDCs is found at *www.wa.gov/esd/work/wdc.htm.*

One-Stop Centers: The Smart Solution for Businesses

The same principles that make a mall a handy place to shop have been applied to workforce development system. Government agencies, community colleges, and local nonprofits have joined forces to create one-stop centers that offer all the job resources, technology, and personal assistance that employers and job seekers need in one place. In Washington, some 50 WorkSource (one-stop) locations are open to the public. (In Washington state see *www.wa.gov/esd/work/oca/connections.htm.*) Although resources vary by location, the following core services are available to employers:

1. **Labor Market Information** — Local and state labor market information is available to employers via self-serve groups or one-on-one services. These include:
    - Occupation descriptions
    - Job and industry growth patterns
    - Economic trends and forecasts
    - Wage levels for various occupations
    - Skill standards
    - Labor force information
    - Economic information (regional and county)
    - Population and demographic information
    - Affirmative action statistics
    - Nonproprietary employer information
    - Education and training outcomes: completion rates, placement rates, and graduate wages

2. **Job Listings** — Employers can list job openings for individuals or groups of qualified workers. Jobs can be listed directly, or staff is available to assist in job listings.

3. **Applicant Referrals** — Referrals of qualified job seekers are given to employers based on the requirements of an employer's open position.

4. **Employee Training and Retraining** — Information and referral, including:
    - Skills enhancement
    - Basic skills
    - English as a second language
    - On-the-job training
    - Apprenticeships
    - Customized or on-site training
    - Employer training incentives
    - Community college and technical college information

5. **Business Assistance Information and Referrals** — Information about a variety of business resources, including:
    - Business registration (Master Business Application)
    - Finance programs for retention, creation or expansion
    - Employment law
    - Fair labor practices
    - Tax information
    - Tax incentives and credit information
    - Audit preparation
    - Other business resources

6. **Unemployment Insurance Access** — Employers can access general information on:
    - Unemployment insurance taxes
    - Benefit charging
    - Experience rating
    - Old Age and Survivor Insurance
    - Tax rates, help with tax wage reporting, and forms
    - Access to unemployment insurance laws, regulations, and eligibility
    - Appeal process information

7. **Internet Access —**
   - 24-hour online access to business information through Work-Source website
   - One-stop resource areas with computers and Internet access

8. **Business Closure/Reduction in Force Information and Referral —**
   - Major layoffs and plant closures
   - Assistance with Worker Adjustment Retraining Notification (WARN)
   - Access to services to help businesses avoid layoffs (e.g., shared work options)
   - Referral to business retention services

9. **Translation Services** (varies by Center)

10. **Job Fairs and Hiring Events —**
    - Opportunities to meet face to face with a pool of prospective job candidates. Events are time-compressed and structured to save employers time.

11. **Other —**
    - Arrange facilities for client interviews
    - Offer quick and easy access to a diverse labor pool
    - Applicant referrals
    - Job readiness workshops
    - Screening of candidates to meet an employer's specific needs

Trade Act:

The federal Trade Adjustment Assistance Program was modified significantly in 1994 by North American Free Trade Act (NAFTA). It helps workers, whose jobs are adversely affected by increased imports, prepare for and obtain employment.

This program allows groups of workers to apply for a variety of benefits and reemployment services if they have lost their jobs or had their wages cut due to increased import activity. After receiving a request, a fact-finding investigation is conducted. If increased imports contributed significantly to job reduction in a company, the U.S. Department of Labor certifies the affected group of workers as eligible for retraining and support service assistance.

Job Skill Program (JSP):

This Washington state program brings together employers and educational institutions to provide customized employee training. State JSP grants, combined with match funds from employers, support four types of training:

1. **New employee training** for prospective employees before a new plant opens or when a company expands.
2. **Current employee retraining** when retraining is required to prevent the dislocation of those employees.
3. **Current employee upgrading** to enhance productivity for advancement opportunities with greater skills and responsibilities.
4. **Industry initiatives** that support development of customized training programs for several companies within an industry.

JSP concentrates its resources in areas with new and growing industries where there is a shortage of skilled labor to meet employers' needs, in economically disadvantaged areas with high unemployment rates, and in areas affected by economic dislocation.

Training may be provided to both new and existing employees. Eligible businesses and industries include private firms and institutions, groups, or associations concerned with commerce, trade, manufacturing, or providing services. Call (360) 733-3650.

Apprenticeship:

Apprenticeship combines classroom instruction and paid on-the-job training under the supervision of skilled journey-level craftsperson or trade professional.

The goal of apprenticeship is to promote development and implementation of structured on-the-job training programs supplemented with related theoretical instruction. Programs provide individuals with the skills to progress from entry-level to fully qualified journey-level workers.

Apprenticeships in Washington are governed by the Washington State Apprenticeship and Training Council and administered by the Department of Labor and Industries. Apprenticeship agreement standards include a progressive increase in scale of wages. Completion standards include minimum total work hours (2,000 hours) and annual minimums for related and supplemental instruction (144 hours). For more information, in call (360) 902-5324.

Tax Credits:

Federal tax credits encourage employers to hire qualified groups of job seekers. Federal tax programs include:

WORK OPPORTUNITY TAX CREDIT (WOTC). This can reduce a firm's federal tax liability by as much as $2,400 per new hire and qualified employee.

WELFARE TO WORK (WtW). This encourages employers to hire long-term public assistance recipients who have received benefits for 18 consecutive months. The maximum two-year federal credit is $8,500 per qualified employee.

EARNED INCOME TAX CREDIT (EITC). This can be subtracted from the amount tax workers owe. Even people who have not filed a return in previous years because their wages were below the minimum income level requirements may be able to get the credit. Employers benefit from the EITC by being able to "boost" an employee's wages at no additional cost.

Alternatives to Layoffs:

Many states have a program that allows employers to reduce employment hours instead of implementing total layoffs for a portion of employees by granting those workers unemployment proportionate to the number of reduced hours. For information on the Shared Work Program in Washington state, call 800-752-2500.

Welfare Reform:

State and federal governments have made concerted effort to help welfare recipients enter the workforce. In Washington state, the welfare reform initiative is called WorkFirst. Services include:

- Employee support services: Job retention services may include short-term financial help for emergencies, such as car repairs or child care, transitional medical coverage, and transportation help; and partial cash assistance to help participants transition into the workforce.
- Tuition assistance: to pay tuition, books, and fees for individual students who are parents and work at least 20 hours a week.

In Washington, call 1-888-734-WORK (9675).

School-to-Work Programs:

School-to-work programs establish a framework to prepare young people for a high-skill, high-wage economy. These programs integrate school-based learning at high school with structured learning experiences in the workplace. This requires partnerships to be developed in the community with employers, educational institutions, and community-based organizations.

A recent survey found that 24 percent of companies with 20 to 99 employers were involved in some form of school-to-work program.

In order to be successful, employers must be able to see the benefits and opportunities that exist when they participate in school-to-work programs. In most cases, this means the program must have a positive impact on the company's bottom line. At the same time, educators must realize curriculums cannot be developed with the intention that all of their students will move on to receive a four-year degree.

Running Start:

The Running Start Program was created by the Washington State Legislature to expand

EMPLOYER PARTICIPATION IN SCHOOL-TO-WORK PROGRAMS

Goals of School-to-Work Programs	Employer Recruitment Strategies	Economic Development Organization Role	Public School Activities	Employer Activities

• Prepare students who do not attend four-year colleges
• Address pressing labor needs
• Enrich high school education in areas of skill shortages
• Cultivate next generation of skilled workers
• Learning is organized around career majors
	• Emphasize programs that serve corporate and community goals
	• Identify private sector champion to recruit other employers
	• Target employers that:
	  – Experience skill shortages
	  – Operate in international markets
	  – Invest in education and training
	  – Have a history of community involvement
	• Build from relationships that already exist
		• Act as intermediary
		• Appoint representative steering committee
		• Administer program
		• Communicate and clarify expectations
		• Broker agreements with labor unions
		• Administer student paychecks
		• Establish and maintain credibility
		• Secure outside funding
		• Facilitate problems or miscommunications
			• Provide counseling
			• Match students with employers
			• Design career days
			• Create curriculum with employer
			• Provide job assistance
			• Integrate work-based learning with academic classes
			• Offer a retraining guarantee to employers
				• Provide funding
				• Create curriculum with school
				• Establish type of program:
				  » Workplace mentors
				  » Career shadowing
				  » Internships
				  » Youth apprenticeships
				  » School visits from businesses
				• Train supervisors
				• Establish training standards
				• Create jobs for graduates

This table was developed from "Employer Participation in the School to Work Transition," by Erin Flynn, *Commentary*, Spring 1994.

educational opportunities for students. Running Start allows eleventh and twelfth grade students to earn college and high school credits simultaneously and earn up to two years tuition-free college credit, so that they get a head start on college. The high school determines which classes at the college are equivalent to the high school requirements. All potential Running Start students are required to take the Computerized Placement Test (CPT).

Other Types of Training:

Training can be customized for firms either on-site or through local community colleges or technical colleges. Skill development approaches can include:

• *Pre-employment training*, where an individual employer or an industry enters into partnership with a local college to design classes that prepare groups of people for specific high-demand jobs.

• *On-the-job training (OJT)*, which allows employers to be reimbursed for up to 50 percent of a qualified employee's wages during formal training on the job.

• *Workplace basic skills, adult basic education*, and/or English as a Second Language (ESL), which help in employment and progress beyond entry-level jobs. Skills to meet the needs of the workplace may include traditional reading, writing, math, and speaking and listening in English, as well as computer literacy, teamwork effectiveness, work readiness, and problem solving.

Businesses that have supported workplace basic skills projects have enjoyed increased productivity, improved team meetings, reduced absenteeism, higher employee morale and improved communication.

For a directory of Washington state workforce programs, see *www.wtb.wa.gov/publications*.

Industry Skill Panels: Addressing Employer Skill Needs

Industry skill panels comprised of employers, labor represtantives, and educators can directly address the skills gap. This is done by determining the skills and level of performance required to function in specific industries and occupations (developing skill standards), identifying skill gaps in the current workforce, and helping to change curricula and assessments to match skill requirements.

Washington has more than 25 industry skill panels that represent more than 65 occupations. The industry clusters covered by skill projects include biomedical, construction, health care, food processing, information technology, metals, plastics, and wood.

One example of a skills panel is the Northwest Alliance for Health Care Skills, coordinated by the Northwest Workforce Development Council and comprised of more than 20 organizations from four counties. This panel identified five priority health care occupations; developed recruitment, training and retention strategies; and established a new radiologic technologist program. Another example is the Inland Northwest Technology Education Center (INTEC), which coordinated a biomedical skills gap project in Spokane that surveyed the growing industry, developed career tracks, created skill standards, and distributed curricula to community colleges and other training providers.

For more details: *www.wa-skill.com*.

WORKFORCE ISSUES

Child Care:

Often, one of the most formidable obstacles an individual must overcome is finding someone they can trust to take care of their children while they look for work or while they hold a job. The availability of good-quality child care is an essential element in any workforce development effort. Employer child care assistance can reduce employee turnover rates, absenteeism, and low productivity. Child care assistance can be offered in a variety of ways:

- Employers can contract for *referral services* to licensed child care providers in their geographic area.
- Employers can develop *flexible personnel policies and benefit plans* that may include flextime, flexplace, job sharing, and extended maternity or paternity and adoption leave.
- The *community* can develop a *child care program* for targeted workers. This program may be implemented through a local church or a coalition of churches or other organizations.
- *Dependent Care Assistance Plan* allows a portion of an employee's pretax salary to be withheld and deposited into an account set aside for care of a dependant.
- Employees can use a *federal child care tax credit* if their income qualifies them.
- An employer may *reserve a number of spaces* in existing licensed child care facilities for employee use. Usually the employer only pays a fee if the space or slot is vacant for more than a month. This method is also effective for employers, as it is not directly linked to individual benefits.
- *Child care vouchers* can be offered by the employer. The employer pays part of cost of care directly to the caregiver of the employee's choice. Child care vouchers may also be available to low-income workers through the state social

service agencies. These vouchers cover all or a portion of the child care costs for qualified recipients.

- Larger employers may provide day care *assistance at their facility*. This service is often provided at or below cost, depending upon the demand and the company's ability to provide.

Child care benefits are found in all kinds of businesses. In Washington state, call (360) 725-4034.

Transportation:

For some workers, just the process of getting to work can be a challenge. The worker may not have a car or has an unreliable vehicle, or they may be unable to drive a car or are too far from buses or other transportation. If the principal challenge is getting the employee to the workplace, communities can address this problem in various ways:

- **Expanded public transportation.** Some communities have created a more personalized public transportation system to help those who cannot transport themselves on standard public vehicles. Systems of this type often address more than the needs of the workers, taking into consideration such targeted groups as the elderly and physically challenged. In Seattle, for example, ACCESS minibuses pick up and drop off people at their doorsteps.
- **Carpooling, vanpooling, and ridesharing.** Some companies set up carpooling to match employees with others who live near them and travel on a similar schedule. Counties may also provide vans or other vehicles for ridesharing to help reduce the number of single occupancy vehicles on the highways during rush hours.
- **Company-provided transportation.** When the need is strong enough, some companies purchase a van and appoint a person to be responsible for picking up and dropping off their co-workers.

Workforce Availability:

Rural areas often need to overcome a stereotype image that businesses may have about limited availability of skilled workers. Some areas have surveyed the workforce in both their county and the broader local labor market pool. This information can be a good marketing tool for businesses with expansion and relocation plans.

Grays Harbor County, Washington, used a methodology developed for U.S. Department of Defense projects to determine civilian workforce characteristics and availability in communities across the nation where military installations were scheduled for closure. This methodology was refined to produce the information needed in assessing communities as locations for new or expanded operations. In this workforce assessment, the consultant firm conducted telephone interviews with individuals throughout the survey area. Those individuals were stratified across age (19-49), gender, household income (up to $100,000), local telephone exchange areas, and zip codes. The purpose was to ascertain availability for work with a new employer, to determine desired pay rates, and to collect information on age, education, commuting patterns, experience and skills.

Skill Attainment: Employability Screening

Employers are concerned that new workers meet desired skill levels. One community developed a tool to be used in the high school to address this need.

The Enumclaw, Washington, School District spent 16 months meeting with business and parent partners to develop a Learning and Employability Profile (LEP). LEP is used to help students and teachers assess student's learning and employability skills.

The model shown in Attachment 9-1 is a simplified version revised by New Vision, the economic development council in

Yakima, Washington, to help employers identify skill attainment by job seekers.

Suggestions For Using the LEP: The ideal model is to discuss the subject of LEP early on in the school year. Clarifying how LEP will be used in the classroom (or district) can help develop clear expectations around performance and process, including influence on grades.

Students and teachers should meet on a regular but varying schedule. One suggestion is to have both the teacher and the student assess the student's competencies and then arrive at a score that represents both of their assessments.

WORKFORCE TRENDS

Changing Demographics:

Many states have seen a slowing in their population growth. Even with continued immigration from other states and countries, workforce growth in Washington slowed to 20 percent during the 1990s. Forecasts suggest that growth will slow to 14 percent in the next decade and to only 8 percent from 2010 to 2020. This presents local communities with an opportunity and a challenge. Good paying jobs will be available to a wider spectrum of people than in the past. But many of the populations that have been underutilized in the past continue to face unique barriers to gaining and retaining employment.

The U.S. Department of Labor projects that workers age 55 or older will make up almost 20 percent of the labor force by 2115. While the total labor force is projected to grow 1.1 percent annually from 2000 to 2010, forecasts estimate that the share that is 55 and older will grow at a rate of 3.9 percent. In addition to there being more retirees, the age composition of those remaining in the workforce will shift. The number of older workers will rise dramatically: one out of every five workers will be 55 or older by 2025, compared to about one in ten in 2000. Some older workers may delay retirement, and some retirees will either want or need to return work to supplement their income. Older workers and retirees will need access to education and specialized training both to mitigate the shortage of skilled workers and to improve their prospects for retaining or obtaining employment.

Incumbent Workers:

By providing training to workers who are currently employed, we can enable businesses to expand and be more competitive, and can sometimes prevent dislocations from taking place.

Alan Greenspan, Chair of the Board of Governors of the Federal Reserve System, has underscored the growing need for greater human capital investment. Pointing out that the enormous advances in technology require workers at all levels to possess higher levels of cognitive skills, he stressed that basic skills alone are no longer enough. Workers must engage, on a lifelong basis, in flexible education and training programs.

Many incumbent (currently employed) workers find they must gain more education to move up a career ladder. Institutions, however, may be unwilling to recognize their previous courses or the skills they have already obtained on the job. If efforts to establish competency-based curricula and assessments are expanded, they may provide a vehicle for granting credit based on prior education or skills learned on the job. A competency-based system would facilitate transfer, though it will require a considerable shift from current practices.

One of the most effective ways to increase the competitiveness of employers is to provide training customized to the specific needs of employers. This will increase the training's efficiency and effectiveness. Colleges can contract with employers to provide customized training, often for incumbent workers, for a fee.

According to a recent Workforce Board's survey of employers, in the previous 12 months, 26 percent of employers had hired new employees who were trained in community college and technical college programs, and 28 percent of Washington businesses have an arrangement with a community or technical college to provide classroom training to their current workers. The majority of contracted training was paid for entirely by the firm, not supported by state dollars. The survey indicated that most firms that used a community college or technical college to train their current workers reported they were very satisfied with the training their employees received.

Nationally, most estimates are that employers invest between 1 and 2 percent of payroll on employee training. A survey conducted by the American Society for Training and Development showed that total training expenditure per employee rose from $499 in 1996 to $649 in 2000.

As Jerry Jasinowski, the President of the National Association of Manufacturers (NAM), stated:

For the United States to maintain its strong leadership position in a growing economy, industry must make greater efforts to prepare workers for the in-creasing challenges of the high-tech era. This may even require them to substantially increase the percentage of payroll that they currently invest in those activities.

The Board of Directors of NAM have called on all 14,300 member companies to invest 3 percent of payroll on training. Investments in employee training pay off in terms of increased productivity and profits. A 1995 study by the University of Pennsylvania, for example, found that investing in the skills of workers had more than twice the impact on productivity as investing in equipment or facilities.

Many workers will still lose jobs and experience difficulty in finding new employment at similar wages because they lack the latest skills desired by growing businesses. The churning of jobs and skills is an inherent feature of a modern growing economy.

Contingent Work:

The need for flexibility and increased competition afforded by digitization requires employers to frequently change the size and composition of their workforce. They are shifing work from "permanent" jobs to contractors, leased employees, and part-time and temporary workers. The world of work may begin to resemble the building trades, where workers move from project to project based on demand.

The term "contingent work" was coined by Audrey Freedman to describe "conditional and transitory employment arrangements as initiated by a need for labor—usually because a company has an increased demand for a particular service or a product or technology, at a particular place, at a particular time."

The term "contingent employees" includes a variety of nontraditional types of workers, such as leased employees, temporary employees, loaned servants, part-time employees, and independent contractors.

The preference by some workers for more flexible schedules has certainly contributed to some of the rise in contingent jobs. Most, however, is a result of changing employer demand. Economic developers need to understand the benefits and risks of this growing trend.

Contingent employment relationships allow some firms to maximize workforce flexibility in the face of seasonal and cyclical forces and the demands of modern methods, such as just-in-time production. This same flexibility helps workers balance the demands of family and work.

On the other hand, contingent arrangements are sometimes utilized simply to reduce the compensation paid by the firm for the same amount of work. Recent court cases have ordered some employers to provide benefits to contingent workers.

In 1997, contingent workers represented an estimated 31.1 percent of the labor force. The percentage of employed workers who have had their current job more than 10 years was 41 percent in 1979 but declined to 35 percent by 1996.

Contingent workers account for almost 60 percent of the bottom decile of wage distribution in the U.S. Temporary workers earn about 14 percent less than permanent workers and are about half as likely to receive any employer-provided health care.

Contingent workers can impact policies in local communities. Employers are less likely to spend money on training if they have a high percentage of contingent workers. Many employers bypass candidates who need extensive training and opt instead for contingent workers already trained or who have a variety of experiences and are able to make an instant contribution.

This decline in job stability and rise of contingent work has resulted in a resurgence of the labor movement. It serves as an intermediary to ensure workers have skills, benefits, and bargaining power with employers. Apprenticeship has served as a training model for contingent workers for hundreds of years. The Taft–Hartley trust has provided benefits to union construction workers who have no single employer.

Telecommuting/Telework:

Today, telephones and computers enable employees to do some of their work from places other than the traditional workplace. When done as a strategy to avoid the commute, it's called telecommuting. Telecommuters work either from their home or from a satellite office or telework center close to their homes.

The term telework, often used interchangeably with telecommute, encompasses a broad range of work styles in which telephones, computers, modems, and overnight shipping enable people to work remotely part- or full-time. Teleworkers may be frequent travelers or employees who live a great distance from the central office, or they may be self-employed, working from their homes or from various locations, such as clients' offices.

Job growth in rural communities has not kept pace with urban areas. In fact, due to depletion of natural resource–based jobs, seasonal occupations, outmigration of the best and brightest high school graduates,

TELECOMMUTING BENEFITS

To Businesses:

- Enhanced employee job performance (productivity and work quality)
- Increased ability to attract and keep valued employees
- Improved employee morale and job satisfaction
- Increased access to new labor markets, including the disabled, semiretired, and rural communities
- Reduced office and parking space requirements
- Less sick leave and absenteeism
- Better corporate image
- Increased ability to meet air quality or transportation demand management requirements

To Employees:

- Greater lifestyle flexibility
- Improved work environment
- Improved morale and job satisfaction
- Enhanced job performance (productivity and work quality)
- Reduced child care costs
- Greater degree of responsibility
- Less commuting time and stress
- Reduced transportation costs

To Community:

- Less traffic congestion
- Less gasoline consumption
- Fewer vehicle emissions
- More job opportunities for disabled, semiretired, single parents, and rural citizens

and insufficient infrastructure, many rural communities are struggling to survive.

Urban regions typically attract and retain skilled employees. But high real estate costs and traffic congestion are forcing many urban businesses to consider relocation or growth outside the region.

Our information-based global economy provides new hope and opportunities for jobs in rural communities. Telework is effective for a broad range of jobs, especially for knowledgeable workers—from word processing and data entry to software engineers. The number of teleworkers nationwide jumped from 4 million in 1990 to 19.6 million in 1999. While the majority of these teleworkers are in urban areas, today's technology makes it possible for this work to occur anywhere.

Examples of telework include call centers, both call-in technical assistance and call-out models; Swiss Air's accounting done in India; Putnam Investments with staff who conduct financial assessments from their homes; and large travel agencies with their reservations done in rural communities.

Rural telework jobs can offer urban employers new opportunities to meet human capital needs and reduce costs. Each job located outside urban areas may mean one less commuter in peak hour traffic—a potentially positive impact on the current infrastructure and environment. Telework jobs benefit rural communities by providing living wage jobs, reducing outmigration, providing year-round employment, and diversifying the economy. It is a win-win solution that benefits everyone. (See Washington Dental Service case study.)

According to the recent Gartner Group research report, *Digital Divide and American Society*, Washington state ranks first in the country in the percent of households with Internet access and second in the percent of households with PCs. These trends, as well as workforce demographics changes, corporate culture shifts, and new ways of doing business, make rural telework a logical next step in Washington state.

For more information, call 360-956-2024.

RURAL TELEWORK
WASHINGTON DENTAL SERVICE

Background:

In the late 1990s, Washington Dental Service recognized the need to expand its operations. "We began to run out of space at our Seattle facility and, at the same time, it was increasingly difficult to attract quality applicants for customer service and claims processing positions," explained Heather Kirton, director of operations. As a result, the company's three-year business plan included an initiative to evaluate expansion alternatives.

Washington Dental Service did not go into the process expecting to locate in a rural community. The company considered alternatives from outsourcing to creation of a second site. Initially, they looked at sites along the Interstate 5 corridor, but costs led them to explore other options. Previous work with the Washington State University (WSU) telework group led the company to consider efforts the state was sponsoring in rural communities.

One of those efforts was the WSU Rural Telework Project, designed to strengthen and diversify the economies of rural Washington communities through telework job creation. To get ready to compete for telework opportunities, Colville had formed the Rural Information Technology Center (RITC) was in 1999. RITC, a locally funded nonprofit corporation, helped the community identify its telecommunications needs and began pursuing solutions. One solution was to collaborate with two local telecommunications providers, Qwest and CenturyTel, to fill gaps in the fiber network and increase bandwidth.

Colville was one of the communities participating in the Rural Telework Project, and Washington Dental Service decided to explore it as a potential second site. Senior management selected Colville for its expansion based on the following business reasons:

- ► Lower cost of living and real estate costs
- ► Quality of the workforce
- ► Necessary technology infrastructure
- ► Supportive economic climate and community

Business Benefits:

- ► Reduced operating costs by more than $1 million over three years due to lower real estate and labor costs
- ► Provided access to a stable and capable labor pool
- ► Alleviated a space shortage in the main office
- ► Supported Washington state community needs and maintained in-state jobs consistent with business vision and image

Community Benefits:

- ► Created 29 professional-level jobs with benefits
- ► Diversified the employment base in the community
- ► Created opportunities for further development of "information economy" jobs

LEARNING AND EMPLOYABILITY PROFILE

Student: _____

Commitment to Quality—*Gives best effort, evaluates work, and completes work to quality standards.*

Minimal / 0–11	Initial / 12–13	Progress / 14–15	Proficient / 16–17	Exemplary / 18–20	Date	Rating
• Minimal effort. • Attempt to evaluate work and utilize feedback is not evident. • Does not regularly complete work.	• Rarely gives best effort. • Rarely evaluates work and utilizes feedback. • Completes work inconsistently.	• Inconsistently gives best effort. • Sometimes evaluates work and utilizes feedback. • Completes work, but does not consistently meet quality standards.	• Usually gives best effort. • Usually evaluates work and utilizes feedback. • Completes work; usually meets quality standards. • Consistently gives best effort.	• Constantly evaluates work and fully utilizes feedback to improve product quality. • Consistently completes work according to the highest quality standards.	1. 2. 3. 4.	1. 2. 3. 4.

Work Habits—*Displays initiative, flexibility, and time management.*

Minimal / 0–11	Initial / 12–13	Progress / 14–15	Proficient / 16–17	Exemplary / 18–20	Date	Rating
• Resistant to begin tasks. • Poor use of time. • Rarely adjusts well to new situations.	• Reluctant to begin tasks without significant teacher intervention. • Needs frequent reminders to use available time. • Has difficulty adjusting to new situations.	• Inconsistently begins and remains on task. • Needs occasional prompting. • Sometimes uses time effectively. • Adjusts to new situations in an inconsistent manner.	• Usually begins and remains on tasks without prompting until the work is completed. • Generally uses time effectively. • Usually adjusts well to new situations.	• Consistently begins and remains on task until the work is completed. • Maximizes time available. • Consistently responds to changing situations in a successful manner.	1. 2. 3. 4.	1. 2. 3. 4.

Communication—Reads with comprehension, writes with skill, and communicates effectively and responsibly in a variety of ways and settings.

Minimal / 0–11	Initial / 12–13	Progress / 14–15	Proficient / 16–17	Exemplary / 18–20	Date	Rating
• Understands and interprets information incorrectly. • Presents information in a vague and unorganized manner. • Refuses to access or use appropriate resources.	• Seldom understands and interprets information accurately. • Presents information in an unorganized manner. • Accesses minimal resources.	• Inconsistently receives, understands, and interprets information accurately. • Demonstrates a limited ability to present information in an organized manner. • Inconsistently accesses appropriate resources.	• Usually receives, understands and interprets information accurately. • Presents information in a clear and organized manner using appropriate methods and resources.	• Consistently receives, understands and interprets information accurately. • Consistently presents information in clear, organized and engaging manner using a variety of methods and resources.	1. 2. 3. 4.	1. 2. 3. 4.

Interpersonal Effectiveness— Works effectively with others and contributes productively as a member of a work team.

Minimal / 0–11	Initial / 12–13	Progress / 14–15	Proficient / 16–17	Exemplary / 18–20	Date	Rating
• Uncooperative and disrespectful in working with others. • Disruptive to group efforts.	• Demonstrates inappropriate group behaviors. • Improvement needed in treating others with respect. • Rarely contributes to group efforts.	• Utilizes a limited number of positive group behaviors. • Generally respectful of others. • Contributes to group efforts in an inconsistent manner.	• Consistently works well with others and is respectful. • Contributes significantly to group efforts.	• Facilitates positive group dynamics and respectful environment. • Demonstrates leadership that plays a significant role in the success of group efforts.	1. 2. 3. 4.	1. 2. 3. 4.

Communication—Reads with comprehension, writes with skill, and communicates effectively and responsibly in a variety of ways and settings.

Minimal / 0–11	Initial / 12–13	Progress / 14–15	Proficient / 16–17	Exemplary / 18–20	Date	Rating
• Understands and interprets information incorrectly. • Presents information in a vague and unorganized manner. • Refuses to access or use appropriate resources.	• Seldom understands and interprets information accurately. • Presents information in an unorganized manner. • Accesses minimal resources.	• Inconsistently receives, understands, and interprets information accurately. • Demonstrates a limited ability to present information in an organized manner. • Inconsistently accesses appropriate resources.	• Usually receives, understands and interprets information accurately. • Presents information in a clear and organized manner using appropriate methods and resources.	• Consistently receives, understands and interprets information accurately. • Consistently presents information in clear, organized and engaging manner using a variety of methods and resources.	1. 2. 3. 4.	1. 2. 3. 4.

Interpersonal Effectiveness— Works effectively with others and contributes productively as a member of a work team.

Minimal / 0–11	Initial / 12–13	Progress / 14–15	Proficient / 16–17	Exemplary / 18–20	Date	Rating
• Uncooperative and disrespectful in working with others. • Disruptive to group efforts.	• Demonstrates inappropriate group behaviors. • Improvement needed in treating others with respect. • Rarely contributes to group efforts.	• Utilizes a limited number of positive group behaviors. • Generally respectful of others. • Contributes to group efforts in an inconsistent manner.	• Consistently works well with others and is respectful. • Contributes significantly to group efforts.	• Facilitates positive group dynamics and respectful environment. • Demonstrates leadership that plays a significant role in the success of group efforts.	1. 2. 3. 4.	1. 2. 3. 4.

CHAPTER 10

TELECOMMUNICATIONS

OVERVIEW*

The world has changed, the Internet has changed it, and the change is just beginning. Like the printing press, electricity, the automobile and the flying machine, the Internet is a transforming technology. To e-mail and telework, to "just-in-time" manufacturing, telemedicine and electronic town halls, it is changing everything about the way we live, work, play, learn, move around and govern. There is no going back. The spread of Internet usage—what the experts call "innovation diffusion"—has been explosive. Measured by the time required to reach 50 million users, the Internet, which took four years to reach 50 million, is spreading more rapidly than radio (38 years), the personal computer (18 years), television (13 years), or any other modern technology.[1]

Business impacts are even more dramatic. The Internet has spawned a whole new way for business enterprises to manage their resources and to do business with each other—what IBM's Lou Gerstner calls "e-business." These new web-based management tools can be used by enterprises of all sizes, provided they have access to the Internet, especially high-speed access.

E-Commerce Trends[2]

E-commerce is the practice of buying and selling of goods and services over the Internet, utilizing technologies such as the

Web, electronic data interchange, e-mail, electronic fund transfers, and smart cards. It has both a retail (home shopping) and wholesale (or business-to-business) component.

Global electronic commerce has exploded in recent years. By 2001, worldwide business access to the Web was expected to grow to 8 million. This growth, coupled with rapid changes in information technology and communication, is having a profound impact on business and the workplace. Increasingly, the use of e-commerce is becoming a condition of trade for the manufacturing and retail industries and is imperative for all industries striving to maintain a competitive edge.

More and more consumers have gone online to make purchases, and for a while companies that were strictly Web based

---

*The text on pages 165 to 169 is an abbreviated version of the Center for New West Points West Special Report, *The "Other" Digital Divide*. Used by permission. For their full 34-page report, see *www.newwest.org*.

were being established. Up until 2001, the proliferation of these "dot-com" companies was so dense that it seemed as if anyone who had an idea simply needed to slap a dot-com at the end of the company name and they had an Internet company. However, between 2001 and 2002, the "Internet Economy" bottomed out. The dot-com companies that were once seen as the wave of the future have gone out of business at a breakneck pace. The measure of success for these companies had been, to a large degree, the number of clicks, or website visits, that they achieved. After the fact, it appears that many of the champions of the "Internet Economy" have come to the realization that solid business principles and practices need to be part of any business to include Web-based companies. The fact that the number of clicks did not translate into the number of sales brought many people to this conclusion. Consumers have mixed opinions as to whether customer service or competitive pricing in relationship to e-commerce is more important. Research has shown there is a specific demographic profile of Internet purchasers and product range currently viable for e-commerce. For example, in 2002, the Federated Department Stores (Macys: Bon and Macys) decided to use their website as a way for customers to "preview shopping prior to entering a store to buy" but they do not sell online.

Digital Divide

Unfortunately, access to the Internet is uneven. The government report, *Falling Through the Net: Defining the Digital Divide*, stated, "Minorities, low-income persons, the less educated, and children of single-parent households lack access to information resources." Even more vexing than the demographic dimension is the institutional dimension—including location and size of an enterprise. This "other" digital divide refers to the gap between large business enterprises, which are largely connected by high-speed on-ramps to the information superhighway, versus small and midsized enterprises—called SMEs[3]—which still use electronic dirt roads.

SMALL BUSINESS

Small business owners have difficulty remaining technologically current. The problems are not only cost, but the learning curve involved. Computer and Internet technologies are good examples. However, it is clear that small business owners for the most part have no choice but to adopt new technologies in some fashion, including computer and Internet technologies. In fact, some argue that the Internet, in particular, offers small businesses a unique opportunity to overcome the economies of scale that often bar them from competing effectively against larger firms. Others view the Internet's impact differently, arguing that brand names enjoy enormous advantages on the Internet and that costs to drive consumers to a firm's website are beyond the capacity of smaller firms. Still, the Internet and business websites are facts of life. Small business owners must compete in a marketplace where the Internet and business websites are ubiquitous and where they are central to the business strategies of many.[4]

Small and midsized businesses face problems in getting good connections to the Internet. It is widely known that most small businesses have computers. By some accounts, four out of five (81 percent) SMEs use computers, and the number is rising,[5] although the rate of growth is slowing.

SMEs are the backbone of the American economy and a foundation institution of American society[6]:

▶ SME payrolls account for more than 50 percent of the existing jobs, and much higher in most communities.
▶ SMEs create 80 to 90 percent of all new jobs.[7]
▶ SMEs pay taxes, especially the income and property taxes that support the physical and social infrastructure—water, sewers, streets, hospitals,

schools, and airports—that are the backbone of America's small cities.

▶ SMEs' corporate social responsibility programs provide the contributions that support community effort.

To put this in context, remember that America has nearly 22 million business enterprises. Only 15,000 are "large" businesses (more than 500 employees); the other 21-plus million businesses are SMEs.

In 2001, virtually all of America's 15,000 large businesses were linked to the Internet, and most had access to high-speed, broadband transport. By contrast, between 57 percent of America's small business enterprises were linked to the Internet in some fashion. Only about one-quarter of small business sold products online.

Most of America's small businesses have a symbiotic relationship with a big business.[8] Sometimes the SME serves as a supplier—e.g., as the maker of bicycle seats supplies a large manufacturer of mountain

Online Functions Performed By Small Business Owners

✓ Order inventories
✓ Transmit data/records from one location to another
✓ Marketing
✓ Search on-line databases
✓ Financial transactions, such as wire transfer
✓ Security
✓ Data measurement

bikes. Sometimes the SME serves as a customer—e.g., as a car dealership is a wholesale customer to an auto maker or a mom-and-pop remodeling business is to Home Depot. (See next page.)

Large business enterprises increasingly prefer to deal with their SME suppliers and/or their SME customers over high-speed Intranets or Extranets (limited access Internets) because business transactions are

faster, cheaper, more timely, and with fewer errors.

Access to high-speed, digital communications is to a business enterprise in the New Economy what good running shoes are to the high-performance marathoner—a necessity, not a luxury.

RURAL BARRIERS

The gap between rural and urban areas to the information highway is another part of the "other digital divide."

The continued survival and prosperity of small towns, suburbs, and rural areas may depend on the ability of business enterprises and public institutions to obtain affordable access to high-speed Internet, just as they depended on access to waterways, railroads, and highways in other eras. The high-speed, broadband networks of the 21st century are essential for attracting and retaining businesses, providing state-of-the-art health care, and offering children the benefits of distance learning and the Internet. But as the value of the computer is increasingly determined by the network one is connected to, the technology needs to upgraded to keep pace with the times.

Telecommunication Opportunities

"TELEMEDICINE"

Challenging weather, long distances, low population density, long travel times and difficult terrain present intimidating barriers to providing affordable health care to Americans in rural and suburban communities. These challenges have led to the development of innovative methods of health care delivery, especially "telemedicine" networks that provide high-speed connections linking hospitals, clinics, care providers, and consumers.

Telemedicine networks offer tremendous benefits—including clinical training, immediate access to medical records and lab

E-BUSINESS AND THE SME:
THE HOME DEPOT STORY

E-business is not just for big business alone. Consider the following: The small contractor or the neighborhood fix-it guy is the quintessential SME. He is self-employed and typically has no employees. This same small businessperson is often supplied by a large business, and many large businesses are moving their operations to the Internet—to create greater efficiencies in their own operations and/or to provide better services to their own customers, the SMEs.

Here's how it works:* Small contractors, who are Home Depot's most valuable customers, are given a log-in and password for a limited access website—an Extranet—full of helpful applications. When the SME building contractor has a new job, he goes to the Home Depot website and enters the specifications of his job—say, a single story, two-car garage or certain dimensions. The website then tells him what materials he needs, how to sequence and schedule the work, and what snags he may encounter. When the contractor makes his order, he finds out immediately if needed supplies are available. Then the Home Depot Extranet will ask whether the contractor would like the materials delivered on-site and whether they should arrive all at once or "just-in-time." If the builder needs, say, a plumber or an electrician, and the people he normally uses are not available, Home Depot will post the details of the job on its site and operate as a labor exchange.

Clearly, a builder with high-speed access to this Internet-based service has a lot of advantages over the builder with no access. He saves time in planning, he saves money by reducing uncertainty which allows him to minimize his stock of extra materials, he improves quality by his access to expert advice, and he eliminates delays by aligning the building schedule with the delivery of supplies and the ability to find help quickly if he needs it. Result: Projects are completed on time and on budget with higher quality and lower overhead. That's a pretty big advantage.**

*Adapted from "You'll Never Walk Alone," *The Economist*, June 26, 1999.

**There are also benefits for the big business. Home Depot reduces its overhead costs by faster throughput and less warehousing. By the information exchanged, it deepens its customer relationship and, if it wants to pass some of that information on to its suppliers, it can also help them to become more efficient by taking much of the guesswork out of their production runs. The services provided also reduce customer turnover. In effect, Home Depot operates as a virtual link between its suppliers and its customers. In the process, Home Depot is transforming itself into a virtual services provider, turning the sale of goods (building materials) into an indispensable business-to-business transaction that supplements the sale of goods with high-value-added business and professional services.

results, and consultations—to health care providers and consumers in rural areas. However, many rural communities cannot afford a high-speed, broadband connection to a telemedicine network.

EDUCATION

Distance learning refers to the many ways computers, software, and telecommunications networks can be harnessed to educate people (both young people and adults) in sparsely populated towns and rural areas as well as in urban centers. The "education on demand" applications include students attending classes remotely, ac-

cessing laboratory equipment, participating in simulations, and conducting research on the Internet. In a few short years, distance learning has evolved to the point where multiple schools can participate in interactive video conferences on a real-time basis.

A major challenge for small-town schools and colleges is the cost of purchasing their own high-speed connections to the networks. However, without adequate funding for distance learning programs and high-cost areas, schools and colleges currently being served will be left high and dry.

FARMING/AGRICULTURE

Farming is a complex and information-intensive business. Jim Burg, farmer and South Dakota Public Utilities Commissioner, described some of the ways that life on the farm is being revolutionized by computers and information technology. The Internet offers farmers a wide range of "electronic commerce" applications, such as buying and selling options, futures, livestock, feed, and other farming supplies. Previously, these transactions could be conducted only in person or through an agent. Using the Internet, a farmer can check the latest market and weather information, research the best feed and fertilizer prices, and even search for tractor parts. Today's high-tech tractors and combines are guided by satellite technology and have onboard computers that monitor crop information such as yield and moisture every 10 feet. This crop information is stored on a computer disk so that it can be analyzed and used the next year to make precise computerized adjustments of fertilizer and insecticide distribution.

ECONOMIC DEVELOPMENT

Competitive advantage in economic development used to be where the asphalt or rails crossed. Today, competitive advantage is where the fiber optic lines cross with high-speed, broadband services.

With tighter labor markets, many companies are looking to expand into small towns and inner cities where costs are lower and the supply of labor is higher—provided these areas can offer the high-speed voice- and datalinks. High-speed communications are basic requirements for any technology-related business or for a business like a call-in center or telemarketing center that uses advanced communications technologies.

High-speed, broadband access to the Internet trumps other quality-of-life amen

The Need for Speed: Bandwidth Requirements for Broadband Applications

Bandwidth Required	(Mbps)
Business Applications	
Telecommuting/SOHO	.014 – 6.0
Internet*	.500 – 1.5
Desktop Video Conferencing	.128 – 1.5
Distance Learning	.500 – 6.0
Local Website Hosting	.500 – 6.0
Telemedicine	.500 – 6.0
Computer Telephony Integration	.128 – 1.5
Consumer Applications	
Internet*	.500 – 1.5
Education	.500 – 6.0
Video on Demand	3.0 – 6.0
Shopping	.500 – 1.5
Interactive Video Games	.128 – 6.0

Source: ADSL Forum.

*In many regions, Internet transport speeds are less than 1 megabyte per second (Mbps).

ities for increasing numbers of people. New technologies give civic leaders new ways to create collaborative and innovative regional policies to solve the old problems of remotely located border towns and their residents. New technologies create new possibilities for where and how people live —and how they work together to solve prob lems.

The digital divide is about social and economic well-being and fundamental economic development—jobs, prosperity, and economic opportunity for individuals, families, communities, and business enterprises —and the ability to participate in America's New Economy. It is critical for economic development staff to advocate the growth of the Internet for business, commerce, education, entertainment, home security, and other functions.

NOTES

[1]From a presentation by Guy Tonti, director, Systems Engineering, Cisco Systems, to the Denver, Colorado, Internet Chamber of Commerce, June 29, 1999.

[2]This section includes updated information from various sources.

[3]SME refers to enterprises with less than 500 employees.

[4]National Federation of Independent Business (NFIB) Small Business Poll, *The Use and Value of Web Sites*, 2001.

[5]See Dennis, William J. Jr. "Most Small Businesses Have Computers; Relatively Few Online," in *Small Business Matters*, Washington D.C.: NFIB Foundation, June 1997.

[6]For a comprehensive overview of the anatomy of America's enterprise sector, see "The State of Small Business," a special report in *Inc.* magazine, May 16, 1995, and especially John Case, "The Wonderland Economy," pp. 14ff.

[7]That is, net new jobs. Many large businesses, especially high-tech enterprises, are creating new jobs in large numbers, but large business enterprises overall are shedding jobs as they downsize, delayer, and increasingly outsource work projects as new technologies shape new approaches to management.

[8]On this point, see James W. Botkin and Jana B. Matthews, *Winning Combinations: The Coming Wave of Entrepreneurial Partnerships Between Large and Small Companies*, New York: John Wiley, 1992.

AUTHORS

Phil Burgess, president and senior fellow of the Center for the New West, is director of the Center's Institute for Information Policy and Culture. Burgess spent 20 years as university professor teaching public policy, management and resource economics.

Florine P. Raitano, a senior fellow at the Center for the New West, is executive director of the Colorado Rural Development Council, served as mayor of Dillon, Colorado, as chair of the Colorado Rural Technology, and on the 10th District Economic Advisory Council of the Federal Reserve Board.

Center for the New West is an independent, non-profit, and nonpartisan policy research institute with headquarters in Denver and a national affairs office in Annapolis, Maryland.

Center for the New West
600 World Trade Center, 1625 Broadway
Denver, Colorado 80202

Phone: (303) 572-5400; (800) 795-WEST
Fax: (303) 572-5499
Web: *www.newwest.org*

MARKETING ECONOMIC DEVELOPMENT ON THE WEB

Economic development organizations need to develop web pages so that businesses and individuals can access the information they need to grow and survive. Many companies and site developers do their initial search on-line of communities and areas to which they hope to expand or relocate. Jim Mooney suggests that EDCs include the following on their informative web pages:

- ▸ Location maps
- ▸ Ten reasons for investing in area
- ▸ Listing of available services
- ▸ Community profile
- ▸ Labor force readiness
- ▸ Key contact information
- ▸ Helpful links

Other interactive options include:
- ▸ Searchable sites and building database
- ▸ Property tax calculator
- ▸ Business tax estimator
- ▸ Personal property depreciation calculator
- ▸ Utility cost estimator
- ▸ Environmental permit selector

TELECOMMUNICATION RESOURCES

Online technology has the potential, depending on the context, to:
- • Reduce customer search costs
- • Allow low-cost customization of the marketing mix
- • Support some market-related activities like auction and brand communities in areas where they were not previously viable

- Give customers access to firms and data (and perhaps visa versa) any time, anywhere
- Abolish some types of intermediary and create other new types
- Strongly reinforce globalization

Examples of business and community resources include:

ONLINE TRAINING FOR SMALL BUSINESS

For businesses to be competitive, they need to be able to market their products through the Internet. Businesses in rural areas, however, often do not have access to website training.

Good on-line training programs are available for businesses. One, the University of Minnesota's Mainstreet electronic commerce curriculum course, helps businesses use the Internet and create websites. Call (612) 624-4900 [item number EP-7530-GO], or visit *www.extension.umn.edu/mainstreet/curriculum.html*.

CENTER TO BRIDGE THE DIGITAL DIVIDE

At Washington State University, the Center provides assistance to people, communities, and governmental entities through education and information, community projects, applied research, and policy analysis. A particular focus is on increasing the ability of community, business, and local government leaders to utilize available telecommunications technologies, to expand business opportunities, and to create jobs. For additional information, contact *bgillis@wsu.edu*.

TELEWORK

Telecommunication infrastructure can expand the possibilities where work occurs. The workplace no longer needs to be a single physical location. Telecommuting or telework is a viable option to address a variety of issues including transportation and child care issues. For more information on Telework, see Chapter 9, page 159.

COMMUNITY ASSESSMENT TOOL

Using the work from Oregon and several other states, Washington state convened a telecommunications work group to develop a community assessment tool. This tool can help communities gather information and define their telecommunication needs, identify their next steps and critical players. (See Attachment 10-1.)

USER SURVEY TOOL

Staff may need hard data to "sell" telecommunication providers on prioritizing investment in upgrading a community's Internet infrastructure. One rural Washington community sent an "Internet survey" (see Attachment 10-2) to 2,600 residents to measure the impacts of Internet and e-commerce on their economy. The goal was to develop the first look at this sectors and develop a starting point for future initiatives and projects.

Using the report on survey results, the local Economic Development Council was able to demonstrate to their local Internet carrier that 78 percent of residents had access to computers and could benefit from upgrade Internet infrastructure. This resulted in the expansion of local Internet services.

SUMMARY

New communications technologies and services are at the core of America's New Economy. Entrepreneurs and traditional freelance professionals—writers, analysts, brokers, accountants, attorneys, engineers, manufacturer's reps—can now live anywhere they want and stay connected to their suppliers and markets through faxes, modems, express mail, and airplane tickets. Access to high-speed Internet and user-friendly, up-to-date community websites could be a critical part of their decision of where to locate.

For a basic guide to telecommunication lingo, see Attachment 10-3.

Office of Trade and Economic Development
TELECOMMUNICATIONS COMMUNITY SURVEY

This survey has two intended purposes: First, for a community to self-assess its readiness to consider how it will make new investments in telecommunications. Second, to identify ways to stimulate new infrastructure and services and help communities create solutions for their telecommunications needs. The information you provide is voluntary, and your answers will be kept confidential.

This survey is divided into four sections. **Section I** focuses on the telecommunications infrastructure in your community, which may make it a candidate for retention of local businesses or recruitment of new telecommunication businesses. Additionally, some questions about infrastructure capacity are technical. **Section II** relates to existing telecommunications businesses. **Section III** focuses upon education a training opportunities in your area, and **Section IV** relates to quality of life issues common to any business interests.

If you are unsure how to answer some of these questions, please work with other organizations and members of your community who may know the answer. Please answer questions as completely as possible. This survey will be tabulated and the results will be shared will all that participate.

Community/county surveyed: _____

Staff person completing form: _____

Telephone number: _____

Section I: Telecommunications Infrastructure

1. Are there long-haul fiber optic lines going through or near your community?
    ☐ Yes ☐ No
    If yes, which company or companies owns the fiber? _____

2. Does your community have access to the fiber?   ☐ Yes ☐ No
    If not, explain: _____

3. Which company provides you access to the fiber? _____

4. Do you know how your community's telecommunications infrastructure is connected to others communities?
    ☐ Yes ☐ No
    If yes, is your connection:
    ☐ Copper wire
    ☐ Microwave
    ☐ Fiber optic   *(check all that apply)*
    ☐ Wireless
    ☐ Satellite

5. Who is your Internet service provider or providers? _____

6. What is the common way to connect to the Internet in your community?
    ☐ Leased line
    ☐ Dial up connection via phone line
    ☐ Cable modem
    ☐ Don't know   *(check all that apply)*
    ☐ Other: _____

7. Do you know what the service rates of the phone/cable line are?
    ☐ Yes ☐ No
    If yes, what are the rates? _____

8. Typically, what speed is your connection?
    ☐ 64 KBPS or slower
    ☐ 128 KBPS
    ☐ 512 KBPS   *(check all that apply)*
    ☐ T1 or faster
    ☐ Don't know

9. What telecommunication services would you want that are not currently available in your community?
    ☐ Dedicated line
    ☐ Faster connection
    ☐ New technology (satellite, etc.)
    ☐ Other (please explain): _____

10. In your estimation, will the businesses currently in your community grow in the next three years in the way you would like them to if they do not have access to wide bandwidth telecommunication services?

☐ Yes ☐ No

If no, what are the community priorities to improve this situation?

_____

_____

11. Have you placed an unfilled order for a T1 line, or do you plan to order a T1 line in the next 12 months?   ☐ Yes ☐ No

If yes, how many T1 lines? ____

12. Please list any specific telecommunication services you have purchased or would like to purchase other than fiber.

_____

_____

13. Do you believe you are lacking in essential telecommunications equipment?

☐ Yes ☐ No

If yes, describe what you believe is missing.

14. Is your community participating in any regional telecommunication efforts?

☐ Yes ☐ No

If yes, describe.

Section II: Telecommunication Businesses

1. How many businesses in your town are telecommunications businesses employing more than 20 people?
   - ☐ Less than 5
   - ☐ 6 to 15
   - ☐ 16 to 25
   - ☐ More than 25

2. Estimate the number of employees in your community working in businesses requiring telecommunication infrastructure.
   - ☐ 0 to 100
   - ☐ 101 to 200
   - ☐ 201 to 500
   - ☐ More than 500

3. Is there a local organization or place for these employees to meet and discuss work-related issues?   ☐ Yes ☐ No

If yes, who is the contact? _____

4. Do you know of any missed business opportunities as a result of not having specific equipment? ☐ Yes ☐ No

5. Are there buildings that are currently used for exclusively telecommunication businesses?

☐ Yes ☐ No

If yes, how many? ____

6. Are there buildings with telecommunications infrastructure that are underutilized?

☐ Yes ☐ No

If yes, how many? ____

7. Are there buildings able to be ready for a telecommunications business with minimum investment? ☐ Yes ☐ No

8. Is there an industrial or commercial business park in your community?

☐ Yes ☐ No

If so, is it ready for telecommunication businesses? ☐ Yes ☐ No

Section III: Workforce Training

1. Is there a trained workforce in your community if new telecom businesses need employees?   ☐ Yes ☐ No

If yes, describe the training that is present in your community. If no, describe what efforts are being made, if any.

2. How is training in telecommunications skills provided in your community?
   - ☐ Private training facilities
   - ☐ Evening classes at the local high schools
   - ☐ Local nonprofit organizations
   - ☐ Community college
   - ☐ 4-year college or university
   - ☐ Other (please describe): _____

List total enrollment for telecommunications courses, if possible. _____

3. Does your community support distance learning?   ☐ Yes ☐ No

4. Is there a center for distance learning in your community? ☐ Yes ☐ No

Section IV: Quality of Life

1. Rate the local business climate as it applies to telecom industries.
   ☐ Excellent   ☐ Indifferent
   ☐ Good   ☐ Negative

2. Does the leadership in your community support expanding or recruiting telecommunication businesses?
   ☐ Yes ☐ No

3. Is your downtown business district viewed as a positive place to locate a telecommunications business?
   ☐ Yes ☐ No

4. Are there any specific local planning issues that affect telecommunications either
   ☐ positively, or   ☐ negatively?
   ☐ Yes ☐ No

5. Are there any specific building permit issues that affect telecommunications, either
   ☐ positively, or   ☐ negatively?
   ☐ Yes ☐ No

6. Is there overnight express mail service available in your community?
   ☐ Yes ☐ No

7. Include a map showing any major highways, airports and ports in close proximity to your community.

8. Describe your community's primary education curriculum (as opposed to technical training) as it may apply to preparing students for training for telecom industries. Include:
   - Number of grade schools: ____
   - Number of junior highs: ____
   - Total number of enrolled students: ____
   - Number of computer courses in schools: ____
   - Type of access to the Internet:
   _____

   _____

   _____

List any telecommunications education awards received by students at your primary schools:

_____

COMMUNITY COMPUTER/INTERNET SURVEY

PLEASE CHECK YOUR BEST CHOICE:

Where do you have access to a computer?
☐ Home ☐ Work ☐ Both ☐ Neither

Do you plan to purchase a computer within the next year? ☐ Yes ☐ No

Do you use the Internet? ☐ Yes ☐ No

Have you ever purchased goods or services from a local vendor online?
☐ Yes ☐ No

Are you interested in local shopping online?
☐ Yes ☐ No ☐ Not Sure

How much do you expect to spend on online purchases between now and the end of the year?
☐ never purchased online
☐ less than $100
☐ $100 to $500
☐ $500 to $1,000
☐ more than $1000

What is your primary reason for making purchases online? (CHOOSE ONE)
☐ Convenience
☐ Better prices
☐ Greater selection

Should the community consider improved telecommunications bandwidth (faster speed) to help local economic development?
☐ Yes ☐ No

Where do you receive most of your news and information?
☐ Newspapers
☐ Newsletters or magazines
☐ Radio
☐ TV
☐ Internet
☐ Other (specify): _____

How interested are you in extended (improved) online access to local information, products, or other services?
☐ Not ☐ Somewhat ☐ Extremely

Are you interested in the services provided by a community portal?
☐ Yes ☐ No ☐ Need more information

What would you be willing to pay for community portal or additional services?
☐ $5 per month
☐ $10 per month
☐ $20 per month
☐ Should be free

What is your age?
☐ 12 to 17
☐ 18 to 29
☐ 30 to 49
☐ 50 to 65
☐ over 65

What is your average annual household income?
☐ less than $15,000
☐ $15,000 to $25,000
☐ $25,000 to $50,000
☐ $50,000 to $100,000
☐ more than $100,000

To take this survey with additional questions, visit: *www.e-ableonline.*

Responses to this survey are anonymous and confidential.

GUIDE TO TELECOMMUNICATIONS LINGO
Commonly Used Terms and Acronyms

Access fees—The charges long-distance companies pay to local telephone company owners for connecting the long-distance network to the local network.

Access lines—The local telephone lines used to connect residential and business subscribers to the local and long-distance telephone networks —and to the Internet. (See Local loop)

Analog—The signal being transmitted is similar to the original signal (electronic pulses).

AT&T divestiture—The court-ordered break-up of American Telephone & Telegraph resulted in the creation in 1984 of the Regional Bell Operating Companies (RBOCs)—sometimes called "Baby Bells." RBOCs account for more than 90 percent of the access lines into America's homes and businesses.

Backbone—The high-traffic-density connectivity portion of any communications network. In telecommunications, a backbone is the major—or biggest—pipe (communications line) in the network.

Bandwidth—Capacity of a network to carry information—text, images video, and sound—in a fixed amount of time. Result: Higher bandwidths, called broadband, can carry more information. Bandwidth is measured in bits-per-second, and a full page of text is about 16,000 bits. Thus, a 33.6 kbps modem can move about two pages a second. (See Broadband, Throughput.)

BLEC—Business local exchange carrier. See CLEC.

Broadband—High-speed digital networks that can rapidly send and receive large amounts of information.

Browser—See Web browser.

btc-commerce(B2B)—Internet-based business-to-consumer commerce. Example: Industry to Industry www.i2i.com (See i-commerce)

btb-commerce (B2C)—Refers to Internet-based business-to-business commerce or e-hubs. Example: www.Amazon.com (See i-commerce)

Bypass—The process by which a large, usually business, customer connects directly to a long-distance network, thus avoiding the local telephone network and avoid paying many of the local, state, and federal taxes on local telephone lines.

Cable modem—Modems that use the CATV provider's coaxial cable link to the home or business. Like DSL over copper wire, the cable modem permits an "always on" high-speed, broadband connection to the Internet.

Carrier of last resort—The obligation of a LEC, usually the incumbent or traditional local telephone company, to provide local telecommunications service to all customers within a specific exchange territory, including consumers and businesses in high-cost areas. (See LEC, ILEC, RBOC)

Cherry picking (See Cream skimming)

Circuit switching (See Switching)

CLEC (pronounced "see-leck")—Competitive local exchange carrier." A CLEC can provide telecommunications services to customers through its own facilities (see Facility-based service provider), by leasing services from the communications network of an LEC (see Interconnection) or by reselling (see Reseller) LEC services.

Common carrier—An entity licensed by the Federal Communications Commission (FCC) or a state public utility commission to supply communications services at established prices, called tariffs. Common carriers cannot discriminate among users and must provide service to all who request it.

Convergence—Coming together of computers, communications, content (e.g. education, entertainment, or shopping), and consumer electronics. Result: Consumers can now get telephone service over cable and video over telephone lines.

Cream skimming—An approach to a market that focuses almost exclusively on the most profitable customers. Also called Cherry Picking. (See CLECs, LECs, Redlining)

Ctb(C2B)—Consumer-to-business e-commerce. Single customer shops a number of businesses for best price. Example: www.Priceline.com.

CtC (C2C)—Consumer-to-consumer E-commerce. Consumers sell goods or service to each other. Example: *www.eBay.com*

Cyberspace—A term used to describe a place formed by computer and communications networks containing a wide range of electronic information and multimedia resources of which the Internet is now a major component. The term originated with author William Gibson in his novel *Neuromancer*.

DDT—Stands for distance, density, and terrain and refers to factors that affect the cost of building and maintaining networks of any kind—railroad, highway, electric power, natural gas pipeline or telecommunications. Areas with a high DDT Factor—that is, with long distances between populations centers, low population density within the population centers, and difficult terrain (e.g., mountains, remote islands, swamps)—will cost a lot more to serve with a network than areas with a low DDT Factor. Current approaches to allocating the burden of what's now called Universal Service requires states to shoulder as much as 75 percent of the cost. This policy greatly favors high-density states and regions can hurt small and midsized businesses and the sparsely populated states of the West and South.

Digital—Uses a binary code to send transmitted information (electronic or optical pulses).

Digital subscriber line (DSL)—This technology uses ordinary copper telephone lines to deliver high-speed information. DSL technologies also enable the telephone company to "split" the voice and data signal coming in to the consumer's premises, giving them in effect two separate lines: one to carry voice signals to the telephone, another to carry the data signals to a computer or other digital device. With this capability, users can leave their computer connected to the Internet constantly (a state called always on in the industry) while still having the option of making and receiving voice telephone calls.

E-business—Refers to all the ways an enterprise (business, government, nonprofits, and individuals) can derive value from the Internet—including customer service, supply chain management, sales channel management, sales

transactions, or even attending a class, booking a flight, or visiting the doctor.

E-commerce—Buying and selling goods and services over the Internet.

Electronic commerce (*See E-commerce*)

Ethernet—One of the most common networking techniques used by business today. Operates on CAT5 lines.

Extranet—A restricted access Intranet used by a business to connect to its suppliers and/or its customers over the Internet. (*See Intranet, Internet*)

Facility-based service provider—A communications provider that builds and maintains its own network. (*See Interconnection, Resellers*)

FCC—Federal Communications Commission. One of several independent federal regulatory agencies. Local and intrastate telephone services are regulated by state public utility commissions. (*See Industrial policy, PUC*)

Fiber optics—Glass threads which transmit signals via pulses of light.

Flat rate—A method of pricing telephone calls so that subscribers pay the same rate per month regardless of how many calls they make or how many hours they use the phone. Subscribers in the data world prefer flat or fixed rates for communications services, the method used for most local calls, especially those that do not cross artificial LATA boundaries, another pre-Internet regulatory barrier enforced by the FCC. (*See LATA, measured service*)

High-speed access—A connection or on-ramp to the Internet that permits high quality voice, data, graphics, and video transmission over digital networks "using any technology" (e.g., coaxial cable, DSL-conditioned copper wires, wireless) that can carry at least 200 kbps. (*See Bandwidth, Broadband*)

HomePNA—Home Phoneline Network allows homeowner to used existing phone lines to share broadband connection with other PCs.

Hyperlinks (*See Web*)

I-commerce—"Internet-based commerce, part of the Internet's evolving nomenclature. When used, I-commerce includes both btb-commerce (business-to-business or wholesale) and btc-commerce (business-to-consumer or retail, sometimes called "e-tailing").

ILEC—Incumbent Local Exchange Carrier *(See Unbundling)*

Implicit subsidy—Fees and "overcharges" mandated by government regulators and charged by LECs. A main source of implicit subsidies is important access fees paid by long-distance companies to LECs. *(See Subsidy)*

Industrial policy—Government's use of taxes, tariffs, regulations, subsidies, or other powers to intervene in the economy to pursue strategic goals in economic policy.

Interconnection—The process of linking one network to another so that telephone calls or data can be transferred. Without interconnection or access, telephone users would only be able to talk to other subscribers of their local telephone company. *(See Resellers)*

Internet—Publicly-accessible worldwide network that uses standard protocols or communications "rules" and methods (see Internet Protocol) to connect individual networks operated by government, industry, academia, and private parties. The Internet originally served to interconnect scientists and laboratories engaged in government research, and has now been expanded to serve millions of users and at least that many purposes.

Internet Protocol (IP)—The method (or protocol) used to route information sent from one computer to another on the Internet or other data networks, such as corporate intranets or industry extranets. The IP is a "connectionless" protocol, meaning there is no set connection between a sending and receiving point on the network. Transmission Control Protocol (TCP) is the method used to reassemble the packets into their original order.

Internet Service Provider (ISP)—An organization that provides access to the Internet. Both individuals and corporations subscribe to ISPs, which provide additional services, including giving each subscriber space on their server (computer) for an electronic mailbox, access to news groups, and maintaining a web page that subscribers can select as their browser's home page.

Internet telephony—Using the Internet, rather than the public switched telephone network (PSTN) for voice or fax communication. Internet telephony appeals to some people because long-distance or international phone calls can be placed over the Internet for the price of the local phone call (placed to access the Internet).

Intranet—A private computer network limited to one company or organization. It can be limited to one building or spread out across the country, using high-speed leased lines provided by the phone company. Access is carefully controlled, and the network is often protected by a firewall, which makes it difficult for hackers to gain access.

IP Network/Protocol *(See Internet Protocol)*

ISDN—Integrated Services Digital Network. Sending voice, video and data over a single telephone line.

IXC—Interexchange carrier—a term for a long-distance company such as AT&T, MCI, or Sprint. Generally speaking, IXCs carry traffic from one LATA to another. *(See LATA)*

LAN/Local Area Network—A short distance communications network, typically within a building or campus, used to link computers and peripheral devices such as printers, CD-ROMs, modems, under some form of standard control.

LATA—Local Access and Transport Area, a (mostly) substate local service region served by an RBOC. As a rough approximation, you can also think of a LATA as an area code boundary, used to separate long-distance prefixes.

LEC—Local exchange carrier. The LEC is the incumbent or traditional local telephone company with an obligation to provide local service to all customers within a specific exchange territory. So the LEC is the "carrier of last resort" and has an obligation to serve those who want to connect to the telephone system.

Lifeline—A program created by federal regulators that waives the monthly subscriber line charge for low-income telephone subscribers. Most states have matching programs. The LECs recover their costs for Lifeline from a subsidy funded by an explicit surcharge on telephone bills.

Local Loop—The line that connects the telephone company's central office to a telephone or some other device (e.g., a computer) located in the home or business of a customer.

Measured service—Also known as toll service or toll charge, a method of charging subscribers based on the time of day, duration or distance of a call. Also called measured telecommunications service (MTS).

Monopoly—In 1848,, economist John Stuart Mill established the principle that there are instances in which a single provider can produce a service or product more cheaply than if there were multiple producers. For most of this century, utilities (including telephone companies) have been considered monopolies.

Networks—A system for connecting various devices. The telecommunications network connects telephones, fax machines, computers (or modems) and other devices.

New Economy—The revolutionary impact that new technologies—especially computers, telecommunications, and related information technologies—are having on organizations and performance of the economy. Sometimes called the "Information Age," the "digital economy," the "information economy," the "knowledge economy" or the "network economy."

Oligopoly—A situation in which a few large players dominate a market and have effective control of pricing. Commonly said to apply to the long-distance market.

Packets or Packet Switching (See Switching)

PANS—Pretty amazing new stuff—such as data services, voice mail, fax forwarding, and other "intelligent" network services—and refers to high-speed, broadband access to the Internet and other advanced telecommunications services. Often contrasted with POTS, "plain old telephone service." (See POTS)

Portal—A gateway to the Internet, usually a website, that includes search engines and a collection of links to other websites or locations on the Internet. Unlike the typical website that focuses on a company, product, or place, a portal is a collection of links to other sites. Examples are information utilities such as America Online (AOL) and CompuServe, which pioneered the concept, or actual websites such as Yahoo!, Lycos, Excite, or Infoseek.

POTS—Plain old telephone service—refers to no-frills voice-grade access to the public switched telephone network, including the ability to place and receive calls and access to directory assistance, emergency services (e.g., 911), and long-distance services. (See PANS)

PSTN—Public switched telephone network. The privately owned U.S. telephone network that links more than 1,200 telephone service providers and their subscribers. Service is nationwide, interconnected (or "interoperable"), and available to all telephone subscribers.

PUC—Public Utility Commission. Refers to the state entity that regulates local telephone service and other utilities. Sometimes called public service commission, department of public services or corporation commission.

Public switched telephone network (See PSTN)

RBOCs—Regional Bell Operating Companies. (See AT&T Divestiture, Carrier of Last Resort, LATA, and MFJ)

Redlining—A risk management practice from the banking sector where bank managers would draw a red line on a map around certain neighborhoods and designate them as off limits for mortgage loan approval. In telecommunications, de facto redlining occurs when government regulations penalize investments in new infrastructure and investments in certain places. (See Cream skimming, CLEC, ILEC, Reseller, Unbundling)

Redundancy—Availability of back-up system in case of failure of the main system.

Regional Development—Government's use of taxes, tariffs, regulations, subsidies, or other powers to intervene in the economy to pursue strategic growth and economic development goals.

Reseller—A business, usually a CLEC, that buys network capacity at wholesale prices from a facility-based provider (or LEC) and then resells it to the public at a profit.

Switches—The machines that switch or route traffic on the telephone network—e.g., from a long-distance network to a local exchange network so you can receive it in your home. Modern switches are digital computers; older switches are mechanical devices.

Switching—The two principal types of switching related to current issues in the communications revolution are circuit switching and packet switching. Circuit switching is used in traditional voice communication and occurs when a switch literally connects two circuits, and these circuits stay connected for the duration of a telephone call or data transmission, even when no one is talking or no data are being transmitted. *(See Internet protocol)*

Tariffs—The published schedule of rates filed by a regulated telephone company with a state public utility commission or the Federal Communications Commission.

Unbundling—The Telecommunications Act requires incumbent local exchange carriers (ILECs) to provide any telecommunications carrier (e.g., a CLEC) access to the ILEC's network elements on an unbundled basis at a discount at any technically feasible point. This means CLECs can lease the ILEC's local loop, the switch and even specific services that are built into the network—such as call waiting, caller ID, call forwarding, etc.—at rates substantially below the retail rates.

Universal service—A national policy, reaffirmed in the Telecommunications Act of 1996, that seeks to provide easy, affordable access to basic telephone service to all who want it. Universal service is an issue today for two reasons: (1) Who should pay the cost of subsidizing subscribers who live in high-cost areas (2) What services should be covered by universal service?

USF—Universal Service Fund. Refers to a program established by federal regulators to subsidize local telephone service in remotely located small towns and other high-cost regions of the country.

Web—The multimedia part of Internet where the user can visit websites anywhere in the world. Developed in Switzerland in 1991, the Web has two main characteristics: 1) hyperlinks, which allow the user to move to another location in the same document or to a document in a different location in the Internet by clicking on any icon, graphic, word or phrase in an electronic document; and 2) support for multimedia data, which permits the user to experience a Web site by live broadcast events, streaming video clips and audio downloads as well as by conventional text and static graphics.

Web browser—The application software that lets a user "surf" the Web—i.e., to search for websites and acquire Web-based information without knowing either the location or the format of the information being sought.

World Wide Web *(See Web)*

SOURCES:

Thomas W. Bonnett, *Telewars in the States.* Washington, D.C.: Council of Governors' Policy Advisors, 1996.

Center for New West Points West Special Report, *The "Other" Digital Divide.*

Matisse Enzer, *Glossary of Internet Terms (www.matisse.net)*, *Computing Dictionary: The Book of Terms and Technologies*, 1996, and *Internet Basics* Sandhills Publishing Company, 1999.

Eric Gagnon, *What's on the Web.* Internet Media Corporation, 1999, 1998.

CHAPTER 11

LOCAL STRATEGIES AND INITIATIVES

KEEPING LOCAL BUSINESSES HAPPY AND HOME

Companies in business today are constantly on the lookout for ways to get and keep the competitive advantage—especially if they expect to be in business tomorrow.

In addition to an effective program to keep local businesses healthy, **a BRE program needs equally effective initiatives to keep businesses local.**

First and foremost, remember that the decision to continue operating a facility or expand local operations is based upon economic viability. Is it going to help the company be more profitable? Is it going to be more profitable to stay in the current location or move? Is there market demand for current product? Has there been a major change in availability of raw products? A company will make its decisions only after balancing all the costs and benefits associated with doing business in the community.

PERCEPTION AND REALITY

"How do you keep 'em down on the farm after they've seen New York?," the song asks. For the purpose of the BRE program, the operative questions are:

- **How do you keep businesses firmly rooted in the community if opportunities to build competitive advantage look better elsewhere?**

- **How do you retain companies targeted by other communities with deep pockets and bags full of enticing incentives?**

It's important to understand that in developing strategies to retain or expand local businesses, the BRE program will be dealing with both *perception* and *reality*—equally compelling, equally dynamic.

Perception: How Things Feel Around Here

In retaining hometown businesses and influencing the decisions to grow and expand locally, markets, business costs, quality of life, and incentives are issues directly connected to *reality*. Many are also elements involved in the saving of businesses at risk of failing or expanding and in the recruitment of new businesses.

But the fact is, while bottom-line realities play key roles in business decisions to relocate or expand, the need by a local company to be recognized as a valuable and valued part of a community is compelling. A friendly, flexible community attitude toward local businesses goes a long way toward keeping businesses local.

Here's where *perception* comes in. And while it represents both tangible and intangible elements of a community's business climate, it's a bit more a matter of style than content.

Reality:
The Way Things Are Around Here

Under the heading of reality, you'll want to conduct an assessment on the strengths and weaknesses of, and opportunities and treats for, retaining and expanding local business. List the reasons companies choose to set up shop in the community and grow. It will include many of the same factors that can spell success or failure for a business—factors a community can foster to prevent local companies from closing their doors, eliminating jobs, and torpedoing stable tax revenues. This information becomes the basis of the program's goals and objectives.

THEY WON'T CARE HOW MUCH YOU KNOW UNTIL THEY KNOW HOW MUCH YOU CARE

Take the issue of compliance. The reality is that no community can do away with local regulation and permitting processes. But the perception the community wants to convey to local businesses is that, while compliance will remain a necessary evil, everyone—from the mayor to the minions—is looking for ways to streamline the process and provide one-stop service.

Conduct an attitude check on those who have direct contact with local businesses on compliance and other public policy matters. **They're the front line in creating a favorable perception of the local business climate:**

- Do these offices have a total quality approach to customer service?
- Do they follow through on details?
- Do they project a friendly, flexible image?

To gauge the level to which the community's business climate is viewed as positive, and where the problems lie, go first to the primary source of credible feedback: the companies that call the community home.

The mail and visitation survey tools of a BRE program (see Chapters 6 and 7, respectively) are used to identify companies at risk of closing or leaving; they will also provide you with leads to evaluate the local business climate. Business visitation programs will give a community an opportunity to put faces to local industry and get an eye-level view of the problems faced by businesses daily. Here's a genuine chance to demonstrate value to local businesses through active problem-solving and solid follow-through efforts.

The personal relationships begun during business visits can yield rewards when companies are faced with relocation and expansion decisions. **If a company remembers the assistance received by the BRE program, the grass may not look so green somewhere else.**

Early warning networks and informal intelligence gathering form the core of BRE programs and initiatives to keep local businesses in a community's own backyard. Early hints of discontent and business climate problems can be dealt with while there is still time to make a difference.

Just ask the businesses that deal with these issues every day and listen—really listen—to the answers.

BUSINESS VARIABLES

As the BRE strategic plan is being developed, keep in mind that a key factor in building competitive advantage is the environment in which businesses operate. **Six variables influence business decisions** and local economic development activities: market, labor, site, cost of doing business, regulatory environment, and quality of life.

MARKET:

The umbrella for all the factors responsible for getting products off the drawing board, into production, out the door, and into the marketplace.

A strong local market reflects a growing economy through the expansion of local businesses. The market-based questions to be answered by BRE staff seeking to retain local businesses and get them to expand their operations within the area include:

- Are current facilities adequate for expanded future production?
- Can local companies tap into research and development facilities to test new products, processes, and innovations?
- Is transportation infrastructure adequate for seamless distribution?
- Are new market opportunities apt to surface?

LABOR:

Labor costs account for the majority of operating costs for businesses.

Businesses are concerned about the quality of the local labor force. They need employees with knowledge, ability, and skills. They prefer communities where the labor force is known for high productivity, low absenteeism, and loyalty. Access to ongoing training or continued education through community and technical colleges is an important benefit to companies and employees.

- Do vocational institutions have training capacity in targeted industries?
- Is a stable, skilled, flexible workforce available?

SITE:

Location that allows a business to successfully conduct trade with its targeted market.

Different businesses have different needs. Some important site considerations include availability and costs of utilities; restriction on requirements for site development; parking areas; site or building design; access to transportation—highways, airports, railroad, etc.; site proximity and accessibility; tax costs; financing; and state and local permitting processes.

- Does the current business site offer easy access to customers, suppliers, and raw materials?
- Is all the necessary infrastructure in place to allow a company to expand?

COST OF DOING BUSINESS:

Factors that influence how many dollars a business can put into its pocket after all it costs to operate go out of its pocket.

High operating costs, coupled with the competitive need to hold product prices steady, can bring moving vans to the door faster than a relocating business can say, "The grass is greener...."

- Is the state and local tax structure conducive to creating and sustaining vital business growth?
- Are labor costs—including wages, work-based benefits, insurance and medical care—comparable to those in other regions?
- Is reasonably priced, buildable land readily available?
- Where do occupancy and construction costs rank?
- Are markets and suppliers near enough to be cost-effective?
- Is the price tag reasonable, in terms of time, effort and cost, for compliance with environmental and other regulation?
- Are utility costs in line with other localities?

- Is there affordable, accessible rail, highway, port, and air transportation?
- Is long-term financing for expansion available?

REGULATORY ENVIRONMENT:

Government rules and procedures that impact the ability to do business.

Regulations are a major concern for businesses. They are concerned about the time required to get permits, number of permits required and cost of permits and the amount of mitigation required.

While regulations can't be eliminated, how the process is handled is very critical to business perception of the community.

- Is the permitting process a nightmare for businesses trying to expand their operations?
- Are issues of turf preservation among city or county government offices causing companies to jump through unnecessary hoops?
- Are the community's compliance forms redundant and overly complicated?
- Do the people in contact positions help or hinder the course of business?

QUALITY OF LIFE:

Factors that influence where and how those in a company—especially top management—live, as well as where and how they work.

Bottom-line factors such as markets and cost of doing business continue to be a priority for relocating or expanding business operations, but quality of life also influences the final decision. Here's what businesses will want to learn and what businesses thinking of relocating out of the area will want to review:

- How does the local crime rate compare with other areas?

- Are health care facilities and professional services accessible and cost-efficient?
- Is housing available and affordable?
- Do public schools rank well compared to local, state, and federal averages?
- Are there adequate sporting, recreational, and cultural opportunities?

BRE staff and partners can identify why it makes good economic sense for local businesses to retain or expand their facilities in the community by understanding the variables that influence business decisions.

INCENTIVES

Incentives are inducements and/or considerations made available by states and individual communities to create and sustain competitive business environments. Incentives can include both tax and non-tax incentives. The attitude and actions of administrative and legislative branches of state government largely determine the business climate. A positive business environment is measured by the degree to which costs and benefits of economic development initiatives are balanced by the diverse needs of individual citizens and communities.

Job creation and retention is often the primary priority for receiving incentives. Some state and local governments require repayment if companies fail to create or retain promised jobs.

STATE BUSINESS INCENTIVES:

Sales and Use or Property Tax Exemptions, Credits, or Deferrals: These may be given to *certain industries* (e.g., Washington state's manufacturing or warehouse tax exemptions on machinery and equipment), to businesses in *certain geographic areas* (e.g., Washington's exemption for qualified construction and equipment costs for manufacturers in distressed areas), or for *employee training or job creation*.

Industrial Revenue Bonds: Tax-exempt or special issue bonds generally available from cities, counties, and state financing authorities to cover land acquisition, construction, equipment, and improvements for special industries, new business attraction, job creation, and expansion.

Low-Interest Loans/Grants: Financial incentives by state authorities and public/private partnerships to fund industrial site improvements, sales tax exemptions, job tax credits for distressed areas, cash grants for job creation, investment tax credits, cash grants to offset lease investment, new job generation projects, business incubator facilities, designated road building funds, small business incentives, research and development initiatives, infrastructure needs, and new product development.

Utility companies can also be instrumental in expansion cases through incentives to reduce energy costs.

Workforce Training: statewide worker training programs can be significant enticements. These programs provide pre-employment and on-the-job training, recruiting and training assistance, plus retraining to meet specific industry needs or expand local workforces. State training programs can vary from cost sharing of training to job tax credit. Washington's Job Skill Program, (360) 753-3650, provides up to half the cost for specific types of customized employee training.

Zones: Foreign Trade and Enterprise programs foster international and domestic business by reducing operating costs.

- *Foreign-Trade Zone* (FTZ) is an enclosed geographic site within the United States which is considered outside customs territory. As a result, FTZs operate as a duty-free area. The Foreign-Trade Zones Act of 1934 was passed to stimulate international trade and create jobs in the U.S. The Act authorized FTZs to function as storage manipulation, trans-shipment, manufacturing and exhibitions centers.

- *Empowerment Zones and Enterprise Communities* (EZ/ECs) are economically depressed areas zones/communities nominated by a government entity and selected by the federal government. The EZ/EC is designated for ten years. Companies located in these zones will benefit from a variety of federal tax incentives, challenge grants, and regulatory relief. EZ/ECs offer assistance to businesses in the form of low-cost capital financing, job recruitment and training programs, tax mitigations, and assistance with relocating. Empowerment Zones have three additional tax incentives available: employment credit, increased Section 179 expensing, and expansion of the Targeted Job Tax Credit. For more information on EZs, check web page: *http://www.hud.gov/cpd/ezeclist.html*.

- *State or Local Enterprise Zone.* Specific eligibility requirements, selection process, and incentives will vary by state or local government. Washington has tax incentives previously available to distressed and timber-dependent counties. These new groups of economically distressed areas are called **Community Empowerment Zones.** For more information about Washington state zones, call (360) 725-4053 or contact the state economic development office.

PRIVATE SECTOR INCENTIVES

Private sector incentives include venture capital corporations, linked deposit programs, applied research funds, export assistance, privately sponsored development credit corporations, infrastructure programs and technology transfer projects.

LOCAL BUSINESS INCENTIVES

Tools for land preparation:
- *Adjustments to zoning* to speed construction
- *Land acquisition* and *swaps* to encourage economic growth
- Help in *negotiating complicated land deals* involving multiple property owners
- Site preparation assistance
- Obtaining road and water improvements from county
- Sale/lease arrangements
- *Property purchase options* to allow communities to acquire land for future development.

Front-end capital and cash flow incentives:
- *Free land or rent* for qualified development projects
- *Temporary space*
- *Land write-downs* to reduce initial capital outlays
- *Land and equipment leases and publicly provided infrastructure* to reduce purchase costs
- *Tax increment financing* to defer front end costs of development
- *Special assessment districts* to help pay for infrastructure and improvements
- *Job creation tax credits* to provide incentives for jobs created by development
- *Relocation expense reimbursement* to ease moving costs.

Tools to lower debt servicing:
- *Industrial revenue bonds* to provide initial funding for expansions and new facilities
- *Loan guarantees/subordinate financing* to secure favorable borrowing rates
- Local *revolving loan funds*
- *Deferred payment mortgages* to reduce initial debt costs
- *Buying down the interest rate* to reduce rates on longer-term loans.

Tools to lower operating costs:
- *Tax abatements* to reduce costs and increase net operating income
- *Payment in lieu of property taxes*
- *Utility incentives* for new investment or high demand users
- *Creation of Foreign Trade or Enterprise Zones* to defer or eliminate specific business expenses and encourage import/export trade.

Workforce development assistance:
- *Pre-employment screening* for new local employers
- *Customized training programs* to upgrade skills for new jobs
- *On-the-job training programs* to subsidize costs of training new workers
- *Job training funds* for new area employers
- *Technology transfer program* to encourage commercialization of new products.
- Some local school districts are now offering business a guarantee that their graduates have basic skills or they will retrain them.

Buyer/Supplier Networks: Some regions have set up a computer database of suppliers by SIC code. By accessing federal and state government and major company needs for services and/or supplier matches can be made. Leads are faxed to local companies. These networks help keep dollars in your community.

Community Awareness of local employers and encouraging local residents and purchasing agents to buy goods and services manufactured in the community.

Caution: Make certain your current employers don't feel neglected.

GRASSROOTS EFFORTS TO HELP KEEP BUSINESSES LOCAL

Effective communications, information distribution, and opportunities to initiate and maintain business-to-business relationships can help local companies succeed. These factors act not only as incentives, but they also build the case that local companies are valued by the community. They can boost awareness of new in-area opportunities, and communicate vital information. Activities BRE staff may wish to implement could include:

Small Business Innovation Research Awards: Introduce local companies to new opportunities to turn their good ideas into new, innovative products.

Match-Market Analysis: Identify existing and potential customers and suppliers for incoming and local companies.

Market Research: Identify existing and potential new markets for local and new businesses.

Manufacturing Councils or Networks: Help local companies build new business relationships and provide a forum for exchange of ideas and mutual problem-solving.

Business Incubation Centers: Provide facilities, business services, and other resources to start-up ventures and entrepreneurs.

The key to success in any appreciation program is sincerity. If you mean it, they'll know. And if you don't, they'll know that too.

For your community to come out on the good side, the BRE staff needs to deal effectively with both the perception and reality of the business environment. BRE programs can play a key role in improving both the perception and reality for the local community.

COMMUNITY SPECIAL RECOGNITION INITIATIVES

Recognition initiatives a community may want to sponsor:

★ **Community-wide Industry Appreciation Days or Weeks** can generate a variety of activities to let local businesses know they're valued.

★ **Industry of the Month Award,** geared to increasing the area's knowledge of local business and enhancing the community's perception of these businesses.

★ **Small Businessperson of the Year Award/Event** to single out special achievement in entrepreneurial or small business ventures.

★ **Local Quality Awards,** to foster high-quality techniques that can help increase production and profitability. Companies often use quality awards as a valuable diagnostic tool.

★ **Plant Tours and Open Houses** to build awareness of local industries.

★ **Proclamations, Certificates, and Plaques** to recognize special business contributions to the community.

★ **Business Advocate of the Year Award** to recognize nonindustry individuals who have worked to build a better business climate.

★ **News Media Programs** to generate awareness of hometown industries and their impact on the local economy.

★ **Display of Manufactured Products** in merchants' windows or in public buildings to spotlight local companies.

CHAPTER 12

UNDERSTANDING BANKRUPTCY AS A TURNAROUND TOOL

Craig S. Sternberg
Sternberg, Thomson Okrent & Scher, PLLC

Bankruptcy does not mean business closure. As a practitioner, it is important for you to understand that bankruptcy is a viable legal tool that can be used to turn around a troubled business. Following is a brief discussion on bankruptcy to help you better understand this technical/legal process.

PROLOGUE

You are a business owner and it is 3:30 p.m. on the Friday afternoon before a warm, three-day, spring holiday weekend. Your banker just called to say that not only has the loan committee turned down your loan request, but that the loan portfolio is being turned over to the special credits department of the bank for a workout.

Out of cash, inventory, and luck, what can you do? To make matters worse, checks were just sent to the Internal Revenue Service and three of your largest, and most important suppliers, who will not ship new product until and unless the checks are received and clear the bank. Without the use of a line of credit facility, which is by no means certain at this hour, how will those checks be covered, to obtain the inventories necessary to make the promised shipments by the end of next week (for which you received substantial deposits)?

Your accountant has warned you about the valuation of inventories, which are maintained on a first-in/first-out basis, since there have been

many and frequent fluctuations in the cost of raw materials. You have a lot of high-cost inventory, which, because the market is down at this time, means that the inventory is overstated. However, the business's equipment was recently appraised at a value significantly higher than the purchase money debt securing it, giving you a good equity. You have a favorable lease on the plant facility and good accounts receivable. Your accounts payable are high and are running 75 to 90 days past due. You have been making payments to all of the larger creditors, and some of the smaller ones are beginning to take collection action.

You certainly have a high level of frustration and fear. So many people who rely on you: 57 employees, your family, customers, and suppliers, to name but a few. You are one of the larger employers in the town and county, and an important supplier of unique and high-quality parts which are sold all over the world.

What shall you do? How will you get by during the next few days and weeks until you figure out what to do?

BRE STAFF'S ROLE

If this manager contacts Business Retention and Expansion staff, they should have ready and potent remedies at their disposal to help. Staff might contact the banker and intervene for this company so that the bank will work with it for a short time. You might recommend that the manager contact the IRS, the suppliers, and other creditors to make or change payment arrangements. You might put the client in touch with financing institutions to arrange for new financing or refer the company to an insolvency or bankruptcy counsel. In any event, an overview of the Bankruptcy Code will help in working with the troubled businessperson.

This chapter is intended to provide a background to the bankruptcy laws which are common throughout the United States. It is intended to give enough information to recognize both the value of the bankruptcy laws as an effective business planning tool, and to advise companies you work with to retain competent and experienced bankruptcy counsel.

The use of bankruptcy, particularly Chapter 11,[1] as a business planning tool has increased substantially since the last major revisions to the Bankruptcy Code in 1979. The revisions made it easier and more palatable for both consumer and commercial debtors to take protection under the Bankruptcy Code. Over time, creditors such as landlords, secured creditors, and consumer credit providers convinced Congress and the courts to strengthen various areas of the Code. Nonetheless, bankruptcy filings continued to rise throughout the 1980s and into the 1990s. During the 1990s, the consumer-type bankruptcy cases seemed to grow and are continuing to grow, while at the same time the business Chapter 11 cases seemed to have peaked and were on a downward trend.[2]

HISTORIC BACKGROUND[3]

The United States has had a bankruptcy law or some provision relating to bankruptcy since the adoption of the Constitution. Article 1 of the United States Constitution provides that the Federal Government shall establish courts in bankruptcy.[4] During the 1800s there were several short-lived attempts at a comprehensive bankruptcy law based on English law of the same era. Filling the void, many states also had some form of debtor relief, although until the latter 19th century most bankruptcy laws were decidedly pro-creditor. In 1898, Congress established the first comprehensive Bankruptcy Act, which supplanted and preempted all state laws relating to this subject. This act was comprehensively amended by the Chandler Act of 1938 and again in 1978. We are currently operating under the 1978 version of the Code, which itself has been significantly amended several times.

The Bankruptcy Reform Act of 1978 (the Bankruptcy Code of 1979) was and continues to be vilified by creditors as being too liberal. During the 1980s and 1990s, the Bankruptcy Code was revised several times to provide additional creditor-oriented remedies. The Bankruptcy Code now seems to favor creditors and nondebtors. For example, there are strong provisions which favor landlords, secured creditors, and the United States Trustee system which keeps a watchful eye over debtors and their lawyers. On the other hand, provisions relating to Small Businesses under Chapter 11, the Family Farmer Bankruptcy under Chapter 12, which has been extended again through early 2003 and the increased monetary jurisdiction for Chapter 13 have helped debtors in those specific areas. Careful pre-bankruptcy planning and attention to detail during the case will alleviate many of the problems for the debtor.

USE OF BANKRUPTCY AS A BUSINESS PLANNING TOOL

There are several different types of bankruptcies. A Chapter 7 bankruptcy is a liquidating tool.[5] The debtor files the petition, and a trustee (court-appointed administrator) takes control of the assets of the estate, liquidates them, and, after paying administrative expenses, distributes the proceeds to the creditors in accordance with the Bankruptcy Code's liquidation schedule.

Chapters 9 (Municipal Reorganizations),[6] 11 (Reorganizations), 12 (Family Farmers),[7] and 13 (Wage Earner Plans)[8] all allow the debtor to remain in possession and pay off debt over a period of time. Businesses would generally file under Chapter 7 or Chapter 11. (Attachment 12-1 provides more explanation on the structure of the Bankruptcy Code.)

Obviously, no one wants to form a business or begin a business venture for the purpose of commencing a bankruptcy proceeding, but, when necessary, a bankruptcy can be employed as a valuable and useful business planning tool.

Among other things, a bankruptcy filing can accomplish the following:

▶ *Stop creditor collection action.* The filing of a petition under any chapter of the Bankruptcy Code automatically stays collection action. This gives the debtor immediate relief and time to reconnoiter.[9]

▶ *Allow for the sale of assets free and clear of liens and claims of creditors.* Since Washington state no longer has a statute governing bulk sales, the Bankruptcy Code is often invoked to allow the sale of assets free and clear of liens. This allows the seller to pass title under the auspices of a Bankruptcy Court to a purchaser for value, free and clear of all creditor claims and attacks.[10]

▶ *Obtain new financing.* The Code allows for the debtor to borrow money and to provide the new lender with superior liens on the debtor's assets, super priority claims or other forms of security. Under certain circumstances, the Code even allows the debtor to "prime" the liens of other creditors giving the lender a first lien on assets which have already been used as collateral.[11]

▶ *Allow for the restructuring of debt.* The provisions of the Code allow the debtor under Chapters 9, 11, 12, and 13 to propose a plan to repay debt. While there may not be a "typical" plan, most plans contain one or more of the following features:[12]

- Extension of payment due dates.[13]
- Rescheduling of payments.[14]
- Sale of assets.[15]
- Infusion of new or additional capital by investment or long-term loans.[16]
- Interim borrowing under court protection.[17]

PITFALLS AND PROBLEMS IN BANKRUPTCY—and how to avoid them

As in any legal proceeding, there are a number of pitfalls and problems in bankruptcy proceedings:

Cost — Chapter 7, 12, and 13 bankruptcies are usually relatively inexpensive and cost-effective. In 2002 terms, most routine business Chapter 7 cases can be handled by competent counsel for $2,500 or less, plus filing fees and related court costs. Most Chapter 12s and 13s can be handled for $3,000 more or less, plus filing fees and related court costs. Chapter 11 attorney fees, however, are usually $10,000 or more. In addition, because of their complexity, and the need to provide periodic reports to the U.S. Trustee's office and creditors, and the information needed to provide the disclosures necessary to accompany the plan, the costs of accountants, appraisers, and other professionals add to the attorneys' fees. Moreover, the U.S. Trustee's office charges a fee of between $250 to $10,000 per quarter, based on a sliding scale depending on the payments made by the Debtor in Possession during the quarter.[18]

Competency of Counsel — Bankruptcy in general, and the Bankruptcy Code in particular, is a complex and complicated area of law. While competent counsel can negotiate around the intricacies of bankruptcy laws, an inexperienced lawyer can cause added costs, loss of a discharge, and failure to confirm a plan, leading to the conversion or dismissal of the case and loss to the debtor and creditors alike.

There are many ways to find competent counsel, including contacting local bar associations, other lawyers, accountants, and bankers. In addition, organizations such as the American Bankruptcy Institute (ABI), most state bar associations, and the American Bar Association maintain a list or registry of lawyers who maintain bankruptcy practices. The American Board of Bankruptcy Certification certifies lawyers both in consumer and business bankruptcies. Information is also available on the World Wide Web from the ABI and other sources, such as West Law. It is not improper to contact or interview more than one lawyer to find the best one for the job. When selecting a lawyer, one should inquire about and understand the lawyer's experience, his or her fee structure, his or her support system (including assistants who can step in to help when the case gets going), and intangibles such as his or her personality and reputation with the court and other counsel. (See Attachment 12-1, Resources.)

The Opposition — Never underestimate the strength, knowledge, or tenacity of your opponents. "Opposition" to a bankruptcy come in a number of ways and from a number of sources. Among those to watch are creditors, the Trustee, the U.S. Trustee, and creditors' committees. Bankruptcy, particularly the Chapter 11 plan confirmation process, is as much a game of politics as it is business economics and law.

CASE EXAMPLE: USE OF BANKRUPTCY TOOLS IN BUSINESS PLANNING

In the case example at the beginning of this chapter, management is about to deteriorate into a near panic! With the three-day weekend pending, management can only imagine what disasters will hit on Tuesday morning.

With luck, management has already been in touch with the company's lawyer, or maybe even a bankruptcy lawyer. Bankruptcy counsel would probably advise the client to meet with the bank to see if a workout is possible. A non-bankruptcy workout has the benefit of being more flexible and usually less expensive than the bankruptcy option. On the other hand, without a bankruptcy, there is no stay of creditor action and no ability to "cram down" nonconsenting creditors.

Over the last decade the number of business bankruptcies, and particularly Chapter 11 bankruptcy filings has dropped substantially. During this time, the costs of filing and shepherding a Chapter 11 debtor through the system has increased substantially, while creditor objections, and the complexities of reports to the United States Trustee have increased sharply. As a result, the changes of a successful Chapter 11 business bankruptcy reorganization have decreased. Thus, it is very important to attempt a non-bankruptcy solution. Such a non-bankruptcy solution might take on any of the following:

MISCELLANEOUS ISSUES OF CONCERN

Among the issues which concern the parties to a bankruptcy are the following:

- **PREFERENCES, FRAUDULENT CONVEYANCES AND OTHER "STRONG ARM RIGHTS."** Under the Code, the Trustee or Debtor in Possession is imbued with certain "strong arm" rights.[19] Among these are the right to set aside transactions and/or recover money for the estate, including payments made to creditors within 90 days on account of an antecedent debt (Preferences),[20] or payments for less than adequate consideration (Fraudulent Transfers).[21]

- **DISCHARGEABILITY ISSUES.** If the debtor is an individual, the Trustee or any creditor can file a lawsuit within the bankruptcy proceeding to determine whether a specific debt will be discharged, or whether the debtor will be entitled to a discharge at all. Most debts are discharged in a bankruptcy. However, certain debts including most taxes, debts incurred by fraud or intentional injury, and most marital claims (support, alimony, and in some cases property settlements) are not dischargeable. In some cases, where the debtor filed false bankruptcy schedules, did not cooperate with the trustee, or committed other bankruptcy transgressions, the debtor may not be entitled to a discharge at all. Where taxes are an issue, the debtor may file the adversary proceeding to obtain a discharge where entitled to do so.[22]

- **PLAN CHAPTER 11 CONFIRMATION ISSUES.** In order to confirm a plan, the debtor must be able to prove each element of the Code pertaining to plans, which includes proof that the debtor complied with the provisions of the Bankruptcy Code, did not obtain the votes necessary by any illegal means, that the plan is fair, equitable, and feasible, and that the reorganization is not likely to be followed by further reorganization. There are many technical rules with which the debtor must also comply.[23]

- **CASH COLLATERAL.** When the bankruptcy petition is filed, in addition to the automatic stay which stays actions by creditors against the debtor and the estate, the filing also results in a prohibition against the debtor from using case collateral—accounts receivable and the like which collateralized a prepetition (prior to filing) loan—without the permission of the secured party. Thus, in order to use cash from the collection of accounts receivable, the debtor must obtain the secured creditor's consent or a court order. In order to gain court approval, the debtor must show that the secured creditor is adequately protected, or must provide adequate protection to the secured creditor by means of additional collateral.[24]

- **ASSUMPTION OF LEASES AND OTHER EXECUTORY CONTRACTS.** Another requirement of the Code is that the debtor assume commercial real estate leases within 60 days of the filing of the case and, at the same time, either cure any prepetition defaults or provide adequate assurance that such defaults will be cured and provide adequate assurance that future lease obligations will be met in a timely fashion. If the lease is not assumed within the 60-day period, the lease is automatically terminated, and the landlord is entitled to immediate possession.[25]

- **RISK OF BEING AN OWNER / MANAGER.** Being a manager in a failing business carries with it certain risks. For example, the IRS may collect unpaid withholding taxes from "responsible officers" of a corporation. Certain other "trust funds" such as collected sales taxes may be traced to and collected from responsible officers. Additionally, creditors may collect from principals who have guaranteed debt. In some circumstances, creditors may claim that managers are liable for obligations incurred when there was no reasonable likelihood of the debt being paid, or where assets of the debtor are transferred to its principals or a successor entity without fair consideration.[26]

- *Reinstatement of the credit line* — If the company can provide additional collateral or guaranties, the bank might reconsider and reinstate the credit line. Alternatively, the bank may consider converting a portion of the debt to a long-term debt and reinstating a portion of the loan.

- *Extension of loan due dates* — An extension of the due date or call on the loan long enough to find refinancing.

- *Sale of assets* — Selling surplus equipment, inventory, or other assets to retire debt. A sale and leaseback of assets or factoring of accounts receivable may also be ways to raise cash.

- *Tax Creditors* — Most tax agencies will allow a short-term workout of tax obligations as long as the current taxes are kept current. The IRS's current policy for employment—trust fund taxes, i.e., withholding and the employee's portion of the FICA (Social Security and Medicare) taxes—is that if the taxpayer does not pay these taxes in full within a very short time, it will close the business. The State of Washington's Department of Revenue takes a similar position with sales taxes. In addition to its other remedies, such as the addition of penalties and interest, and filing of liens, the State Department of Revenue will move to revoke the delinquent taxpayer's business license. Both the IRS and the State Department of Revenue can proceed against responsible officers to collect the "trust taxes."[27] In a Chapter 11 bankruptcy, the taxing authorities are deemed to have accepted the debtor's plan, if the plan provides for payments of the tax debt over a period of time which does not exceed 72 months from the date the tax was assessed or the filing of the petition, whichever is later.[28]

- *Unsecured Creditors* — Management may have already made agreements with the larger creditors. The scheduled payments may be continued or renegotiated. The main problem with a non-bankruptcy workout is that there is no effective way to bring nonconsenting creditors into line.

TIME AND COST FACTORS

Bankruptcy reorganizations are expensive. The fees of attorneys, accountants, appraisers, and other professionals often can sink the very company the professionals are working so hard to reorganize. In addition to the debtor's own fees, the courts will often award fees to creditors' committee professionals and to the professionals for individual creditors in some circumstances.

One of the contributing factors is that the bankruptcy professional must often drop everything else he or she is doing to take over the reorganization case. Another is that the proceedings are adversary and technical and require meticulous detail and documentation. After the case is filed, the lawyer and other bankruptcy professionals cannot be paid more often than every 120 days, without special approvals, and all fees have to be approved by the Court after notice to creditors and a hearing.

In the Seattle area in 2002, qualified bankruptcy counsel charged between $200 and $350 per hour. Fees in a routine case will run $15,000 to $40,000. It is not unusual for fees to run over $100,000. Virtually all bankruptcy counsel will require a retainer or payment of fees in advance. All fees, including fees paid in advance and after the commencement of the bankruptcy proceeding, are subject to Bankruptcy Court review, regardless of the source of payment.

Most bankruptcy professionals will try to use more informal workouts rather than to file a Chapter 11 bankruptcy. Since there are no mechanisms to "cram down" errant creditors, however, informal workouts could become a significantly expensive process with no positive results.

In each case, the business should be sure to understand the fee structure and obtain an estimate of fees in advance. The business must understand, however, that such estimates are subject to many external pressures. The debtor may also object to the bankruptcy attorney's fee application in the formal Chapter 11 proceeding.

In preparing to negotiate with the creditors, the business needs to:

- Identify the source of the problem.
- Identify and consider the debtor's debt structure, i.e., secured, unsecured, trade, employees, taxes. In doing so, keep in mind the statutory priority scheme of the Bankruptcy Code, and the way in which the Code treats certain creditors.
- Review the debtor's financial information, to see how up to date and accurate it is.
- Compare probable outcomes—sale, liquidation, reorganization—and determine the likely outcome for each of the creditors under each scenario.
- Analyze the risk of third party exposure.
- Determine adequacy of the secured creditor's documentation and perfection.

From this information, a business needs to create a plan. In dealing with creditors, the business should keep an eye on the Bankruptcy Code for two reasons: 1) Most savvy credit administrators have sufficient understanding of the Bankruptcy Code to make it the universal language in creditor/debtor workout negotiations; and 2) If they end up in a bankruptcy, they might as well have created a structure upon which to build a formal plan. Thus, when negotiating with the creditors, get the agreements in writing, and in the settlement agreement have the creditor agree to vote for the plan that is being negotiated.

A LESSON

In our example, management is presented with a number of problems which will require the quick collection and mobilization of its resources.

The *first thing* management should do is call the bank and tell the banker that there are critical checks outstanding the bank is expected to honor, and that these checks would not have been released but for the fact that there was sufficient credit on the line of credit, after current collections of accounts receivable.

The *second thing* would be to contact the top officers, the shareholders and directors, as well as the lawyers and accountants, to set up at the very least a conference call (if not a meeting) either over the weekend or first thing after the weekend. It is hopeful that between the lawyers and accountants, management will find a qualified bankruptcy lawyer and accountant to give advice through these perilous times.

Next, if possible, inventory figures and accounts receivable should be checked. It will be important to have figures as accurate as possible. Inventories are converted to sales which become accounts receivable and ultimately cash. All together, these assets, to the extent they are collateral for loans, are "cash collateral." Confidence in the accuracy of these figures will be vital in an informal work. In a Chapter 11 case they will be necessary both to provide "adequate protection"[29] to the secured creditor to support interim working capital, and as a defense to a secured creditor's motion to modify the automatic stay to allow it to foreclose on its security.[30]

Management should also review back orders, employee schedules, and needs and make a list of where expenses could be cut and how cash can be raised quickly. For example, which employees can be laid off? What purchases can be postponed or canceled altogether? What assets can be sold and which accounts can be collected for immediate cash, subject to bankruptcy court approval?[31]

Finally, management should factor this information, along with projected sales and expense savings information, into operating budgets weekly for the next four weeks and for the next ninety days, and six months.

Armed with all this information and the lawyers and accountants, they can present a plan to the bank to revitalize their business and account. Believe it or not, many companies have survived a visit to the "special assets" department of their banks. Some banks will even support the business through a rollback or even an informal compromise and extension of debt program, as long as the collateral remains intact and management remains honest.

If not, the second approach should be presented: Chapter 11 bankruptcy reorganization. Here, the bankruptcy lawyer takes over. With his or her assistance, the debtor-to-be prepares the necessary financial information, including a schedule of all debts (with the names and addresses of all creditors), all assets, and a "statement of financial affairs" which gives an historic and current view of the business. The lawyer will also assist in the preparation of the "first-day orders," including authority to act as counsel for the Debtor in Possession,[32] and the motion to use cash collateral,[33] pay the outstanding payroll, and the like. All this, of course, after the fees have been paid and or arranged.

The first-day orders are often presented *ex parte* with notice to creditors to follow. For example, the orders approving the retention of professionals generally do not require notice to creditors but do require notice to the U.S. Trustee, whose duties include the oversight of attorneys' and other professional fees.

The motion to use cash collateral is generally set at the "debtor's convenience" after shortened and limited notice, usually to the bank and any other person who holds a security interest in the assets which are cash collateral, the U.S. Trustee, and the 20 largest creditors.[34] Since the Bankruptcy Code prohibits the debtor from using cash collateral without permission of the secured creditors and a court order, it is the debtor's obligation to: (1) bring the hearing, (2) notify those creditors and "parties in interest," i.e., those who have an interest in the proceedings, and (3) show that the cash is needed for survival and that the secured creditors' interests are not denigrated by the debtor's use of the cash collateral, i.e., that the secured creditors will remain "adequately protected."[35] The court generally limits a cash collateral order for the first three or four weeks, until the debtor can provide notice to all creditors and convene a full-fledged hearing.

Other first-day orders may include permission to sell surplus assets not usually sold in the ordinary course of business, and permission to pay certain obligations such as prepetition wages and employment taxes to maintain the workforce.

Soon after the case is commenced, management, the lawyers, and accountants will start working on the disclosure statement and plan of reorganization.[36] The disclosure statement is a document which contains sufficient historic, business, and financial information about the debtor and information about the plan, so that a party in interest can make an informed decision about the proposed plan. The disclosure statement must be approved by the Court, after notice and a hearing, before it and the plan can be disseminated to the creditors.

The plan is the "contract" between the debtor and its creditors. It includes the classification of claims, and the manner and method of repayment of the debt. Plans are approved by a vote of the creditors. In order to be confirmable, the plan must receive a majority in number and two-thirds in amount of all claims voting in an impaired class of creditors. If just one class votes, the debtor or other plan proponent may bring the plan on for a confirmation hearing. At the confirmation hearing the debtor must prove that the plan is fair,

KEEPING BUSINESS HEALTHY, HAPPY, AND LOCAL

feasible, and equitable and that it meets the requirements of the Bankruptcy Code.

Once confirmed, the plan binds the debtor and all creditors.[37] If all goes well, the case will be closed and the newly reorganized debtor will continue its business under the Plan.

The Plan itself under a Chapter 11 may take many different forms. It may:

- provide for the compromise or reduction of some or all of the debt with payment over time;
- provide for the sale of the assets to a third party; or,
- for the infusion of new capital either by way of an investment or "take-out loan."

One caveat, however, especially in a small closely held business: Unless all claims of a class of creditors which is entitled to a priority are paid in full, or all in such class agree to a different treatment, a class with a lower ranking priority cannot be paid. Thus, unless all creditors are paid in full with interest, the shareholders cannot retain their interest unless they agree to an infusion of capital.

CONCLUSION

In the context of helping a failing business, an able insolvency or bankruptcy counsel can be invaluable. While a little knowledge of bankruptcy laws can be more dangerous than helpful, knowledge in the hands of a professional can be the difference between a successful reorganization and a total loss.

ABOUT THE AUTHOR

Craig Sternberg is the senior member of Sternberg Thomson Okrent & Scher, and has practiced law in Seattle since 1970. His practice emphasizes insolvencies, reorganizations, and business bankruptcies. He is a member of the Washington State Bar Association and the American Bankruptcy Institute, and holds a certificate in business bankruptcy from the American Bankruptcy Board of Certification. Craig Sternberg can be reached at (206) 386-5438.

REFERENCES

[1] Chapter 11 of the Bankruptcy Code, 11 U.S.C. Secs. 1101-1146. All references herein are to the Bankruptcy Code, unless otherwise clearly noted.

[2] Federal Reserve Statistics. *See also,* Judge Lisa Hill Fleming and Craig A. Hart, *Measuring Chapter 11: the Real World of 500 Cases,* 4 ABI Law Review 119, Spring 1996; and Jagdeep S. Bhandari & Lawrence A. Weiss, *The Increasing Bankruptcy Filing Rate: An Historical Analysis,* 67 Am. Bankr. L.J. 1 (1993) (reporting a 185 percent increase in bankruptcy filing rate from 1980 to 1991).

[3] For additional information, see Charles Jordan Tabb, *The History of the Bankruptcy Laws in the United States, 3 ABI Law Review 5 et seq. (Spring, 1995).*

[4] U.S. Constitution, Art. I, Sec. 8, Clause 4.

[5] Chapter 7 of the Bankruptcy Code, 11 U.S.C. Secs. 701-766.

[6] Chapter 9 of the Bankruptcy Code, 11 U.S.C. Secs. 901-946.

[7] Chapter 12 of the Bankruptcy Code, 11 U.S.C. Secs. 1201-1231.

[8] Chapter 13 of the Bankruptcy Code. 11 U.S.C. Secs. 1301-1330.

[9] Sec. 362.

[10] Sec. 363.

[11] Sec. 364.

[12] See, generally, Secs. 1123, 1222, and 1322.

[13] See, confirmation provisions of Chapters 9, 11, 12, and 13 discussed herein.

[14] See, *supra.*

[15] Sec. 363 of the Bankruptcy Code.

[16] See, confirmation provisions of Chapter 9, 11, 12, and 13. See, also Sec. 364.

[17] See, Sec. 364.

[18] 28 USC Sec. 1930(a)(6) as amended by HR 3610 (Pub. L. 104-208) September 30, 1996.

[19] See, Sec. 543.

[20] Sec. 547.

[21] Sec. 548.

[22] Sec. 523.

[23] Sec. 1129.

[24] Sec. 363.

[25] Sec. 365(d)(4).

[26] See, IRC Sec. 6672.

[27] 26 USC Sec. 6672 and RCW 82.32.300 and WAC 458-20-21(6).

[28] Sec. 1929(a)(a).

[29] Sec. 361.

[30] Sec. 362.

[31] Sec. 362, 363.

[32] Sec. 330.

[33] Sec. 363.

[34] Sec. 363BR2001.

[35] Sec. 361.

[36] Sec. 1121, 1129.

[37] Sec. 114a.

SUMMARY OF
BANKRUPTCY CODE CHAPTERS

The Bankruptcy Code is divided into several chapters which control the rights, duties and procedures of debtors, creditors and other parties in interest. The first three chapters (1, 3, and 5) deal with basic and administrative matters; while the final four chapters (7, 9, 11, and 12) deal with the various bankruptcy options.

Chapter 1 — Basic Provisions

Chapter 1 sets forth the "basics" such as the definitions of terms used in the Bankruptcy Code, powers of the court and the like.

Chapter 3 — Case Administration

Chapter 3 sets forth the administrative provisions of the Bankruptcy Code, including how to commence and the effect of commencing a case; the appointment of a trustee and duties and obligations of a debtor in bankruptcy. This Chapter also establishes the automatic stay of or injunction against creditor proceedings while the case is pending and establishes the power of the Trustee or Debtor in Possession to use, sell or lease property of the estate, defines and proscribes the use of "cash collateral" and establishes the powers to borrow money for the operations of the estate, particularly under Chapters 9, 11, 12, or 13 of the Code.

Chapter 5 — Creditors, Debtors, and the Estate

Chapter 5 deals with the relationships between the creditors, debtors, and the estate. It establishes the procedures to file, contest, allow and value claims. It provides for exemptions and a method to contest the dischargeability of a particular claim against the Debtor. Chapter 5 also deals with the so-called "strong arm" provisions for the Trustee which allows the Trustee to set aside preferences and fraudulent conveyances, for example.

Chapter 7 — Liquidation

Chapter 7 is often thought of as the "basic bankruptcy." Under Chapter 7, the debtor allows the Trustee to take over his or her assets, and liquidate them, distributing the proceeds in accordance with the strict distribution scheme established under this chapter in the Code.

Chapter 9 — Adjustment of Debts of a Municipality

Chapter 9 is used by municipalities, such as Orange County, California, when default approaches.

Chapter 11 — Reorganization

Chapter 11 is used by corporations, partnerships, and individuals to adjust/reorganize debt. Chapter 11 may be and has been used by giant corporations, such as Texaco, several airlines, and Johns-Manville, for example, and numerous small companies and even individuals to stay litigation, and execution on judgments and to reorganize the company's debt structure. This is the most prevalent in the larger business restructuring, but may be used by smaller companies and even individuals to restructure even personal debt.[1]

This Chapter 11 makes provisions for the special issues raised in the Chapter 11 case, such as the establishment of a creditors' committee, the debtor-in-possession and the disclosure statement and plan. Chapter 11 allows the Debtor to remain in possession and to operate its business during the proceedings.

Chapter 12 — Adjustments of Debts of a Family Farmer with Regular Annual Income

Chapter 12 is a relatively new provision of the Code which was added as a result of the farming crisis in the mid-1980s. This provision allows a family farmer to retain and operate the farm property, while reorganizing its debt. The Chapter 12 has special rules for handling farm cases.

Chapter 13 — Adjustments of Debts of an Individual with Regular Income

Chapter 13 is the so-called "wage earner" provision of the Code which allows an individual, but not a corporation or partnership, to retain assets while retiring debt over a period of time usually three years, but up to five years. Chapter 13 is also used to retire debts which otherwise might not be discharged in a Chapter 7 bankruptcy. It is ideal for the family which, or a businessperson with regular income who, desires to repay its creditors in an orderly fashion over time. Similar to Chapter 11, the debtor proposes a plan, but the procedures are shortened and streamlined to save money and provide more certainty of outcome. Under Chapter 13 a trustee is appointed to collect money, usually by wage assignment, and to make the Chapter 13 plan payment.

The 1994 revisions to the Bankruptcy Code also increased the debt limitations for a debtor to qualify for protection under Chapter 13 of the Bankruptcy Code. The increased debt limitations allow debtors including businesspeople and unincorporated businesses to take advantage of the provisions of Chapter 13 as long as the total debt does not exceed $1,000,000, of which no more than $750,000 may be secured debt.[2]

---

[1] Fleming and Hart, *Measuring Chapter 11: the Real World of 500 Cases,* supra.

[2] Sec. 1.

RESOURCES TO IDENTIFY BANKRUPTCY ATTORNEYS

American Bankruptcy Institute
44 Canal Center Plaza, Suite 404
Alexandria, VA 22314-1592

    phone: (703) 739-0800
    fax: (703) 739-1060
    e-mail: abi@pipeline.com
    Web: www.abiworld.org

American Bankruptcy Board of Certification
44 Canal Center Plaza, Suite 404
Alexandria, VA 22314-1592

    phone: (703) 739-1023
    fax: (703) 739-1060
    Web: www.abiworld.org

American Bar Association
750 North Lake Shore Drive
Chicago, IL 60611

    phone: (312) 988-5648
    fax: (312) 988-5711
    Web: www.abanet.org

Washington State Bar Association
2001 Sixth Avenue
Seattle, WA 98101

    phone: (206) 727-8200
    fax: (206) 727-8320
    Web: www.wsba.org

BUYING A BUSINESS OUT OF
A BANKRUPTCY OR WHEN INSOLVENT

Following is a simplification of the pitfalls and benefits to acquiring a business out of a bankruptcy and without a bankruptcy.

Issue	Bankruptcy[1]	Non-Bankruptcy
Title	Will have a court's order, which will both clear and "guaranty" title both to personal as well as real property.	No assurance of clear title except for real estate and titled vehicles and boats.
Cost	Usually more expensive.	Sometimes, you get what you pay for!
Time and Timing	The Bankruptcy Code has specific notice and time requirements. Beyond that, and third party "interference," the parties control the timing.	Generally, the parties control the timing for the transaction.
Notices to Third Parties	Required.	No specific legal requirement, unless a foreclosure or shutdown of a business.
Protection from Creditors	Yes.	None.
Fraudulent Transfers A Fraudulent Transfer is a conveyance or transfer of property for less than full and adequate consideration.[2]	Will not be a problem because of the "notice and opportunity to be heard" requirements of working within the Bankruptcy Code.	Could be a problem. Advice: Have the property valued by an independent appraiser. Note: If the deal is too good to be true, it probably is!
Sales Free of Liens	Authorized by the Bankruptcy Code in certain cases.	Only if bought from a secured creditor in a foreclosure sale.[3]

As a general proposition, when dealing with a business with lots of personal property assets—furniture, equipment, inventories, accounts receivable, and the like—there is no sure way to "guaranty" or insure title, as with real property, where you can obtain title insurance for a modest fee. However, in a bankruptcy, the debtor in possession or trustee will be required to provide a notice and an opportunity for all creditors and other parties in interest to be heard before the Bankruptcy Judge. After hearing, the judge will issue an order which will, in effect, "insure" that the Buyer will acquire title free and clear of all liens, claims, and encumbrances.

NOTES

[1] See, generally, Bankruptcy Code, Sec. 363.

[2] Note: The Bulk Transfer Laws of the State of Washington were repealed in the early 1990s.

[3] See Washington State Deed of Trust Statute (RCW 61.24) and Uniform Commercial Code.(RCW 62A).

BUYING A BUSINESS WITHOUT BANKRUPTCY PROTECTION

As with anything one does in a business without bankruptcy protection, working outside a bankruptcy with an insolvent seller may be precarious. However, if these minimum precautions are taken, the sale should go smoothly:

- Obtain title insurance for any real property or leasehold interests.

- Obtain a Uniform Commercial Code Information Check, which can be done online or through sources such as CT Corporations Systems.

- In spite of the fact that there are no longer Bulk Transfer laws in Washington state, the business might consider giving notice to all creditors advising them of the sale, the consideration and other information similar to what was required under the Bulk Transfer statute or even the Bankruptcy Code.

- The business needs to check with both their state's Department of Revenue and the local County Treasurer regarding any taxes owed as these taxes may follow the assets.

EVALUATING BUSINESS RETENTION AND EXPANSION PROGRAMS

Rebecca A. Livengood
Principal, Rebecca Livengood,
Community and Economic Development Planning

Marion Bentley
Utah State University

INTRODUCTION

Business retention and expansion (BRE) as an economic development component consists of all local development efforts to assist and encourage local businesses to grow and expand. This includes technical assistance, financing, management training, federal procurement, marketing, custom fit training, tax credits, and other subsidies.

Because BRE consists of so many different elements, it is important to determine what works and what doesn't. The success of any BRE program can be measured by a community's businesses expansion and growth. Therefore, it is important to understand which elements lead to those goals.

WHY EVALUATE?

Accountability to sponsors and other parties investing in business retention and expansion may be a primary motivation for undertaking program evaluation, but the evaluation process and results can provide other benefits:

- Provide a rational basis for the allocation of resources,
- Identify areas for management improvement,
- Obtain feedback from the "customers" of the programs which can be used in program planning;
- Determine the effectiveness of the economic development strategy behind the programs; and
- Provide high-quality results which can be used to market the utility of economic development programs specifically and in general.

EVALUATION ISSUES

Issues common to most BRE program evaluations include:

- Developing measures for programs that differ in type of assistance and purpose;
- Measuring the individual program impact of projects with multiple program funding sources;
- Determining the length of time a program must be in operation before program impact can be measured;
- Determining whether individual programs have had the intended impact;
- Separating the process of program implementation from its impacts;
- Assessing the availability of data and the methods for collecting it; and
- Meeting the needs and expectations of the variety of audiences of the evaluation.

Evaluation of business retention and expansion programs can determine the worth, value, usefulness, quality, or effectiveness of the process and outcomes of local program activities.

The *two primary purposes of evaluation* are: *1) formative*—to improve, and *2) summative*—to prove. *Formative* evaluation is conducted during the process of the BRE program to provide information to participants, program staff, and administrators, and other interested and involved partners. It is reported as timely feedback and supports decisions to modify, change, or continue activities that will improve the BRE process and its outcomes. *Summative* evaluation is conducted at the end of the program and provides information to decision makers and potential consumers regarding use or adoption, continuation, or termination and is reported and documented as summative judgments.

Evaluation of BRE programs can be *conducted by internal or external sources*. *Internal* evaluation has the advantages of familiarity with program features and participants, proximity, and usually trust and cooperation. The main disadvantage of internal evaluation is a perceived lack of objectivity and credibility. *External* evaluation, on the other hand, has the advantage of objectivity, credibility, and usually higher competence on the part of external evaluators, but lacks familiarity and cooperation and generally costs more.

PURPOSES FOR EVALUATION

	FORMATIVE (IMPROVE)	SUMMATIVE (PROVE)
Audience	Project Staff	Potential Customer
Major Characteristic	Timeliness	Convincing
Measures	Often Informal	Valid/Reliable
Frequency of Data Collection	Frequent	Usually once or twice
Sample Size	Often Small	Large
Questions Asked	What is working? What needs to be improved? How can it be improved?	What results occur? With whom? Under what condition? With what training? At what cost?
Design Constraints	What information is needed? When?	What claims do you wish to make?

Formative evaluation—used to improve—is most commonly collected and assessed by internal sources, usually program operators. This practice is useful and appropriate. Rarely, however, is formative evaluation conducted by external sources—a valuable and potentially useful partner in the BRE process. On the other hand, summative evaluation—used to prove—is all too frequently collected and interpreted by internal sources—a practice that is perhaps generally inappropriate because of familiarity and bias and should be relegated to appropriate external sources.

CUSTOMER FEEDBACK

Many economic development practitioners do not take the time to stop and listen to their marketplace (existing business). Direct customer feedback can be a valuable source of market intelligence. First, it is straight from the customer—unfiltered and unadulterated. It may even be the only real truth, because everyone else may have a vested interest in the BRE process. Secondly, it is readily accessible and provides staff feedback on program services and willingness of firms to tell their peers about the program (marketing). The sample evaluation questionnaires from North Dakota (Attachment 13-1) and Washington (Attachment 13-2) could be the starting point for customizing and creating customer feedback instruments. These sample questionnaires, administered after the BRE activity is completed, are for the most part internal formative tools which look at how to improve the process. Similar instruments can be designed and administered at important milestones or stages of the BRE process—following volunteer visitors training or firm visitations, for example—and external partners could help design and implement the evaluation questionnaire.

EVALUATION APPROACHES

Two examples of evaluation strategies are presented in this chapter. The first, an evaluation of New York state economic programs, is primarily summative, conducted by an external contractor. The second is a study of BRE programs by the University of Minnesota and is largely formative; it involves both internal and external evaluation.

NEW YORK STATE EVALUATION

The state of New York legislatively mandated biannual external evaluation of its economic development programs. The first two state evaluations were designed and conducted by Knowledge Systems and Research, Inc. (KS&R).

An overall, unified design for evaluating the economic impact of New York state programs was possible because of the basic underlying goal common to all programs. The New York design is well suited to evaluating any set of programs with a common purpose, including the purpose of business retention and expansion. The approach to this evaluation design is based on the key premise of a *focus on program impact and a common definition of areas of such impact*. The evaluation addresses the fundamental question: Are the programs achieving their intended purpose?

The evaluation design includes eight areas of potential program impact:

1. *Impact on business*. Many programs were expected to have positive impacts on businesses in New York state. The effects to be measured included impacts on sales, sales per employee, increased purchases from suppliers, exports, business profitability, competitiveness of products or services, new product capacity, or impacts on the labor force quality, availability, or productivity.

2. *Targeting to economically distressed areas*. Several of the programs had objectives related to providing assistance in economically distressed areas of the state. Measures of impact included the number of businesses and individuals assisted in those areas.

3. *Providing assistance to targeted businesses*. Many of the programs were targeted to specific types of businesses, e.g., small businesses, manufacturing businesses, minority or women-owned businesses. The degree to which these businesses were reached by the pro-

grams was an important area of program impact.

4. *Impacts on jobs created or retained.* Most programs had a job creation or retention objective. The impact evaluation's focus in this area was on permanent jobs created or retained because of their long-term effect. Permanent jobs anticipated to be created or retained were also reported. Where feasible, secondary job creation was also estimated using employment multipliers to estimate the full range of job creation.

5. *Coordination and leveraging impact.* To the degree that programs coordinated with other programs or services and/or otherwise leveraged other resources, including other public sources and private capital investments, their ability to have an impact increased.

6. *Capacity impact.* Some of the programs sought to build regional capacity for achieving economic development by providing resources to regional agencies. The evaluation of their impact included consideration of capacity-building.

7. *Impacts on targeted individuals.* Some programs were targeted to serving special populations such as dislocated workers, minorities or women. The degree to which these individuals were reached by the programs was another important area of programs impact.

8. *Resulting economic growth and project costs.* The ultimate purpose of all of these state programs was economic growth in New York state. Measurement of this growth in relationship to costs was an important part of evaluating economic impact. Measures included estimates of increased revenues to the state through increased income and state taxes, reduction in unemployment and public assistance payments, and repayment of loans. (For businesses that are hesitant to provide tax information, a process to estimate taxes is described in Attachment 13-4.)

The application of each of those measures to the 12 New York state economic development programs is illustrated in the accompanying matrix. Each of the eight impact areas listed is shown across the top of the matrix, including in addition, a "program specific" category to include impact measures unique to individual programs. The 12 economic development programs are listed on the left side of the matrix. The check marks indicate which impact areas apply to each program.

Information Collection Activities

KS&R collected both quantitative and qualitative information related to program impact:

▸ **Structured interviews** with managers of the program and other key staff.

▸ **Program- and project-specific information** from centralized files, both manual and automated.

▸ **Surveys of representatives of funded projects.** For programs where substantial numbers of completed projects existed, contacts were primarily with representatives of *completed* projects. Surveys were mostly by telephone, although some contacts were in-person.

▸ For programs where project funding was to an intermediary, **telephone or mail surveys** of a sample of individuals or companies that received assistance or services from the programs.

▸ **Telephone interviews** conducted with a sample of members of relevant program **advisory committees** or similar entities.

▸ **Telephone interviews** conducted with **directors** of the state's regional economic development offices.

▸ Contact with local and statewide **economic development experts,** including New York state legislative staff and a sample of industrial development agency and local development corporation directors.

IMPACT OF NEW YORK ECONOMIC DEVELOPMENT PROGRAMS

	Business	Targeting to Distressed Areas	Assistance to Targeted Businesses	Jobs Created & Retained	Coordination & Leveraging	Capacity	Targeted Individuals	Economic Growth & Project Costs	Program Specific
Infrastructure	✓	✓		✓	✓			✓	✓
Export					✓			✓	✓
Entrepreneurial Assistance	✓	✓	✓		✓		✓	✓	
Small Business Loans	✓	✓		✓	✓			✓	
Small Loans Regional	✓	✓	✓	✓	✓	✓		✓	✓
Large Business Loans	✓	✓	✓	✓	✓			✓	✓
Regional Loans & Grants	✓	✓	✓	✓	✓	✓		✓	✓
MWDE Loans	✓	✓	✓	✓	✓	✓	✓	✓	✓
Urban Development		✓		✓	✓	✓		✓	✓
Labor Force Training	✓		✓		✓		✓	✓	✓
Industrial Productivity	✓		✓	✓	✓			✓	✓
Research & Information									✓

▶ **Labor market information** from NYS Department of Labor and statewide business statistics were obtained from the state data center and other appropriate sources.

Sample of Program Evaluation

Key findings of the Industrial Effectiveness Program (IEP) impact survey can be summarized as follows:

Job creation and retention

- *On average, IEP recipient companies reported that there would have been somewhat fewer employees at their current location if they had not received IEP assistance. However, several respondents noted that efficiency gains, due to their IEP projects, have resulted in fewer employees because of their ability to now produce more with fewer employees.*

Impacts on business

- *Most company representatives report that it is unlikely that their IEP project would have proceeded in the absence of state assistance.*
- *IEP productivity assessment projects are estimated to have resulted in a $98.6 million increase in company sales annually.*
- *75 percent of respondents reported the program improved company productivity compared to industry norms.*
- *Nearly all respondents reported increased sales, profits, and productivity as a result of the program.*

Targeted business

- *92 percent of companies had 500 or fewer employees, and 44 percent had 100 or fewer.*

Coordination and leveraging

- *Regional and local economic developers find IEP to be a very useful tool for assisting manufacturers that need to be more productive.*

LESSONS LEARNED IN
NEW YORK EVALUATION STUDY

Although the methodology discussed here was developed for and applied to a set of state-wide programs, its flexibility makes it suitable for the evaluation of local and regional economic development programs as well. The methodology lends itself to cross-cutting conclusions and recommendations, and allows for comparisons where appropriate. The surveys of economic development professionals permit the testing of awareness of the selected programs and their suitability to local needs. Similarly, the survey of program beneficiaries allow the exploration of customer satisfaction, as well as the documentation of program performance.

Because these surveys were administered by an organization independent of the agencies offering the programs, respondents were assured of impartiality and anonymity. Agencies conducting their own program reviews should take care to create a similar impartial environment in order to minimize any influence on the results.

Data Collection

Data collection is a significant undertaking in this methodology. Data collection should be planned ahead and, where possible, incorporated into the routine information collection and administrative process of each program.

Data required for measurement of business performance and impact on economic growth was problematic in implementing this methodology. While conceptually feasible, the calculation of state and local taxes generated and purchases made by firms in the local economy proved impractical, given the resources available for the study. Other economic development agencies may find that it is possible to collect key data which will permit these calculations. New York state, however, found that:

— Many businesses do not collect information in a way that allows them to report these impacts easily or consistently;
— Most firms view administrative costs associated with the program approval and reporting process as burdensome;
— Some businesses may be reluctant to provide data that they feel is proprietary; and
— For programs of substantial size, the volume and frequency of firms submitting information makes 100 percent monitoring a burdensome and expensive undertaking.

This situation can be remedied by recognizing the data needs of the evaluation model at the beginning of the evaluation period, coordinating and standardizing the data collection, and maintaining a data base. For many programs, a review of the data already collected will reveal areas where data collection can be streamlined and areas where new data is required.

Benchmarks

In many of the impact areas, the measures used to qualify program performance do not have standards or benchmarks against which they can be measured. Economic development agencies should establish these benchmarks at the outset of the program, review performance on a regular basis and make changes accordingly. While program history can provide some basis of comparison, active goal setting and benchmark development will strengthen any evaluation. There may be some reluctance to establish benchmarks which are comparative because of fears that program performance will fail to measure up. This fear may be addressed by keeping benchmarks internal while reporting on overall performance.

Length of Time

For many programs, the **length of time for impact** to be apparent is longer than the two-year interval between evaluations practiced in New York. Each agency undertaking evaluation should schedule its efforts around anticipated impacts. Loan programs, for example, would be more appropriately measured every three years.

Finally, this methodology can produce useful results even when "perfect" data is not available. The framework established numerous measures for each program, creating a good indication of program performance, even where information for specific measures are not available.

Using the NY Methodology

Key to the successful use of this methodology is its incorporation into the program planning and implementation process, and the recognition of its value by the staff involved in planning and implementation.

It is likely that the planning process in any given organization will need some enhancement in order to support the evaluation effort. Often the planning process may be informal, except where related to budget formulation. From one year to the next, planning may consist of providing activity reports for each program as justification for increased funding. By integrating the basic elements needed for evaluation into the planning of the overall approach to economic development and into individual program planning, the information required and the basis for evaluation will be in place.

The basic elements needed for evaluation are the measurable objectives which are expected to be achieved in a given period of time. These objectives in turn should support a defined strategy for addressing the problems of the community. All the measures used in this methodology were developed to measure objectives defined for a specific program. For example, the objective of "enhancing areas of the state which are in danger of becoming substandard" (the wording comes from enabling legislation) is measured by the number and percent of services (in this case loans) provided to areas defined as distressed. Formulating

objectives and appropriate measures can be difficult but is worth the effort in being able to subsequently see how performance stacks up to expectations.

Once objectives and measures have been developed, the information required for the measures needs to be collected. The more information collected routinely in program operations through application forms and regular reporting, the less will have to be collected during the evaluation process.

The evaluation itself can be undertaken in parts: program by program, or by impact areas across programs. Agencies can do much of the work themselves, especially if the data is routinely collected. New York state found advantages in hiring an outside contractor because of the perceived need for an independent view.

The state also found that staff and management better understand the overall goals and how the programs address those goals as a result of the evaluation. This understanding then leads to a further strengthening of the goals and commitment to appropriate changes and innovation.

BRE VISITATION EVALUATION

The second evaluation example is based on research conducted by the University of Minnesota on Business Retention and Expansion visitation programs in six states.

This study highlighted that one natural evaluation indicator is the BRE program's immediate employment impacts. Immediate employment impacts, however, provide an incomplete picture of success, since a program performing well in this area may fail to develop a network of concerned citizens that will continue to work for a strong, stable local economy.

Although immediate employment effects are not the principal focus of BRE visitation programs, any job created or saved by addressing a firm-specific problem indirectly helps assure success on long-term objectives. At the community level, these immediate "success stories" provide the citizens who have donated their time with evidence that the program does provide benefits to their community, encouraging them to continue their involvement in planning and networking activities. Similarly, at the state level, they translate into higher enthusiasm for the program, making the task easier to convince new communities to try the BRE visitation approach. Since immediate job creation and job saving can have such influence on overall program outcome, it is worthwhile investigating differences between programs that did and did not report success in this area. A survey of local visitation coordinators explored such differences.

The long-term goal of BRE visitation is a stable, strong local economy developed through improving the competitiveness or efficiency of local firms. The program addresses this objective by enhancing communication and strategic planning. In the long run, the change in local employment after a successful BRE visitation program could be negative, if an noncompetitive firm uses the resources it learns about through the program to become more capital-intensive in its method of production. In this scenario, the program prevents the firm from going out of business, but some jobs are lost after the plant is retooled. Thus, use of secondary employment or income data to evaluate BRE visitation is not straightforward.

An alternative to measure the effect of a program is to solicit evaluations from program participants. In using such a strategy, it is necessary to examine specific program objectives, capturing participants' perceptions of how well the program worked in each area. Specific program findings from the Minnesota study are reported in Chapter 7.

CONCLUSION

Evaluation of business retention and expansion activities is not easy to develop and implement, but is worth the effort. By incorporating the evaluation activities and the development of appropriate measures into the program planning and budgeting process, the evaluation will enable the goals embodied in the measures to be more effectively accomplished.

BRE programs that report evaluation data, of either formative or summative variety, are in a much better position to "improve" their program and "prove" its impact.

REFERENCES

Livengood, Rebecca. "Evaluation of the Impact of Economic Development Programs," *Commentary*, Summer 1993.

Loveridge, Scott, Thomas D. Smith, and George W. Morse. "Immediate Employment Effects of Business Retention and Expansion Programs," Staff Paper Series, Department of Agricultural and Applied Economics, February 1992.

ABOUT THE AUTHORS

Rebecca A. Livengood holds a masters degree in City Planning from the Massachusetts Institute of Technology. She has more than 20 years experience in economic development. She served as Director of Economic Development for the City of Syracuse, New York, and for the past thirteen years has been providing consulting services to economic development agencies in strategic planning, market analysis, program design, and evaluation. She may be reached at 315-478-6938.

Marion Bentley was the Director of the Utah Business Resource Network, an outreach business assistance and consulting unit housed in the College of Business at Utah State University. He was also an Extension Business and Economic Development Specialist and Associate Professor in the Department of Economics at USU. He may be reached at 435-797-2284.

MEASURING PERFORMANCE RESULTS

HOW TO MEASURE RESULTS

- Collect "baseline" information when you start implementing project/actions (to compare with later when you are assessing results).
- Regularly and frequently collect information about your projects ("track progress").
- Use a variety of methods and sources: survey, focus groups, document review, "stories," self-assessment diaries.
- Involve community stakeholders in collecting and interpreting evaluation information.
- Don't just measure—identify factors contributing to or hindering achievement of desired results.
- Carefully select indicators (measures) of success:
  - ▸ Information describing observable, measurable characteristics/changes.
  - ▸ Answer question: "How will I know desired result has been achieved?"
  - ▸ Indicators should be:
    - — valid (measure what you are trying to measure)
    - — directly relevant to project goals
    - — understandable/meaningful
    - — affordable, accessible, and timely

LEVELS OF BRE RESULTS

- **Impact/End Results:** Changes in the economic, physical, or social environment in the community that are attributable to BRE, sometimes referred to as "long-term outcomes."
- **Applications and Adoptions:** Changes in practice/policy as a result of BRE.
- **Learning:** Changes in knowledge, attitudes, skills or aspirations ("KASA") through BRE.
- **People Involvement and Reactions:** Number of participants/businesses, degree of involvement, and their level of interest, approval, satisfaction, or support for BRE activities.
- **Activities:** Information and delivery methods used to interact with program participants (BRE businesses, volunteers, staff).
- **Inputs:** Personnel/time/money/equipment used for BRE.

(Evaluation terminology can be confusing. The key is to be consistent with what you mean by different terms.)

SAMPLE BRE MEASURES

Issue: Lack of skilled labor for leather factory/tannery.

Project: Design/deliver new leather-working training/apprenticeship program at community college.

- ▸ *Immediate Result (output):* Number of courses and content, number of trainees entering program.
- ▸ *Short-term Result (outcome):* Number of people completing training and apprenticeships; number of graduates hired by leather factory.
- ▸ *Long-term Results (outcome):* Increase in production, efficiency (cost of inputs to outputs), and profits.
- ▸ *Impact:* Increase in the number of jobs, workers' wages, and level of satisfaction of business owner and employees.

EVALUATION OF RETENTION AND EXPANSION BUSINESS VISITS

County/Community: _____

1. What was your role in the local business retention and expansion program?
    (Circle all that apply.)

    1. Leadership Team member
    2. Task Force member
    3. Volunteer interviewer
    4. Individual interviewed during firm visit

2. What is your employment affiliation? *(Circle all that apply.)*

    1. Elected public official
    2. Appointed public official
    3. Education official
    4. Economic development professional
    5. Private employer
    6. Private employee
    7. Retired
    8. Other (please specify)
       _____

3. How successful was this program in demonstrating a pro-business attitude?
    (Circle one.)

    Not Very Successful   **Very Successful**
    1   2   3   4   5

4. How successful was this program in helping business firms learn about local, regional and state resources for business? *(Circle one.)*

    Not Very Successful   **Very Successful**
    1   2   3   4   5

5. How successful was this program in helping local leaders understand the strengths and weaknesses of the community from the perspective of local businesses? *(Circle one.)*

    Not Very Successful   **Very Successful**
    1   2   3   4   5

6. How important was it that University economists analyzed the data collected on the firm visits? *(Circle one.)*

    Not Very Important   **Very Important**
    1   2   3   4   5

7. Overall, in your judgment, how effective have the recommendations and the implementations (BRE) plans been for improving local business competitiveness?

Very Effective	Effective	Uncertain	Not Effective	Harmful
1	2	3	4	5

8. What have been the most important accomplishments?

_____

_____

9. Overall, in your judgment, how effective will the BRE plan be in improving local business competitiveness in the next two to five years?

Very Effective	Effective	Uncertain	Not Effective	Harmful
1	2	3	4	5

10. What is the most important recommendations that needs to be accomplished?

_____

_____

11. Please rate the following factors of the BRE program:

	Excellent	Good	Fair	Poor	Don't Know/ Not Applicable
1. Content of the questionnaire	1	2	3	4	5
2. Length of the questionnaire	1	2	3	4	5
3. Maintenance of confidentiality	1	2	3	4	5
4. Resolution of local problems	1	2	3	4	5
5. Support from state staff	1	2	3	4	5
6. Development of plan	1	2	3	4	5
7. Implementation of strategic plan	1	2	3	4	5

12. If you were asked by a business or government in a neighboring community whether or not that community should establish a BRE program, would you recommend it?

Yes Definitely	Yes Probably	Uncertain	Probably Not	Definitely Not
1	2	3	4	5

SOURCE: North Dakota BRE Program

Business Retention and Expansion Program

OUTCOME QUESTIONNAIRE

**Washington State
Department of Community, Trade and
Economic Development**

*Please return your completed questionnaire
in the envelope provided to:*

*Business Retention and Expansion Program
2001 6th Avenue, Suite 2600
Seattle, WA 98121*

KEEPING BUSINESS HAPPY, HEALTHY AND LOCAL

County Business Retention and Expansion

Program (BRE) is committed to providing a quality service. Your opinion on BRE services provided to your company would be greatly appreciated. Please take a few minutes to complete the questionnaire, and return in the envelope provided. If you have any questions, call (206) 256-6112.

Q1 What basic services did the program provide to you?
....
....

Q2 Which specific services did you find most valuable? Why?
....
....

Q3 How do you rate the quality of service provided by the BRE with regard to:

	EXCELLENT				POOR
Ease of obtaining help?	1	2	3	4	5
Timeliness of service delivered?	1	2	3	4	5
Communication in clear, nontechnical terms?	1	2	3	4	5
Competence of BRE personnel?	1	2	3	4	5
Professional treatment?	1	2	3	4	5
Identification of problems?	1	2	3	4	5
Identification of practical solutions?	1	2	3	4	5
Overall program assistance?	1	2	3	4	5

For any services you rated as *poor*, please tell us why you rated them as low as you did.
....
....

Q4 How did you find out about the Business Retention and Expansion Program?
....

Q5 What factors caused you to seek assistance?

1 Need for financing   2 Change in market
3 Local infrastructure   4 Competition
5 Other (please specify) ....

Q6 Do you consider your company still at risk from these factors?
1 Yes   2 No

Q7 If yes, what additional issues need to be addressed?
....
....

Q8 If no, to what extent to you credit the turnaround or expansion to BRE?

COMPLETELY.............................NOT AT ALL
   1   2   3   4   5

Q9 What is one thing the BRE could do to improve the services it provided to your business?
....
....

Q10 Would you recommend the program to a business associate?
1 Yes   2 No

Q11 (optional)   Name: ....
          Telephone: ....

Thank you for taking the time to complete the questionnaire. If there is anything else that you would like to comment upon regarding BRE, please so on the back.

BRE CUSTOMER SATISFACTION SURVEY

Your input is the critical contributor to improving our future service.

Client: _____   **Project Manager:** _____

Project Number: _____   **Project Resource:** _____

Project Name: _____

	Very Satisfied	Satisfied	Neutral	Dis-satisfied	Very Dissatisfied
	A	**B**	**C**	**D**	**F**
1. Are you satisfied with the quality of services you received?	☐	☐	☐	☐	☐
2. How would you rate the ease of obtaining help?	☐	☐	☐	☐	☐
3. How would you rate the professionalism with which you were treated?	☐	☐	☐	☐	☐
4. How well did we deliver what we promised?	☐	☐	☐	☐	☐
5. How would you rate the quality of our services?	☐	☐	☐	☐	☐
6. How would you rate the value of the project relative to the cost?	☐	☐	☐	☐	☐
7. How well did we meet deadlines?	☐	☐	☐	☐	☐

8. How did you find out about this program? _____

9. What factors caused you to seek assistance?   ☐ Need for financing   ☐ Change in market
                                                   ☐ Local infrastructure   ☐ Competition
                                                   ☐ Other (*please specify*): _____

10. Is your company still working with these issues (listed above)?   ☐ Yes ☐ No

11. If Yes, what additional issues need to be addressed? _____

12. How did this experience compare with your expectations?_____

13. If we did not meet your expectations, where did we fall short? _____

14. What suggestions do you have about how we could serve your needs better in the future?

_____

15. Would you recommend us to others?   ☐ Yes   ☐ No

If yes, to whom would you recommend or refer us?
    Company Name: _____
    Contact: _____

Please send the survey back to Business Retention and Expansion Program by fax (206-256-6125) or by mail (2001 6th Avenue, Suite 2600, Seattle, WA 98121).

Feel free to call Ginger Rich, WA State BRE Project Manager at 206-256-6112 or your Project Manager regarding your responses to this survey or any other issue with which we can help you.

Revised 06/16/02

_____ ***KEEPING BUSINESS HAPPY, HEALTHY AND LOCAL***

HOW TO CALCULATE TAX IMPACT

Ideally, you can get information directly from the company on estimated taxes. However, in case when companies are unwilling to share information, use the following methodology to estimate taxes. Three resource books are helpful for calculations.

What you need to know:
- SIC Code
- Employment Level

Example:

*Mobile Home Manufacturer (SIC 245)
100 Employees*

Business & Occupational Tax

From **Census of Manufacturers or Annual Survey of Manufacturers**, calculate sales and wages per employee. For SIC 245, sales per employee average $118,875. For 100 employees, sales total $11.89 million. B&O Tax Rate = .004664 X Sales = <u>$55,455 B&O Tax</u>.

Property

From **RMA Statement Studies**, find ratio of Sales/Net Fixed Assets for firms in correct sales category ($11.89 million sales). The ratio is 9.8, so for sales of $11.89 million, the average capital investment is $1.213 million.

The property tax rate from County Assessor would be $14.729/1000 assessed value—so the annual property tax is <u>$17,866</u>.

Other resource book: **R. W. Means Construction Cost Index**.

Unemployment Insurance

Average rate = 3.14% X maximum $21,300 X 100 workers = $66,541 experience rating from .36 to 5.4%.

Labor & Industry

Composite rate = $1.51/hour worked
Average 49 weeks X 40 hours X $1.51 X 100 = $295,960

Sales Tax

Difficult to calculate. A manufacturing study by Washington State Department of Revenue provides some estimates for manufacturers.

INDEX